How to Be Like **Rich DeVos**

How to Be Like Rich DeVos

Succeeding with Integrity in Business and Life

Pat Williams
with Jim Denney

Health Communications, Inc.
Deerfield Beach, Florida

www.hcibooks.com

Library of Congress Cataloging-in-Publication Data
is available from the Library of Congress.

ISBN-13: 978-0-7573-0158-2
ISBN-10: 0-7573-0158-4

Publisher: Health Communications, Inc.
3201 S.W. 15th Street
Deerfield Beach, FL 33442-8190

*Cover photo courtesy of RIKU+ANNA/*www.rikuanna.com
Cover design by Larissa Hise Henoch
Inside book design by Lawna Patterson Oldfield

To my daughter Caroline and her husband,

Navy chaplain Dimitry Givans.

I pray that the principles in this book will

brighten the path before you.

Contents

Foreword by Charles W. Colson ix

Chapter One: **My Friend, Rich DeVos** 1
Chapter Two: **Stand Up and Lead!** 9
Chapter Three: **Be a Risk Taker!** 41
Chapter Four: **Speak Up!** 53
Chapter Five: **Be Wise!** 73
Chapter Six: **Be a People Person!** 81
Chapter Seven: **Be a Life Enricher!** 103
Chapter Eight: **Be a Mentor!** 119
Chapter Nine: **Get Out and Sell!** 139
Chapter Ten: **Give Till It Feels Good!** 155
Chapter Eleven: **Love Your Family!** 181
Chapter Twelve: **Love Your Country!** 199
Chapter Thirteen: **Have Faith!** 217
Chapter Fourteen: **Keep an Upward Look!** 245

Afterword: Here's to You, Rich! 273
A Final Word from the Author—and from Rich 293
Acknowledgments 295

Foreword

I WAS DELIGHTED TO hear that Pat Williams was working on a book about Rich DeVos. Rich is one of the most remarkable and admirable men I've known in my lifetime. I first met him in 1975, when I spoke at a Gospel Films banquet in Michigan. I didn't know much about Amway at the time (although when I was in the Nixon White House, my limousine driver was an independent distributor and I bought Amway products from him when he drove me home at night).

> *"As a Christian, an American and an entrepreneur, Rich DeVos is a singular personality."*
>
> William F. Buckley Jr.
> Founder, *National Review*

I stayed in touch with Rich over the years, seeing him at a variety of events and corresponding with him from time to time. I once read a newspaper article that said he kept a copy of my book *Born Again* on his boat, on which he cruised the Potomac and hosted many politicians. I wrote and thanked him, and we corresponded frequently from then on.

As I got to know Rich DeVos better and better over the years, I became increasingly impressed by his humble and generous spirit, coupled with a dazzling personal charisma. He was not at all what I expected a billionaire corporate leader to be. When I heard him speak, I discovered that he is one of the best public speakers of our age.

One time I was in West Michigan and dropped by his headquarters. That visit gave me a wonderful insight into Rich DeVos.

A number of Amway distributors were gathered in the lobby in a receiving line that day, and Rich interrupted our meeting so that he could greet them. I followed him down the stairs and watched him with them—he greeted every one of them as if they were best friends. The time he spent with them didn't tire him—it energized and inspired him! I was impressed to see how, throughout that encounter, he radiated sincerity, enthusiasm and love for those people.

Rich has been a generous supporter of our ministry, Prison Fellowship. In 1996, I visited with Rich and his wife Helen at their home in Manalapan, Florida. Sitting with them in their living room, I was struck by the evidence of their simple, humble Dutch roots. For all of his enthusiasm and inspiration, for all of his wealth and success, Rich is still what he has always been since the beginning: a boy at heart, full of enthusiasm and dreams, full of love for God and love for people. He worked his way up the hard way, and he has respect and affection for all hard-working people.

Rich and Helen had just given a very generous gift to Prison Fellowship, and I thanked them for it. Instantly, they both protested, "No, no! Don't thank us! Thank *you* for what you're doing! You're the one doing the important work. We just wrote a check, and that's nothing more than we're supposed to do!"

Helen talked about learning to tithe as a teenager. "In my home," she said, "we always tithed. We always set apart the first 10 percent for the Lord's work." Helen, the lovely, gracious former schoolteacher, just wants to give back to God a portion of what she has received. In fact, when you accept her check, she makes you feel as if you are doing *her* a favor by helping her to practice her faith! It's really quite extraordinary.

Wealthy, prominent people often use their money to get their way—even when they donate to a good cause. Not so with Rich and Helen DeVos. They never use money to gain power over others. They use their money simply to serve God and help people.

We have a ministry to the children of prison inmates called Angel Tree. When I told Rich that we had decided to name our Angel Tree summer camp scholarships "The Rich and Helen DeVos Scholarships," he got teary-eyed. "I really don't deserve this honor," he said—and he was sincerely humbled. To this day, Rich is in awe of the fact that God has blessed him so richly and that he has been able to use his wealth to help other people.

On New Year's Day 1997, I called Rich to wish him a happy New Year. He told me he was leaving for England where he was hoping to have a heart transplant operation. His voice was melancholy, and I don't think he expected to come home alive. I wondered if I would ever see him again on this Earth. Before I hung up, I reminded him, "Christians never say good-bye, so let's just say *au revoir*—'until we meet again.'"

Seven months later, I had the joy of visiting Rich in his London hotel suite soon after his amazing heart transplant operation. We had a fabulous time rejoicing over the second wind that God had given him in life. He was like a new man—like Lazarus called forth from the grave by the voice of Jesus himself. All of his old strength, determination and optimism were fully restored. Added to that was a new depth of insight into the meaning of life. "God has kept me around for a purpose," he told me. "I'm spending the rest of my life on what really counts for him."

> *"The best part of my job is that I have gotten to know Rich DeVos. He's the single most important man I've ever met, a great man. He's had a big impact on me. I can't get enough of him. I call him a 'Halley's Comet,' because he's the kind of man who comes along only once every seventy-five years. People ask me, 'What's he like? Is he really that great a man?' Yes, he is."*
>
> JOE TOMASELLI
> VICE PRESIDENT AND GENERAL MANAGER,
> AMWAY GRAND PLAZA HOTEL

Rich DeVos will certainly be remembered as one of the great entrepreneurs of our age. He and his partner, Jay Van Andel, started from scratch and built a company that has provided meaningful business opportunities for literally millions of people. That company has given birth to a whole new form of individual enterprise. The company they founded continues to be one of the extraordinary social and cultural phenomena of our times.

Despite all that Rich has accomplished, I believe his greatest contributions to the world are still to come. Some of those contributions will be made, no doubt, as people read this book. Thank you, Pat Williams, for giving us this chronicle of Rich's life, along with the spiritual lessons and life principles that we can learn from Rich. And thank you, Rich DeVos, for being the generous, humble, godly friend and leader you are.

—Charles W. Colson

Chapter One

My Friend, Rich DeVos

I WILL NEVER FORGET the moment I first met Rich DeVos. I had flown halfway across the country just to spend forty-five minutes with this man. I put out my hand and said, "Mr. DeVos, it's a pleasure to meet you."

He shook my hand firmly, flashed a broad grin and said, "Skip that 'Mr. DeVos' stuff. I'm Rich."

I thought to myself, *I know you're rich! That's why I'm here!*

And that was true. I had flown from Orlando, Florida, to West Michigan for a chance to talk to one of the richest men in the world. But at that moment, I had no idea how much that first handshake, that first introduction, was going to change my life. In the years since that meeting, my friendship with Rich DeVos has enriched my life in ways I never dreamed possible.

Let me go back to how it began, how I first came to know Rich DeVos. It was 1990, and the Orlando Magic had just played its first season as a National Basketball Association franchise. At that time, I served as the team's first general manager. Having just launched a pro basketball team, I wondered, *Why not start a major league baseball team in Orlando?* The owners of the Magic (whose major investor at that time was Bill DuPont of the Wilmington, Delaware, DuPonts) were interested in making the move into baseball, so we began pursuing that dream.

Building a major league team is unbelievably expensive. The expansion fee alone was $95 million—and that didn't include all the start-up costs. Our application to the league had to be submitted by Tuesday, September 4, 1990, the day after Labor Day. In July, just six weeks before the deadline, Bill DuPont came into my office. "I've decided not to continue with the baseball effort," he said.

My heart flopped onto the floor, quivering like Jell-O. "But—why?" I asked.

He explained that his real-estate business had made some investments that hadn't panned out. He was not in a position to take on new projects—especially anything as costly as a major league baseball expansion team.

So I quietly went in search of a new principal owner—but there were no takers. By mid-August, the deadline was fast approaching. One name kept coming to mind—Rich DeVos, cofounder of Amway Corporation and one of the wealthiest men on the planet. I knew him only by reputation. I didn't have a clue how to reach him.

I talked to my longtime friend Bobby Richardson, the former Yankees second baseman, and I told him my tale of woe. "Bobby," I said, "the guy I need to get to is Rich DeVos."

"Oh, that's easy," Bobby said. "You can get to him through Billy Zeoli."

Billy Zeoli! I had known Billy for years as a speaker, author and president of Gospel Films (now called Gospel Communications International). It turned out that Rich DeVos was chairman of the board at Gospel Films, and Billy, who goes by the nickname Z, was a close confidant of Rich DeVos.

So I called Billy and told him what we were trying to accomplish. "Z," I said, "do you think Rich DeVos would be interested in owning a baseball team?"

Z is very intense, and when he speaks his sentences are like machine-gun bursts. "I dunno. I dunno," he said. "I'll get back to ya."

A week went by, and I chewed my fingernails down to the elbow. Finally, Billy called. "Rich is interested," he said. "Let me set up a meeting." It took a few more days to set up the meeting. Finally, Z called me and said, "I've got it set up. You'll meet with Rich on August 30 in Grand Rapids, Michigan."

August 30! That was cutting it close!

"You'll be staying at the Amway Grand Plaza Hotel in downtown Grand Rapids."

"Okay, Z," I said. "Just tell me what to do, and I'll do it."

A $95 Million Decision

I dropped everything and flew to Grand Rapids. Billy Zeoli picked me up at the airport and took me to the hotel. Early the next morning, we drove out to the Amway Corp. headquarters in Ada, Michigan. There I met with Bill Nicholson, the company's chief operating officer and a very sports-minded guy. He listened to my pitch for an hour or so, and things seemed to be going well. . . . Then Billy Zeoli came into the room. He was ashen-faced. "There's a problem," he said. "Rich is at his summer home in Holland, and he's not coming in today."

I blinked. "He has a place in the Netherlands?"

"Holland, Michigan," Z replied.

"Ah."

Well, Z was in a frenzy. He got on the phone and actually *scolded* Rich DeVos! I thought, *Gee, maybe that's not such a good idea! Shouldn't we be handling this guy with kid gloves?*

"Rich," Z told him, "you've got to come! This guy came here all the way from Orlando!"

When Billy Zeoli got off the phone, he heaved a sigh of relief. "He'll be here," Z said. "Now, Pat, when Rich gets here, I want you to stay out of sight. When he comes in the lobby, don't let him see you!"

"Why is that?" I asked.

"Because Rich DeVos loves people and he loves to talk," Z said. "If he spots you in the lobby, he'll start gabbing with you on the spot, and we'll never get you guys upstairs for a meeting!"

At about 1 P.M., Z took me to the lobby and had me stand behind a potted plant in the corner. Moments later, I heard the *thrum-thrum-thrum* of helicopter rotors. I peeked around the plant and saw the helicopter set down on the grass in front of the building. At the same time, there was a big commotion in the lobby—people talking at once and racing outside to see who would step out of the helicopter.

About a dozen Japanese Amway distributors who had made their pilgrimage to the company's headquarters surrounded the helicopter as the door opened and their hero, Rich DeVos, stepped out. Their cameras flashed along with Rich's broad smile. He shook hands all around, then entered the lobby.

Following Billy Zeoli's instructions, I made myself invisible behind the plant as Rich strode across the lobby, went upstairs and disappeared inside his headquarters on the second level. A few minutes later, Billy Zeoli returned and ushered me up to Rich's office. Z introduced us.

We sat down at a conference table and got down to business. Normally, when you are talking about a business deal involving tens of millions of dollars, you make a multimedia presentation, replete with bound notebooks filled with marketing data and demographic studies. But I had come into this meeting with only one thing in my hand: a notepad on which I had drawn a pie-chart with a ballpoint pen. That hand-drawn chart was my one and only visual aid. It showed the structure of the proposed ownership group for the baseball team. I have that piece of notepaper framed and hanging on my office wall today.

My conversation with Rich lasted no more than forty-five minutes. I didn't know it then, but it was the beginning of what would become a warm and lasting friendship between Rich DeVos and me. He listened carefully, then said, "Tell you what—would you step out into the hall for a few minutes? I just want to talk it over with my associates, then I'll give you my answer."

So I waited out in the hall while they talked, but I didn't have to wait long. About ten minutes later, Rich, Z and Bill Nicholson came out. Rich said to me, "Tell the National League I'll go forward with them. Have a nice weekend."

And with that, he left.

> *"My teammates and I all like Rich DeVos. The Magic organization is a family, and Rich is like a grandfather to the team. When he speaks to us, we listen because of the wisdom he imparts."*
>
> Pat Garrity
> Orlando Magic Player

I stood in stunned amazement for several seconds, then I turned to Z and said, "What just happened here?"

"You heard him," Z said. "He told you he's going to do it."

"You mean," I said, completely awed, "Rich DeVos made a $95 million decision—just like that?"

"Just like that," said Z. "He's with you 100 percent."

I exhaled. "Wow!"

And that was my introduction to Rich DeVos.

From Presidents to Parking Attendants

Z drove me to the airport. I felt so energized and ecstatic that I could have flown all the way to Orlando without an airplane! As it turned out, the expansion plans for baseball in Orlando never materialized. The National League bypassed Orlando in favor of Denver and Miami.

But something good still came of those efforts. Rich DeVos and other members of the DeVos family became enchanted with the magic of Orlando, Florida—and with the Orlando Magic. In August 1991, the DeVos family purchased the Magic, and Rich became my employer—and my friend. As I write these words, it has now been more than thirteen years that I've been able to study the life of this amazing man.

Before coming to Orlando, I worked as a general manager of NBA teams in Philadelphia, Chicago and Atlanta. I have worked for several brilliant, capable owners, people I have admired and respected. But I have to say that Rich DeVos is in a class by himself. He has not only made a great mark on professional sports, but he has made a profound mark on my life. I am proud to call him my friend.

In the fall of 2001, I wrote a book called *How to Be Like Mike* for Health Communications, Inc. That book, exploring the character traits and success secrets of Michael Jordan, did so well that my publisher, Peter Vegso, asked me to consider other ideas in a *How to Be Like* series. I met with Peter and showed him a list of eighty famous people who have lived extraordinary and exemplary lives. Peter looked at that list and picked out a few names—then he pointed to one name in particular.

"I want to do a book on this guy," he said. "Can you do it?"

The name he pointed to: Richard M. DeVos.

I thought, *Can I do a book on Rich DeVos? Can I do a book about a man who is not only my employer but my mentor and my friend?*

"Peter," I said, "if Rich would give his blessing to the project, I would be honored to write the book."

At that time, Rich had recently been through heart-transplant surgery in London—the latest campaign in a twenty-plus-year battle against heart disease. He had just published a new book of his own, *Hope From My Heart: Ten Lessons for Life* (J. Countryman, 2000). I went to Rich and asked his permission to write this book. He not only agreed, but he gave me complete access to his world. He pointed me to people who knew him well—former United States presidents, CEOs of *Fortune* 500 companies, church leaders, NBA stars, janitors and parking-lot attendants. The list of Rich's admirers is long and represents the broadest spectrum imaginable.

I spent many months tracking down hundreds of people who know Rich DeVos well, and they generously shared their stories with me. The result is a book that I'm sure will profoundly affect your life, just as knowing Rich DeVos has affected mine. In these pages, you will discover an American original, one of the most admirable and exemplary people who has ever lived.

> *"Rich DeVos is his own man—no fancy stuff. He is the man he appears to be. With Rich, there is no pretending because he walks the walk. Rich's character and his values never change, and that is why his message never changes."*
>
> DONALD BUSKE
> GRAND RAPIDS BUSINESS LEADER

Here are just a few reasons why Rich DeVos is unique: Rich started at the bottom and became self-made. He has enjoyed a lifelong friendship and business relationship with one partner, Jay Van Andel; that partnership has lasted nearly sixty years. He has enjoyed more than fifty years of marriage to one woman. He has built his business on a foundation of helping people. He has maintained a strong faith in God through numerous obstacles, trials and setbacks. In his climb to success, he has remained true to the values and principles he was taught as a boy. Rich has given millions to good causes, and his generosity and philanthropy continue to this day. Rich and Jay have successfully passed leadership of their company to their children—and they have wisely stayed out of the way, allowing the next generation to build a new legacy.

Other business leaders have achieved greater wealth than Rich DeVos. Other business leaders have achieved greater fame than Rich DeVos. But how many business leaders of Rich's affluence and influence can say that they have maintained such excellent and rewarding relationships with their spouses, children, grandchildren, colleagues and employees? How many are so universally loved and applauded for their faith, generosity, compassion, courage and sterling character? How many have achieved such peace and satisfaction in life? Most famous people have a hard time living up to their public reputations; Rich's reputation, unblemished as it is, doesn't begin to do him justice.

> *"The uniqueness of Rich DeVos has nothing to do with his wealth and power. It has everything to do with his love for God and his love for people. Rich is a beautiful human being."*
>
> JOYCE HECHT
> GRAND RAPIDS COMMUNITY LEADER

When you apply all of the criteria by which a human life can be measured, you have to conclude that Rich is far and away one of the most successful human beings who has ever lived. His character, attitudes and actions have made him a person well worth studying and emulating. That is why I have written this book.

Each of the coming chapters in this book explores one facet of Rich's character, one quality that has allowed him to overcome huge obstacles and achieve the highest level of success and fulfillment. The good news is that we can all build these qualities into our own lives. We can all become more like Rich DeVos—and in the process, we will achieve undreamed-of heights of success and fulfillment in our own lives.

So let's take a good look at this amazing life. Let me introduce you to my good friend, Rich DeVos.

Chapter Two

Stand Up and Lead!

"OWN YOUR OWN BUSINESS, son. That's the only way to control your own future. Own it, work hard at it, set high goals for yourself and never give up, no matter what obstacles come your way." From the time he lost his job in the Depression until the day he died of a heart attack at age fifty-nine, Simon DeVos repeatedly reinforced that message to his son Rich. And Rich DeVos took that message to heart, building not just a business but an empire.

Richard Marvin DeVos was born on March 4, 1926 in Grand Rapids, Michigan—three years before the stock-market crash that triggered the Great Depression. When his father lost his job during those times, his family lived in the attic of Rich's grandparents' house. By living there rent-free, they were able to rent out their own home and maintain the $25 monthly mortgage payments.

Rich's parents, Simon and Ethel DeVos, raised him in an atmosphere of love, family togetherness and a positive attitude toward life. "We grew up poor," Rich recalls, "but we were certainly no poorer than most other people in the Depression. During the week, my father sacked flour in a grocer's back room, and on Saturdays he sold socks and underwear in a men's store."

Although his family struggled financially as Rich entered high school, his parents sacrificed and wore second-hand clothes to send him to a private religious school, Grand Rapids Christian High School. Nothing about Rich's academic achievements outwardly marked him as a future business leader—he was an average student earning mediocre grades.

"Rich tells the story of the man who owned his own farm. This man put headlights on his tractor so he could work at night. Would he do that if he worked for another man who owned a farm?"

PETER SECCHIA, GRAND RAPIDS BUSINESS AND COMMUNITY LEADER

"During my first year in high school," Rich recalls, "I spent a lot of time chasing girls and goofing off. I'm the kind of person who has to apply himself to get good grades—and I didn't apply! Though I didn't actually flunk any classes, there were a number of classes where I just did the minimum for a passing grade. For example, I passed Latin—barely. My teacher said, 'I'll give you a D if you promise never to take it again.'

"My dad was very unhappy with my grades. He said, 'Son, if this is all you're going to accomplish in a private school, why should I knock myself out to pay your tuition? You can goof off in public school, and it won't cost me anything.' So the following year, my dad sent me to public school to learn a trade and be an electrician. At public school, I was labeled 'not college-bound.' I was miserable that whole year in public school. For the first time, I realized all that I had lost by goofing off in school.

"So I decided to go back and finish my high school education at Christian High. That was the first time I ever made a decision with consequences. When I told my dad what I wanted to do, he said, 'Who will pay for it?' I said, 'I will. I'll do odd jobs to earn the extra money.' The second time around at Christian High, I was serious and I made better grades."

To this day, Rich is grateful for the privilege—a privilege he *earned*—of attending a school that reinforced the lessons of faith, optimism and hard work that he was learning at home. He is also grateful because it was at Christian High that he met Jay Van Andel, who would become his best friend and business partner for almost sixty years.

> *"We are all created by God and are all equal in his sight. That's the foundation of my business."*
>
> RICH DEVOS

Jay owned a car, but Rich, who was two years younger, didn't. So Rich paid Jay twenty-five cents a week for a ride to school and back. During those drives together, Rich and Jay discovered they had many interests in common, including a shared dream of becoming independent businessmen. Jay's parents raised him with the same positive attitudes and strong work ethic that inspired young Rich DeVos. The possibility of working for an employer never entered the minds of Rich and Jay. They saw themselves as leaders, not followers; as entrepreneurs, not employees.

Rich and Jay attended Calvin College in Grand Rapids. They did tours of duty in the Army Air Corps in separate parts of the world. They kept in touch by V-mail during the war, making plans to go into business together when the fighting ended. In fact, the Air Corps gave them the idea for their first business venture: a flying school and charter flight service.

After the war, Rich and Jay returned to the States, convinced that civil aviation was the wave of the future. They believed the time would come when every American home would have an airplane in the garage, and millions of people would learn to fly. So they went home to Michigan and founded Wolverine Air Service.

Although Rich and Jay were both Air Corps veterans, neither was a pilot. "We didn't let anything dampen our enthusiasm," Rich later recalled, "not even a little detail like not knowing how to fly."

Rich and Jay hired some of their Air Corps buddies and other experienced pilots to do the flying while they stayed on the ground and did the selling.

Wolverine Air Service was an idea whose time had come. Rich and Jay tapped into an exploding public interest in civil aviation with the slogan, "If you can drive a car, you can fly a plane." They pooled their savings, bought a secondhand Piper Cub airplane and began building an air service. Right from the beginning, perseverance and creative problem-solving proved to be the keys to success in the aviation business. When the construction company told them that the runways would not be completed in time for Wolverine's grand opening, Rich and Jay equipped their plane with pontoons and used the Grand River as their runway—problem solved. Wolverine Air Service opened its doors right on schedule.

> *"Rich and Jay built their business from scratch. They did it the hard way. They know what it's like to be poor. It's impossible to replace that experience."*
>
> Dexter Yager
> Independent Business Owner

Other air services were trying to get off the ground in the Grand Rapids area, but Rich and Jay got there first and beat the competition. Within months, they expanded from a single Piper Cub to a fleet of a dozen airplanes. Wolverine Air Service became hugely successful—and inspired their second successful enterprise.

Rich and Jay noticed that people enjoyed coming to the airport to watch the planes take off and land. Their air service business had become an attraction! So why not take advantage of the crowds they created? So they decided to open a restaurant. The fact that they knew nothing about the restaurant business didn't even give them a moment's pause.

While on a trip to California, they had seen a completely new kind of eatery called a drive-in restaurant. Customers parked, gave their orders to a "car hop" waitress, and she brought the food to them in their cars. So Rich and Jay started a restaurant adjacent to the airport—the Riverside Drive Inn, the first drive-in restaurant in that part of Michigan.

Opening night at the Riverside Drive Inn was almost aborted when the power company failed to show up as promised to connect the electricity. Many people would have simply canceled the ribbon-cutting—but not Rich and Jay. They had advertised a big, splashy opening for their new venture, and they were going to deliver. So they dashed into town, rented a gasoline-powered generator and opened right on schedule, using home-cranked electricity.

> *"It was fun to watch Dad and Rich together. When they were in the same room, there was electricity all over the place."*
>
> DAVE VAN ANDEL
> JAY'S YOUNGEST SON

Rich DeVos and Jay Van Andel always looked over the horizon. They could see that, while their businesses were thriving today, the public's interest in aviation could fizzle tomorrow. Concluding that the aviation boom would not go on indefinitely, Rich and Jay decided to sell Wolverine Air and the Riverside Drive Inn.

It was time to take off in a new direction—but *which* direction? They began looking for a new venture that could bring them success for decades to come—and it wasn't long before they found it.

The Amway Story

In 1948, Rich DeVos and Jay Van Andel sold Wolverine Air Service. They then bought a thirty-eight-foot schooner and took off for the Caribbean. Following their year-long adventure (more about that later), they began distributing nutritional supplements for a California-based company called Nutrilite. Rich and Jay purchased a Nutrilite sales kit and began selling Nutrilite vitamins and nutritional products in their spare time. During the early 1950s, they attended Nutrilite business seminars and visited the Nutrilite manufacturing facility in Buena Park, California.

By the late 1950s, problems developed within the Nutrilite organization. The manufacturing and marketing arms of Nutrilite were two separate corporate entities and some difficulties developed.

Rich and Jay were dismayed to see themselves and other distributors being hurt by the clashes within Nutrilite. Sales and profits seemed to be in jeopardy.

So, in 1959, Rich and Jay did the logical, entrepreneurial thing: They founded their own company. They called their new company Amway, which was short for something near and dear to both of them—the American way of life. Building on what they had learned as Nutrilite distributors, Rich DeVos and Jay Van Andel adapted and refined the classic Nutrilite marketing plan and came up with a plan that was uniquely Amway.

"If you hang out with failures and adopt the attitudes of failures, you will also be a failure. If you look to successful people as your model, if you listen to what they say, if you work hard and persevere the way successful people do, you'll make it."

Rich DeVos

Rich served as president of the company, Jay as chairman of the board. Though they had shared goals and interests, they had different personalities and abilities. It was a well-balanced partnership because they complemented each other's leadership strengths while compensating for each other's weaknesses. Decision-making responsibility was shared fifty-fifty.

"The reason we got along so well," Jay Van Andel recalls, "was because of our absolute trust in each other. Rich and I always thought about each other's best interests. Sometimes we might agree to disagree, but no matter how we differed on this or that, we both knew we could count on each other's complete loyalty. We had a tremendous working relationship and friendship, and we learned a lot from each other. We shared common experiences in business and family life, and we shared a common faith. Our friendship was the basis of our successful partnership."

"Whenever we had a new idea, we could never say if it was Rich's idea or mine. New ideas seemed to come to both of us at the same time. We knew each other so well, we could practically read each other's minds. We would sit and talk and bounce ideas back and forth, and every new concept seemed to have its genesis in that synergy between us. We had such a great mutual trust that whatever I said was binding on Rich, and whatever he said was binding on me. Nobody could ever play one against the other, because we knew each other and trusted each other completely."

Although they continued selling Nutrilite products, they added their own products to the line, starting with a concentrated, biodegradable household cleaner called Frisk, which was later renamed Liquid Organic Cleaner, or L.O.C. for short.

Rich and Jay recruited a network of distributors who sold products by demonstrating them in the consumers' own homes. In 1960, their first full year of business, they sold over half a million dollars' worth. The following year, they opened their own manufacturing plant near Grand Rapids. Rich and Jay had learned from the Nutrilite fiasco. They exercised firm leadership over the entire organization and kept manufacturing and marketing all under one roof. As a result, Amway never experienced any internal clashes like the one that nearly destroyed Nutrilite.

Casey Wondergem, a former Amway executive, spent more than two decades observing Rich and Jay in their respective leadership roles with Amway. "The harmony between Rich and Jay was remarkable," he recalls. "I was in hundreds of meetings with them, and I never saw them angry with each other. They may not have always agreed, but they were always amiable.

"One day, an interviewer asked Rich if he would consider running for governor of Michigan or president of the United States. Rich replied, 'I will run if Jay will serve.' That answer describes Rich and Jay perfectly in their leadership roles. Rich enjoyed being out front—the salesman and the cheerleader. Jay was the executive, the manager—he wanted to be on the inside, making the company function smoothly. It was the ideal marriage of talents and abilities."

"Jay was one of those students who could make straight A's without ever opening a book. His mind stores and processes information like a computer. He can look at a problem, size it up, lay out all the pros and cons, and give the facts to back up his point of view. He's really amazing."

RICH DEVOS

U.S. Congressman Vern Ehlers also marvels at the unique leadership chemistry of these two longtime friends. "Rich and Jay always maintained a deep respect for each other," he recalls, "and they shared the same values. Both are devout Christians and very active in church. Jay was the quiet guy who handled the nuts and bolts of running a successful business, and Rich was the dreamer, the preacher, the guy who inspired audiences and sold the Amway concept to millions of people. Rich and Jay are great business leaders because they divided their duties well."

Amway employee Joan Williamson has known Rich and Jay for many years. "As leaders and executives," she says, "Rich and Jay have always complemented each other so well. In addition to being business partners, they have always been good friends. They were so alike in their commitment, their values and their Christian faith, yet they contrasted with each other in their personalities and skills. It was the ideal match—each one supplied what the other lacked, and that's one reason Amway became so successful."

Independent business owner Jerry Meadows offers this observation on the way Rich and Jay meshed their leadership roles: "Rich and Jay went into business with a deep friendship and a concern for each other. They respected each other's talents and abilities. If either one voted no, the proposal wouldn't happen. They always presented a united front, and the distributors needed to see that. As independent business owners, we didn't always agree with the decisions Rich and Jay made, but we always knew that they were working together to do the right thing for us all."

> *"Rich and Jay's partnership is a reflection of the character of both men. They are both remarkably unselfish. They have always worked together for the good of the whole."*
>
> GEN. ALEXANDER M. HAIG JR.
> FORMER U.S. SECRETARY OF STATE

Throughout the 1960s, Amway continued to expand, adding products such as cookware and cosmetics. It also expanded its territory, spreading across the United States and into Canada. In 1972, the company purchased Nutrilite Products, Inc.—and the food supplements that Rich and Jay sold as they built their multilevel marketing business in the '50s became one of Amway's biggest product lines.

Exploding sales resulted in 1980 being designated Amway's first "Billion Dollar Year." During the decade of the '80s, the company expanded its world headquarters in Ada and constructed a new cosmetics plant. In the 1990s, a new generation took over the operation of Amway as Dick DeVos succeeded his father Rich as president, and Steve Van Andel succeeded Jay as chairman. Today, Rich's youngest son, Doug, is president.

The company started by Rich and Jay in their basements continues to grow as it moves into the new millennium. In October

2000, Amway became one of three subsidiaries under a new parent company, Alticor; the other two subsidiaries are Quixtar Inc., a Web-based business opportunity in North America, and Access Business Group LLC, a manufacturing and logistics provider to Amway and Quixtar, as well as other companies. Alticor worldwide sales in 2003 totaled $4.9 billion in nutrition and wellness, body and beauty, home, and other products and services through 3.6 million independent business owners in more than eighty countries and territories.

> *"For over twenty years, I've watched the enthusiastic way people respond when they are in Rich's presence. It's not his money and power they're responding to. It's his personal energy and leadership."*
>
> Bob Kerkstra
> Retired Amway Executive

Rich DeVos attributes the phenomenal growth of the company to the fact that Amway products are distributed through independent business owners (IBOs) whose earning capacity is limited only by their desire and hard work. Using the Amway principles, many IBOs earn six-figure incomes. (The term "independent business owner" replaces the former term "distributor" to describe the millions of people around the world who embrace the business opportunity originally created by Rich and Jay.) Alticor and its subsidiaries employ nearly eleven thousand people worldwide.

Some of the most famous motivational and leadership speakers in the country have addressed Amway business meetings, including former United States presidents Gerald Ford, Ronald Reagan and George Bush.

But the most important friends Rich DeVos has made were not the entertainers and presidents he knew, but the thousands of ordinary people who have known and loved him. The success story of Rich DeVos is built on the thousands of success stories of independent business owners and Alticor employees around the world.

As an employer, Rich DeVos was never "the boss." He was always a leader and a friend. Whenever he walked through the production plant in Ada, Michigan, the people who worked for him would smile and call out, "Hi, Rich!" They greeted him by his first name, and he greeted them the same way. People who worked with Rich viewed themselves as members of his team, partners in his mission, friends and colleagues in his enterprise. That is one of the keys to Rich's leadership style—and to his extraordinary success.

> *"After working with Mr. DeVos for eight years as a flight attendant, I can honestly say that there is not a better man to work for."*
>
> MISSY CONROY, FLIGHT ATTENDANT, MAGIC CARPET AVIATION

An Example of Bold Leadership

In September 1991, Rich, Helen and other members of the DeVos family bought the Orlando Magic for about $80 million. Why did Rich want to take on the headaches of running an NBA franchise? Because Rich DeVos is a *leader*. He knew that the world of professional sports would give him a larger platform for influence and leadership in our society. He knew that being an NBA team owner would vastly increase the audience for his message of success through faith, optimism, perseverance and hard work.

"One of the reasons we bought the Magic," Rich recalls, "was to expand the opportunity to share our values with our players, the Orlando community and the world at large. We wanted to have a positive impact on all of these people.

"In January 2002, about four and a half years after my heart transplant, I decided to quit the sports business and take life a little easier. We publicly announced that the DeVos family had decided to sell the Orlando Magic. But within weeks, I began to have second thoughts.

"Soon after I put the Magic up for sale, I attended a party in Palm Beach. There, I ran into sports announcer Curt Gowdy, and he said to me, 'I hear you're selling the team. Is that true?' I started to say, 'Yes,' but I found it almost impossible to speak—I almost choked on that one word. That's when I realized that I couldn't part with the Magic. So I went home and told my wife, 'I've changed my mind. I can't sell the team. We're going to keep it.'

"In March, we announced that the DeVos family had decided not to sell the team. Not long after that, I saw Bill Walton at a game. He came over to me and said, 'Don't ever get out of this business. We need you. We need your values as part of the NBA.'"

"Rich likes to spend time with the team in the locker room. He talks to the team as a whole, and he takes time with the individual players. He's very open about his Christian faith and values. He's the guy who writes the paychecks for all of these millionaire basketball players, but he'll come to them very humbly and say, 'I am a sinner saved by God's grace.' And those guys listen."

JOHN GABRIEL, GENERAL MANAGER, ORLANDO MAGIC

In the NBA world, Rich DeVos is truly unique. There is no other owner like him. Former Magic head coach Brian Hill put it this way: "When Rich speaks to the players, they listen to him. Why? Because he makes you feel like you're the most important person in the world. When he comes to the locker room to talk to the team, the players never think, 'Oh, here comes the owner to give us another rah-rah speech.' It's always, 'We love this guy because of the way he treats us. We truly like being in his presence.'"

Rich DeVos has a special place in his heart for young people, and he wants today's youth to understand the same lessons he learned as a young man: Anyone can be successful in a land of opportunity like the United States of America—if you are willing to work hard and pay your dues. "You can own a large corporation," Rich once said, "and most young people aren't impressed. But when you own the Orlando Magic and get your picture taken with Shaquille O'Neal, kids listen!"

How to Solve Problems Like Rich

One of the reasons Rich DeVos is such a great leader is that he is a great problem-solver. His friend, Paul Conn, author and president of Lee University, recalls a situation that illustrates Rich's simple, direct approach to problem-solving:

"One time, Rich came to Lee University as a guest of honor. We held a reception for him and invited faculty, staff, alumni and other guests. As people stood around the food tables, chatting and socializing, one of the faculty members started whining, 'How can you eat these little wienies when there are no forks?' He went on and on like this, to the point where the people around him found it embarrassing.

"Rich heard this and said to the man, 'I'll get you a fork.' He went over to a waiter, requested a fork, brought it back and handed it to the faculty member. The man took the fork and began to eat his little wienies. In his simple, quiet way, Rich was trying to teach the man something, but I don't think this fellow ever got the point.

"I'm sure Rich was thinking the same thing I was thinking: *I wish this guy would just shut up.* But Rich, being the problem-solver that he is, figured that it was easier to get the fork and stop the man's whining. This anecdote gives you a glimpse into the kind of problem-solver Rich DeVos is. His attitude is, 'Let's just solve the problem, even if the solution is as simple as getting a fork.' It didn't matter to Rich that he was the guest of honor, that he had flown all that distance in his private jet. He's a servant and a problem-solver, and he's not too important to go get a fork."

When problems arise, how do you respond? In a crisis, there are two kinds of people in the world: whiners and problem-solvers. Which kind are you? Rich is a problem-solver. If you want to be like Rich, you've got to be a problem-solver, too. From interviews I've conducted with people who know Rich well, I have identified seven essential features that mark Rich DeVos's approach to problem-solving:

1. Be Proactive

Rich DeVos doesn't wait for problems to find him. He is proactive. He seeks problems out. He makes sure he catches problems while they are small, before they start to get out of hand. Former Alticor employee Steve Hiaeshutter recalls an incident that illustrates Rich's proactive approach to problems.

"Rich conducted 'speak-up sessions' at Amway," Steve recalls. "You could sit with him and air out your feelings, complaints or suggestions, and Rich would listen and respond to your concerns. I was nineteen and working in the plant when I attended my first speak-up session. There were about twenty-five people sitting around a table. I was sitting next to Rich.

"Rich opened the session, and then we just went around the table, speaking up and voicing our complaints or problems. One person said, 'There's no 7 UP in the vending machines.' Another said, 'The color of these uniforms clashes with the color of the walls.' I listened, and I couldn't believe the silliness of it all—every complaint was completely trivial.

"I made some snide comment, and Rich turned to me and said, 'May I ask, what is your problem?' I said, 'All these complaints are so minor, they're not worth mentioning. This is a big waste of your time.' Rich said, 'It doesn't matter how big or small the complaints are. If it's a problem at all, I want to hear it.'

"Later, Rich came to see me and took me aside. 'Let me explain something to you, Steve,' he said. 'Those meetings are my measuring stick. I go looking for problems, and I hope every problem I find is as trivial as 'there's no 7 UP in the vending machines.' If that's the biggest problem we've got, I'm pleased. That means that the company is doing well.'

"I never would have thought of that. It was so simple—pure genius. I never forgot that lesson: Be proactive. Go looking for problems before problems get too big."

2. Define the Problem

Once a problem has been identified, you must define what that problem is in order to solve it. That means you must gather your facts and examine all the elements of the problem so that you have a clear picture of what the problem is. Rich's daughter, Cheri Vander Weide, has grown up with the master problem-solver. She recalls, "Dad has always said, 'Defining the problem is 90 percent of the task. Once the problem is defined, the solution usually presents itself.' Dad would define the problem by gathering people together, getting all the facts on the table and asking for everyone's viewpoint. Sometimes, just laying out the problem would cause a consensus to form. At that point, Dad would offer a simple solution. It all starts with defining the problem. A problem-solving leader has to be willing to listen to his people."

3. Keep It Simple

Complexity paralyzes thinking. Simplicity brings clarity. Once the clutter of complexity is cleared away, the simple solution to the problem often becomes clear. Bob Schierbeek, a business advisor to Rich DeVos, says, "On business matters, Rich is quick to grasp a concept, simplify it, repeat it back, make the decision that needs to be made and move on."

Brian Hill agrees: "Rich DeVos has the ability to quickly size up a complex problem, reduce it to its essentials, then give you a simple solution for handling it."

Adds Rick Breon, a health-care CEO in Grand Rapids, "Rich DeVos sits on our board, and he functions as a catalyst for problem solving and decision making. He doesn't dominate a discussion. Mostly, he listens. But when he speaks, people pay attention because he has a unique ability to sift through all the complexities, get to the heart of the matter and offer a simple, practical solution."

4. Take It Step-by-Step

Once you have identified a simple, practical solution, it is important to implement that solution in a careful, step-by-step fashion. "Dad's wisdom," says Rich's son, Dan, "is to stick to the basics, keep the process clear and uncomplicated, and do everything in the proper order. Start with A, then go to B, then proceed to C. Every big problem can be solved once it is broken down into simple, bite-sized chunks."

5. Take Your Time

It sounds trite, but it's absolutely true: Haste really does make waste. Rarely does a problem need to be solved in a panic—and panic-driven solutions usually make the problem worse, not better. Rich's son-in-law and Orlando Magic CEO Bob Vander Weide observes, "Even though Rich is the ultimate Type A personality, he can be very patient. Sometimes, when he sees people trying to rush or force a decision or a solution to a problem, he'll say, 'Take your time. Sleep on it. We'll know more down the road.' Rich never loses his composure in a crisis. I've never once seen him hit the panic button. Rich is calm and deliberative because of his inner discipline, his consistency and the strength that comes from his core values."

6. Listen to Your Intuition

After you have defined the problem, simplified it to its bare-bones essentials and boiled the solution down to a series of practical steps, ask yourself, *What does my intuition say? Is there a still, small voice inside of me, trying to get my attention and warn me? Or do my intuition and my intellect agree?*

Rich's chief business advisor, Jerry Tubergen, says, "Rich has great instincts, and he relies on those instincts to make good decisions. He bases a large part of his decision making on intuition. He has a good head for facts, but he likes his facts laid out simply. He likes things uncluttered—not a lot of homework to do, no information overload. His style is to quickly sift the relevant from the irrelevant, listen to his intuition, make a decision and move on. He doesn't stew on things. He doesn't look back. He trusts his instincts."

7. Stay Cool Under Pressure

One of the most important qualities a problem solver needs is the ability to remain cool in a crisis. Panic clouds the mind and paralyzes the will, making it impossible to solve problems. In my interviews with people who know Rich DeVos, I heard again and again that he has an amazing ability to remain calm and clear-headed in an emergency.

One evening in the summer of 1996, Rich and Helen DeVos were vacationing in Nantucket. "Our boat was tied up stern-to," Helen recalls, "so we had to reach the shore by walking down our gangway. On this particular evening, we had been to a party down the dock. The weather was chilly, and we were wearing jackets—in Rich's case, a pile-lined jacket. Rich's heart problems were severe at the time, causing him to tire easily, so we left the party early and returned to the boat.

"We reached the gangway, and Rich said, 'Ladies first.' So up I went. As I stepped onto the boat, Rich started up the gangway along with his security aide, Jim Shangraw. There was a cracking sound, and the gangway just broke under the weight of Rich and the other man. Both of them went into the water."

Jim Shangraw picks up the story. "That water was cold!" he recalls with a shudder. "It was really dangerous for Mr. DeVos, because he had been in poor health since his heart attack in 1992. It was night, so it was dark and cold, and when I came up sputtering, I couldn't see Rich at all. He was underwater."

"Rich was wearing that pile-lined jacket," Helen adds, "and it was soaking up the water. The weight of it was pulling him down. Finally, Jim Shangraw grabbed hold of Rich and pulled him to the surface—but it was all he could do to keep Rich and himself afloat. There was so little room between our boat and the seawall that it was hard to get any help to them."

"We were splashing around," says Jim Shangraw, "trying to keep our heads above water, trying to find something to grab onto. I remember looking at Rich's face, and there wasn't a trace of panic in his eyes. In fact, he looked at me and said, 'Helen's going to be mad at me! She told me I'm not supposed to get wet!' There I was—freezing, soaking and wondering how to keep the two of us from drowning—but I had to laugh."

"That's Rich for you," Helen concluded. "Here's a man with a serious heart condition splashing around in freezing water, and he's *joking* about it! His grace under pressure helped ease the tension until we could get someone to help pull them out."

Bill Nicholson, former COO of Amway, told me, "Rich is the guy you want to have at your side in an emergency. He stays calm in a crisis. He stays focused on what needs to be done. He keeps a positive attitude. He figures out the problem and he solves it."

If you want to be a leader like Rich, then do what Rich does: become a problem solver.

For decades, Rich has been a national leader, a tireless advocate for American values. As a public speaker, he has shared his message of success, hope and "compassionate capitalism" with audiences around the world. One of his recorded talks, "Selling America," was honored by the Freedom Foundation with the Alexander Hamilton Award for Economic Education.

Rich has also been a leader in the business world, having served on numerous corporate boards, such as Gospel Communications International and Butterworth Health Corporation. He has demonstrated the social conscience and compassion of a leader, having generously donated time and money to such humanitarian efforts as the National Organization on Disability, the Presidential Commission on AIDS and the Salvation Army. His work has earned him dozens of prestigious awards, including the Adam

Smith Free Enterprise Award (American Legislative Exchange Council), the William Booth Award (Salvation Army), the Humanitarian Award (House of Hope), and many other honors. He has also received numerous honorary doctorate degrees from colleges and universities across the country.

Rich DeVos is also a spiritual leader. He has a passion for telling people about his friend, Jesus Christ. He has boldly shared his Christian convictions in three powerful books: *Believe!* (1975), a motivational and spiritual classic; *Compassionate Capitalism* (1992), published a year after his second heart-bypass operation; and *Hope From My Heart: Ten Lessons for Life* (2000), a gift book containing many life lessons and reflections following his miraculous heart-transplant operation.

> *"I have reflected for many years on the subject of leadership, on the qualities that make a man a good leader, and I have concluded that respect for other people leads the list. Without respect for the people one is to lead, it is impossible to be an effective leader."*
>
> RICH DEVOS

Still amazingly active and vigorous after a stroke, a triple bypass followed within weeks by a staph infection requiring three more surgeries in 1992 and a heart transplant at age seventy-one, Rich DeVos refuses to retire from life. He remains a leader in the Alticor world and the Orlando Magic organization—and he remains an example of bold leadership to all Americans. My own life has been profoundly changed because I have had the privilege of knowing Rich DeVos as a mentor, leader and friend.

Principles of Effective Leadership

What are the qualities of Rich DeVos that have made him a great leader in so many spheres—business, politics, society and religion? Over the years, I have made an intensive study of leadership. In my book, *The Paradox of Power* (Warner Books, 2002), I distilled the art of leadership down to seven essential principles of an effective leader:

> *"Rich is a man of great vision, and he has the communication skills to motivate you toward your own vision."*
>
> BEURT SERVAAS
> PUBLISHER, *SATURDAY EVENING POST*

1. Vision
2. Communication Skills
3. People Skills
4. Good Character
5. Competence
6. Boldness
7. A Servant's Heart

Rich DeVos exemplifies every one of those seven principles. Let's take a closer look at these seven qualities and see how you and I can learn to lead like Rich DeVos.

Leadership principle no. 1: vision

Vision is the ability to imagine a bright and optimistic future. All great leaders have the ability to envision a better tomorrow, then energize and motivate people to turn that dream into a reality. Alticor today is a multibillion-dollar corporation because Rich DeVos had a vision of a company that would enable thousands of individual business owners to realize their own personal dreams of a better future. But in a very real sense, the founding of Amway was not only the result of Rich's vision, but of his father's vision.

Reflecting on his boyhood, Rich recalls, "My father said to me many times, 'Rich, one day you'll own your own business.' He put that dream in my mind. I never doubted that my father's dream would come true. I believe we were created by God to dream big dreams."

For most of his boyhood, young Rich DeVos did not look or act like someone who dreamed big dreams. "I was barely making it through school," he says. "I earned unimpressive grades, and I didn't have any concrete goals for my life. I had a fuzzy idea that I was going to own my own business, but I didn't have any idea how I was going to make it happen."

One day, at a high school assembly, something happened that instantly changed young Rich DeVos into a visionary. "A young man came to our school to speak to us about setting goals for our lives. He told us that he had set twenty 'almost impossible goals' for his life. One of those goals was to travel all the way around the world by the time he was eighteen. Then he presented a slide show of his trip. I was amazed. This fellow was a world traveler at eighteen! That very night, after the assembly, I began to write down goals and dreams for my life. From that day on, I had a focus and a vision for the future—and my life was never the same."

> *"I was in high school with Rich. He was aggressive and confident, but always affable and friendly to everyone. I couldn't have predicted all of the incredible success he's had—but it doesn't surprise me, either."*
>
> Dr. Louis Helder
> Longtime Friend of Rich DeVos

Shortly before he graduated from Grand Rapids Christian High School, Rich had one more experience that reinforced his vision of himself as a future business leader. "I had a teacher named Dr. Leonard Greenway," Rich recalls. "At the end of my senior year, he signed my yearbook, 'To a clean-cut young man with talents for leadership in God's Kingdom.' He sensed something in me that I never realized before. I never forgot those words.

"Forty years later, I went to a class reunion, and there was Dr.

Greenway. I had been the senior class president, so I emceed the event. I said, 'Dr. Greenway, you wrote something in my yearbook. Do you remember what it was?' Amazingly, he stood up and quoted it perfectly. I often wondered if he had written that in every student's yearbook—but I don't think so. Dr. Greenway's vision enabled me to see my own potential as a Christian leader."

Rich knows how his life has been shaped by a sense of vision, and he encourages people everywhere to dream big dreams and envision a brighter future. Some years ago, Rich's son Doug brought several of his college friends home for spring break. As Doug and his friends sat around the dining-room table, Rich asked each of Doug's friends, "What do you want to do with your life?" One of Doug's friends, Greg Bouman, answered, "I want to run a small business." Rich replied, "A *small* business? Why not a *big* business?" That is so typical of Rich DeVos—he always encourages people to dream big dreams.

> *"Leadership is not conditioned on where you live and what education you have. You can start where you are. Anyone can become a leader."*
>
> RICH DEVOS

Rich is quick to point out that it is not enough merely to dream a big dream, to envision a grand vision. Our big dreams and bright visions will come to nothing if we do not stay focused on them and see them through to completion.

"Having a dream helps fortify your confidence," Rich says. "But along with the dream you have to set tangible, realizable goals and stick to them. Too many people get intrigued by the grass on the other side of the fence, and every two or three years run off to some new opportunity. And while there's nothing wrong with seeking opportunity, in order to find it you've got to be a builder. Those who keep flitting from one dream to the next are what I call 'opportunity seekers,' not builders. People who go into something new all the time spend their whole lives starting over."

Edwin J. Feulner, president of The Heritage Foundation, told me, "Rich DeVos has inspired countless people around the globe to dream big dreams. He has made a permanent impression on The Heritage Foundation and on my family and me. After visiting with our staff at our headquarters, Rich pulled me aside and said, 'What this organization needs is a vision statement. You and your team need a shared vision if you are going to have a lasting impact on social policy in America. A bold but practical vision will help you to reach those long-term goals you've been telling me about.'

"I knew he was right because I have watched his phenomenal success as a businessman and a leader. I was so captured by his enthusiasm that I began working with the Heritage leadership on a vision statement. We worked away at it for almost three years, producing dozens of drafts until we got it just right. We received counsel and advice from employees, trustees, donors and several congressmen and senators. Every time we revised that statement, we knew we weren't just changing words around—we were shaping the future of our institution.

"My wife Linda and I were able to visit Rich in London and pray with him while he was waiting for his heart transplant. As ill as he was, he wanted to know how we were coming with our vision statement! After his successful surgery, he returned to the States and began making speeches again, inspiring thousands of people with his personal testimony of how God had miraculously given him a new heart and a new life.

"A week after the Board of Trustees approved our final vision statement, I got together

"People who dream impossible dreams and strive to achieve them raise man's stature a fraction of an inch in the process, whether they win or lose."

RICH DEVOS

with Rich at a huge convention where he was one of the featured speakers. I showed him the finished statement—seventeen words representing three years of work. I said, 'You know, Rich, that statement of vision is going to guide everything our organization does from now on—and we owe that statement to you.'

"Rich was so moved and touched by the impact he had made on our organization that he decided on the spot to change the speech he was scheduled to deliver. He sat down and scribbled a few notes, then he went out and gave a rousing speech that he called 'Our Vision for America.' Because of the vision of Rich DeVos, The Heritage Foundation and its two hundred thousand supporters are focused on the goal represented by this vision statement: 'The Heritage Foundation is committed to building an America where freedom, opportunity, prosperity and civil society flourish.' God bless America—and God bless Rich DeVos!"

> *"Rich DeVos is a leader of influence because he is outspoken and passionate about his faith, his politics and his business beliefs."*
>
> Mike Jandernoa
> Grand Rapids Business Leader

Every organization, corporation or team needs a vision. Without a vision, how will you know what success is? More importantly, how will you know how to get there? Your vision is your definition of success. It seizes your imagination and pulls you along. Your vision is what you struggle for, compete for, fight for and sacrifice for.

Great leaders like Rich DeVos are people of vision.

Leadership principle no. 2: communication skills

A great leader is also a great communicator. What good does it do to have a shining, optimistic vision of the future if you cannot communicate that vision to the people around you? A visionary leader must be able to articulate that vision promote that vision and sell that vision to his or her employees, partners and teammates. "My vision" must become "our vision," a shared vision, so that everyone in the organization can move in formation toward a single goal.

Rich DeVos is a great leader largely because he is a great communicator. We'll take a closer look at his communication skills in chapter 4, but for now it is enough to observe that his success and influence as a leader come from his amazing ability to communicate hope, enthusiasm, energy and confidence to the people on his team—whether that team is independent business owners or Alticor employees or the Orlando Magic. Rich continually communicates optimism—and his optimism is contagious.

Of course, talking is only one-half of the communication equation. The other half is *listening*. "My company went public in 1993," recalls Rich's friend, Peter Secchia, Grand Rapids business and community leader and former U.S. ambassador to Italy. "Rich was on my board of directors. He'd come to the meetings and sit quietly, just listening to the discussion. When he finally spoke, all heads turned his way. He has the ability to hear all points of view, then distill all the elements of a discussion to a few clear, simple observations. His listening skills are the equal of his speaking skills. That's why he's such a great leader."

> *"Leadership is like respect. You can't demand it. It must be earned. You rise to a position of leadership."*
>
> RICH DEVOS

"Rich DeVos is a leader who listens," says Jon Nunn, a community leader in Grand Rapids who knows Rich well. "When Rich goes to the Amway Grand Plaza Hotel, he'll talk to the doorman, the bellhop, the maître d'. He'll ask questions: 'How do you like working here? What can we do to improve your working conditions? How can we improve service to our guests?' That kind of 'listening leadership' really encourages team spirit in an organization."

Joe Tomaselli, vice president and general manager of the Amway Grand Plaza Hotel, agrees. "Rich is such a great listener, and he's so disarming that sometimes I have to remind myself, 'This is my boss!' You tend to think of him as your friend. When you have a conversation with him, he leaves you feeling terrific. He tells you, 'You're doing a great job. I'm proud of you.'"

Great leaders know that authentic communication is two-way. Leaders don't just talk. They listen.

Leadership principle no. 3: people skills

J. Paul Getty, the great oil industrialist and philanthropist, once said, "It doesn't make much difference how much knowledge and experience you possess—if you are unable to achieve results through people, you are worthless as a leader." Rich DeVos is successful and influential today because he is able to achieve results through people. He has the best people skills of anyone I know.

Rich's people skills spring from his genuine love for people. Writer Frederick L. Collins once observed, "There are two types of people—those who come into a room and say, 'Well, here I am!' and those who come in and say, 'Ah, there you are.'" Rich DeVos is in the second category. He is a genuine lover of humanity.

> *"I love Rich's entrepreneurial spirit. I was impressed by the way he used his yacht and resorts as employee incentives. I started doing exactly the same thing in my company."*
>
> TOM MONAGHAN
> FOUNDER, DOMINO'S PIZZA

A leader with great people skills is always respected and admired by the people who serve under him. You can hear the respect and admiration in the voices of those who serve under Rich DeVos. "Rich always has a positive attitude toward everything in his life, and that rubs off on others," observes Marvin Van Dellen, a friend since high school. "He's a real disciple of Dale Carnegie. Everywhere he goes, Rich makes friends and influences people. There's a magic to his personality, and he has built his empire on that."

"Rich DeVos loves people," agrees Patrick Broski, a longtime employee of Rich and Helen DeVos. "I see him first thing in the morning and it's always, 'Good morning, Patrick!' And it's genuine and enthusiastic. He treats everyone equally, from U.S. presidents to cab drivers. He has a genuine concern for all people."

Rich believes that the way we treat people is crucial to our success as leaders. How does that work? John Weisbrod, chief operating officer of the Orlando Magic, explains: "Many leaders tell their people, 'You need to do this and that in order to make me look good.' And they use intimidation and punishment as motivation to get their people to produce results.

"But Rich teaches that there is a much better way to motivate people to produce results. He says, 'Make sure your employees know you care for them as people, that you care for their families. Treat them fairly and compassionately, and they will be inspired to do their best for you. They will produce so much more for you because they love you and don't want to let you down. Love is a much more powerful motivation than fear of punishment.' That's a valuable leadership insight, and I've never forgotten it."

We'll take an in-depth look at the people skills of Rich DeVos in chapter 6.

Leadership principle no. 4: good character

A leader must have good character in order to inspire other people with his vision for the future. As leadership guru John Maxwell observed, "People buy into the leader before they buy

> *"I resent anyone who says about a nonprofessional worker, 'He is just a mechanic' or 'just a salesman' or 'just' anything—he is a warm, giving, highly complex human being, cast in the image of God himself. He is the backbone of this country. I practically burst with pride in his achievement and respect for what he is."*
>
> Rich DeVos

into the leader's vision."

I once heard General Norman Schwarzkopf speak at an event in Orlando, and he said something that has stuck with me ever since: "People choose their leaders based on character. I judge character not by how men deal with their superiors, but by how they deal with their subordinates. That's how you find out what the character of a man truly is." Rich DeVos has many admirable character qualities: humility, integrity, honesty, compassion, generosity, perseverance, courage. But one of his most outstanding character traits is the one General Schwarzkopf identifies: *respect* for those who serve under him.

I've talked to scores of people who have been in Rich's employ, and they all paint a consistent portrait of a man who respects his people, and who is respected and loved by them. Several people have told me about Rich's visits to the Ada, Michigan, production plant where products are manufactured. He would walk through the facility, greeting people by name, pausing to chat with individuals, asking about their families, taking extra time with those who had a sick spouse or other family problem. His employees would greet him with smiles and a hearty shout of "Hi, Rich!"

The business world is full of bosses. But to the employees of Alticor and the Orlando Magic organization, Rich is not a boss. He's a *leader*—and a friend. The people around Rich DeVos buy into his vision and his leadership because he is a person of strong character.

Leadership principle no. 5: competence

No matter what your leadership arena may be—an organization, corporation, military unit, church or sports team—the people around you will only follow your leadership if they have complete confidence in your competence to lead them. Notice that the first seven letters of the word "competence" are C-O-M-P-E-T-E. The people you lead need to know that you are a *competent* and *competitive* leader. They need to believe that you will fight hard to help them be winners. They need to see that you have the wisdom, skill and experience to shape them into a competent, competitive team.

> *"Rich is a great delegator. He hires you to do a job, then he leaves you alone to go do it. His example has shown me that great leaders don't micromanage details. Great leaders inspire people to do their best."*
>
> John Weisbrod, Chief Operating Officer, Orlando Magic

Rich DeVos has proven that he is a competent leader. He demonstrated his competence and competitiveness through:

1. *A strong track record.* People know Rich DeVos is competent because he has experienced success; people are willing to follow him because he is a proven winner.

2. *The ability to delegate.* Rich doesn't try to do it all himself. He is the visionary, the keeper and custodian of the Big Picture. As a master delegator, Rich trusts other competent people to see to the details, and he holds them accountable to carry out their tasks. Their success becomes his success.

3. *A commitment to excellence.* Rich DeVos sets high but realistic standards for himself and his organizations. He is never satisfied with "good enough." He continually works to improve the services and products of his organizations.

4. *A commitment to continual personal growth.* Rich DeVos is an avid reader, a sponge for new information and innovative ideas. Competent leaders continually have their antennas up for new concepts and trends.

5. *A commitment to hard work.* Rich learned the lessons of hard work early in life, and he always made sure that no one in his organizations ever worked harder than he did. A competent leader continually strives to reach the next level of his or her potential.

6. *A commitment to winning.* Rich loves to compete because he loves to win. One of Rich's friends shared a story with me that illustrates Rich's competitive drive: "One day I was playing tennis with Rich at his home in Grand Rapids. I have to admit that tennis is not one of my favorite sporting activities. When I play, it's more of a pastime than a competition. But Rich plays to win. So as we started playing, he noticed that I was dogging it. He said, 'You don't really want to win, do you?' Well, that spurred me to elevate my game! Rich taught me something that day: Whatever you do, compete to win. Totally align your behavior with your goal."

"Rich is a terrific ping-pong player, and I'm good, too. Even when Rich had his bad heart, he still beat me four out of five times."

BILL BRITT
INDEPENDENT BUSINESS OWNER

Leadership principle no. 6: boldness

If a leader isn't bold, he isn't a leader. A bold leader takes risks and encourages risk taking throughout the organization. No football team ever got to the Super Bowl by punting on every fourth-and-one situation. In military campaigns, victory usually goes to the side whose leaders devise bold, imaginative battle plans. And in the business world, the top corporations are usually those led by bold, innovative executives.

The boldness of Rich DeVos is legendary—and we'll take a closer look at the bold nature of this audacious and enterprising leader in chapter 3.

Leadership principle no. 7: a servant's heart

Shortly after Rich's heart-transplant surgery, we had a meeting of the RDV Sports organization, the parent company of the Orlando Magic. The meeting was held in Grand Rapids. Rich, who was in London recovering from his surgery, joined the meeting by satellite TV. The first item on the agenda was the Magic Fan Attic team store. It had become clear that the store needed to be downsized, which meant the elimination of sixteen jobs.

We debated the issue for about twenty minutes. Rich remained silent throughout the debate. Finally, he spoke up. "This funeral has gone on long enough. It's time for the burial." It was Rich's metaphoric way of saying that it was time to end the discussion and make a decision. Then he asked, "What happens to the sixteen employees who are going to be downsized?"

Several suggestions were offered.

"Whatever it takes," Rich said, "I want them taken care of. Relocate them in the organization if you can. If not, make sure they get severance packages and help in finding new jobs. Just make sure they are taken care of."

Rich didn't personally know any of the people who worked in the Magic Fan Attic, but that didn't matter. He cared about his people, even those he had never met. And he considered himself the servant of his people—not their boss.

I spoke to a Grand Rapids business leader who served with Rich on the board of a charitable organization. This man made a fascinating observation about Rich's leadership style: "If Rich is part of an organization," he said, "and he sees that the leadership in place is performing effectively, he's content to be a follower. He lets others lead. In other words, Rich is not only a great leader but a great follower. He does not feel compelled to take over the proceedings or force his way into the leadership position." This man is describing a rare quality among leaders—and particularly among leaders at Rich's level of success and accomplishment.

"Rich DeVos believes we're all children of God, and he's committed to breaking down barriers of race and color. After the Amway Grand Plaza Hotel opened, he made sure that his hotel manager put plans into effect to hire significant numbers of minority applicants. He wants to make sure that people have opportunities to succeed, regardless of their race or ethnicity."

Paul Collins
Award-Winning Artist

Rich DeVos understands that authentic leadership is not about being the boss. It's about being a *servant*. He patterns his leadership style after the greatest leader—and the greatest servant—of all time: Jesus Christ. Jesus once sat down with the twelve men in his organization and told them what leadership is all about: "You've observed how godless rulers throw their weight around . . . and when people get a little power how quickly it goes to their heads. It's not going to be that way with you. Whoever wants to be great must become a servant. Whoever wants to be first among you must be your slave" (Mark 10:42–44, *The Message*).

If you want to be like Rich, you must lead. And if you want to lead, you must serve. If you don't understand servanthood, you don't understand leadership. Rich not only understands servanthood, he exemplifies servanthood—and that is why he is a great leader.

Chapter Three

Be a Risk Taker!

AFTER SELLING WOLVERINE AIR Service in 1948, Rich DeVos and Jay Van Andel decided they needed a vacation. They had read a book by a man who sailed the Caribbean before World War II. Inspired by dreams of adventure on the high seas, Rich and Jay bought a thirty-eight-foot, wooden-hulled Nova Scotia schooner that was dry-docked in Connecticut. Their plan was to sail down the east coast of the United States to Florida, then over to Cuba (this was in the days before Castro), and then across the Caribbean to South America.

Their schooner (named the *Elizabeth,* which means "God is good fortune") was just barely seaworthy—but Rich and Jay loved every leaking, creaking, peeling inch of her. They assumed that *all* sailboats needed a lot of bailing to keep them afloat! Knowing next to nothing about navigation, they repeatedly got lost and ran aground as they made their way down the East Coast. At one point, they sailed the wrong way up the New Jersey Intracoastal Waterway and got stuck in a swamp.

"We were so lost," Rich later recalled, "that even the Coast Guard couldn't find us! What does it say about your navigational skills if you can't even find the Atlantic Ocean? We ended up way back in the inland marshes, miles from the ocean. The Coast Guard searched all day for us, and when they finally located us, they couldn't believe where we were."

Rich and Jay eventually made it to Florida, bailing and pumping all the way. They set a nightly alarm to wake them after midnight so that they could turn on the bilge pumps. If they failed to do so, the decks would be nearly awash by morning.

Leaving Florida for Havana, Rich and Jay thought they had the leak situation under control. While sailing along the northern coast of Cuba, however, the boat began taking on water. They stopped for repairs, spending two weeks in Cuba while their boat was recaulked. Then they set out to sea once more—and the boat began to sink. The new caulking was even more leaky than the original caulking!

> *"I have seen many people fail because of fear. People are afraid of going into business because they are afraid to take risks. When we started out in the flying business, Jay and I didn't know a thing about flying—and we succeeded. Later on, I bought a boat despite the fact that I had never sailed before. Sure, my first boat sank—but soon I was racing yachts and winning! How can you ever win if you never take a risk?"*
>
> RICH DEVOS

Sometime past midnight, as they wallowed in the Bahama Channel, the *Elizabeth* sprang multiple leaks and began to go down. The bilge pumps strained to keep the boat afloat, but to no avail. Realizing their boat was a goner, Rich and Jay fired flares and blinked SOS messages with their flashlights. At 2:30 in the morning, they were plucked from the deck of their sinking schooner by an American freighter, the *Adabelle Lykes.* Minutes later, the *Elizabeth* slipped beneath the waves.

Living the Adventure

"After the *Elizabeth* went down," Rich recalls, "our friends and family back home thought, *Well, their little adventure's over. They'll come home now.* But Jay and I hadn't come all that way just to turn back. Sure, we'd lost our boat, but we still had a lot of the world to see."

The American freighter dropped Rich and Jay off in Puerto Rico, where they signed aboard a tramp tanker as deckhands. They worked their way to Curaçao in the Netherlands Antilles, then hopped a small plane to Venezuela. From Venezuela, they journeyed through Colombia, traveling by paddle-wheeled steamboat along the Magdalena River, then transferring to a narrow-gauge railroad that took them to the Pacific coast. From there, they traveled all the way down the coast through Chile, where they booked a flight over the Andes to the Atlantic coast, and then they traveled by land and water back to the Caribbean coast.

"That trip changed my life," Rich says. "It taught us both a lot of life lessons that served us well in the years to follow. Every business venture I've been involved in since those days has benefited from the lessons I learned on that once-in-a-lifetime adventure.

"That trip also reinforced one truth that Jay and I already knew: If you're not taking risks, you're not living. You've got to take risks and make your own opportunities. You've got to try new experiences and see what happens. It doesn't matter how old you are, or whether you're rich or poor. You have to leap into life and live the adventure.

"All of life is a risk. When you start a business, you take a risk. Get married, that's a risk. Parenting is highly risky. Making friends is risky. When you take a risk, there's always the chance that you will lose. But if you never take a risk, you forfeit the chance to win, the chance to succeed. So to win, you must risk. If you never gather

> *"Rich DeVos is always living in the present and thinking about the future. He rarely looks back and second-guesses himself. He always focuses on what's next."*
>
> Jerry Tubergen
> Chief Business Advisor

your courage and set off in a new direction, then a day will come when you realize that your whole life has slipped away from you."

If there is one common factor among all successful people, it is a high capacity for risk. Successful people take chances. That doesn't mean they are reckless—far from it. They take *calculated* risks. They gather information and consider the odds. They plan for contingencies. But at the same time, they refuse to be paralyzed by fear and indecision. When it is time to act, they act—and they act boldly.

Life-Changing Risk Principles

Here, then, are some life-changing principles we can learn from Rich DeVos and his sailing adventure:

Risk-taking principle no. 1: be decisive

"You'll never learn to sail by standing on the shore," Rich says. "Make a bold decision and see it through."

Those timid souls who delay a decision until all the facts are crystal clear usually decide too late. Successful people know that the advantage goes to those who decide quickly, firmly and boldly. When you need to make a decision, don't wait to get all the facts. Settle for 75 percent or even 50 percent of the facts. Size up the situation as best you can, take a quick check of your instincts and intuition—then launch out boldly and decisively.

"You'll never have all the information you'd like," Rich says, "but that's okay. Make a decision anyway! Go for it! Be bold! Be aggressive! Don't let your lack of confidence hold you back. Confidence comes from doing."

"Wherever you see a successful business," says management guru Peter Drucker, "someone once made a courageous decision." That can certainly be said of Rich DeVos and Jay Van Andel and their successful company.

> *"There's as much risk in doing nothing as in doing something."*
>
> TRAMMELL CROW
> REAL-ESTATE DEVELOPER

Every decision involves an element of uncertainty and risk. If there was no uncertainty, there would be no need to make a decision. A decision is required precisely because the best course of action is not obvious. Successful people make the best decisions they can, even when the outcome is far from assured.

Decisiveness requires courage and boldness. You must be willing to make a decision, accept the consequences of that decision and keep moving forward. There's no time to stop and wring your hands, wondering if you made the right decision. You must keep looking ahead to the next decision. What if you made the wrong decision? Simple: Make another decision, correct your mistakes and keep moving forward.

The Rich DeVos Guide to Good Decision Making

Over the years of working for Rich DeVos in the Magic organization, I have seen him make many bold, risky, multimillion-dollar decisions. From watching him and talking to him in those moments of decision, I have identified eight principles Rich uses whenever he has a difficult decision to make. These eight principles have made him one of the most effective and successful decision makers of all time.

1. Pray

Prayer is two-way communication, so talk to God and ask him for wisdom—then listen for his answer.

2. Define the Decision That Must Be Made

Ask yourself: *What am I trying to achieve with this decision? What is the problem that must be solved? What are my options?* Avoid looking at the decision in either/or terms. There are often three or more options to any decision, so think creatively and expand your options.

3. Gather Information

Get as much information as possible—but don't wait too long to decide. Avoid getting caught in "the paralysis of analysis." Usually a good decision can be made with considerably less than 100 percent of the available information; 50 to 75 percent is usually sufficient.

4. Make a List of Pros and Cons

This will help you to think clearly and logically about the decision you must make.

5. Listen to Your Instincts and Intuition

This does *not* mean, "Trust your feelings." Feelings are never a good substitute for clear-eyed analysis. But most decisions are improved by listening to your intuition as well as your logic.

6. If Still Undecided, Consider Your Worst-Case Scenario

What is the worst thing that can happen if you decide this way or that way? Considering your worst-case scenario will help you identify the uncertainty and anxiety that keep you from deciding—and it will bring clarity to your thinking.

7. Seek Counsel from Trusted Advisors

Proverbs 11:14 (KJV) tells us, "In the multitude of counselors there is safety." Sometimes an outside perspective can bring clarity to the situation. You don't have to take the advice of other people, but it is wise to listen and at least consider it.

8. Make a Decision

Don't stall, don't procrastinate—*decide.* Then act on your decision and trust the guidance God gave you in answer to your prayer.

Theodore Roosevelt once observed, "In any moment of decision, the best thing you can do is the right thing. The next best thing is the wrong thing. And the worst thing you can do is nothing." The successful person looks at a problem that everyone else calls "impossible" and sees only a bold decision that needs to be made. In fact, here's a good rule of thumb for successful decision making: *The bolder the decision, the more successful the outcome.* Alvin Toffler, author of *Future Shock,* put it this way: "It is better to err on the side of daring than the side of caution."

If you want to be like Rich DeVos, then don't wait to strike when the iron is hot; make it hot by striking! Don't worry and fret about whether you're on the right track or not; just make your own track! Be bold, be decisive—and you'll become a little more like Rich.

Risk-taking principle no. 2: be flexible

"On that Caribbean trip," Rich says, "I learned the importance of improvising and adjusting to changing conditions. If your boat sinks, learn to swim. If a door slams in your face, open a window. When you face a challenge, be flexible. Use your ingenuity. Don't say, 'Oh, no! An obstacle! An impossibility! What do I do now?' Instead, say, 'Oh, boy! A challenge! An opportunity! Here's a chance to see how creative I really am!'"

My son David is a sergeant in the United States Marines and a frontline veteran of Operation Iraqi Freedom. The Marines have two mottoes—one official, one unofficial. The official motto is *Semper fidelis,* or "Always faithful." The unofficial motto is *Semper gumby,* which means "Always flexible." In other words, the Marines are like Gumby, that flexible clay animation puppet on TV. Marines are creative, adaptable, eager to try new approaches and methods. They bend and stretch any which way to get the job done.

"I'm staggered by the story of Dad and Jay sailing the Caribbean in that leaky boat. They didn't know a thing about sailing, but they went out on the open sea! What were they thinking? If my kids ever do anything like that, I'll knock their heads together!"

Doug DeVos, Rich's Youngest Son and President of Alticor

You can't be successful if you're stuck in a rut. You can't be like Rich if you are rigid and inflexible. Does Rich DeVos set schedules, agendas and objectives? Absolutely! Is he a slave to schedules, agendas and objectives? Absolutely not! When an opportunity or a human need comes up, Rich is quick to shift gears, quick to change direction, quick to flex.

If there's one thing that is constant in life, it is change. Life is full of surprises. If you are rigid and stubborn about sticking to your schedule and your agenda, you are doomed to frustration. But if you are always open to change, if you don't let surprises throw you, then you'll be able to adjust and adapt to whatever comes your way. As Chuck Smith, senior pastor at Calvary Chapel of Costa Mesa, California, has so wisely stated, "Blessed are the flexible, for they shall bend and not be broken."

So if you want to be like Rich, then *semper gumby!*

Risk-taking principle no. 3: don't let others stomp out your dream

Remember the Sinatra song, "That's Life"? One line talks about people (and I'm sure you've met a few) who think it's fun to stomp on other people's dreams. The world is full of dream stompers. Many of them go around stomping on other people's dreams out of envy, because they have no dreams of their own. Don't let them get you down. Stay true to your dreams. Take risks for your dreams. Make your dreams come true. Imagine how good you'll feel when you accomplish the very goal that everyone was telling you couldn't be done!

Rich DeVos puts it this way: "There is never a shortage of people who stand on the sidelines and tell you, 'It can't be done!' There are plenty of people who think they are doing you a favor by telling you to give up and stop trying. Sometimes they don't have to tell you in words—the look in their eyes or the tone of their voice is enough to discourage you. Don't listen to those people! Don't be afraid of their criticism or rejection. Don't let them plant their fears in your mind. If you have a dream, dare to believe it, dare to do it, dare to make it come true. If God has lit the flame of a dream inside you, don't let anyone stomp it out.

"The greatest assets you own are your dreams. Don't let anyone take them from you. Associate with others who support your dreams and can help you make them come true. Whatever your dream, always believe you can do it."

Risk-taking principle no. 4: think "I can!"

Henry Ford once said, "If you think you can or you think you can't, you're right." Bestselling author Harvey Mackay put it another way: "Optimists are right. So are pessimists. It's up to you to choose which you will be."

When you take a risk, make sure you do so with an optimistic, "I can!" attitude. Optimists have the confidence, enthusiasm and energy to achieve successful outcomes. Pessimists are defeated before they start, because they go into a risky situation with an attitude that says, "This probably won't work. My goal is really not attainable. I'm probably going to fail." If you begin a venture with self-imposed limitations in your thinking, then you are starting out with two strikes against you and a fastball coming straight at your head.

"Dad is an entrepreneur. Risk taking and hard work are in his blood. Dad has never had a boss in his life, so he has a hard time thinking like an employee because he's never been there. It's hard for him to understand the security-versus-risk struggle of the normal guy. To him, you are not really living unless you're taking a risk."

DICK DEVOS
RICH'S OLDEST SON

So begin with an attitude of "I can!" Your "I can!" is more important than your I.Q. Your "I can!" may be just the edge you need to turn your dream of success into a reality.

Rich DeVos recalls, "My father always taught me to believe in the unlimited potential of individual drive and effort. When I was a boy, every time I said, 'I can't,' he'd stop me and say, 'There's no such word as *can't*.' He was right! Think about it: Is there a good use for the word 'can't'? Not one! 'I can't' is a self-defeating statement; 'I can' is a statement of confidence and power."

Risk-taking principle no. 5: learn the lessons of failure

When you take a risk, you have to accept the very real possibility of failure. In fact, if we live as risk takers, we will *certainly* fail from time to time—but failure is never final unless we fail to learn from it. Proverbs 24:16 (NIV) tells us, "Though a righteous man falls seven times, he rises again." That is the Rich DeVos story in a nutshell. Though he is one of the most successful men who ever lived, Rich knows what failure is like. Before he and his friend, Jay Van Andel, founded Amway Corporation, they suffered a string of failures.

Immediately after their schooner, the *Elizabeth,* sank in the Caribbean, Jay and Rich began laying plans for their next big business venture. They decided that, on their return to the States, they would open an import company to bring wood carvings from Haiti into the United States. They pursued this new venture with great optimism and youthful energy—and their import company fell flat on its face!

> *"I wouldn't have applied to Princeton if I hadn't learned to take risks. Grandpa inspired me to be a risk taker. That's how he lived his life. He always tells us, 'Go for it!'"*
>
> Elissa DeVos, Rich's Granddaughter (Dick and Betsy's Daughter)

Next, they opened an ice-cream shop—which promptly failed. After that came a factory that produced wooden rocking horses—and again they failed. At this point, Rich and Jay probably began to wonder why they ever sold Wolverine Air Service and the Riverside Drive Inn—the only businesses in which they had truly succeeded. They had failed as sailors and as entrepreneurs—yet they didn't let failure keep them down.

"I look at failure this way," Rich says. "Failure is a learning experience. You learn much more from failure than from instant success. So when you fail, you should learn everything you can from your failure. If you learn a billion-dollar lesson from a million-dollar flop, then it was well worth it—a cheap education. You just have to approach failure with a teachable attitude."

To Rich and Jay, failure was just a learning experience on the way to greater success. They knew that with perseverance, imagination and courageous risk taking, they would succeed again. And—as the Alticor story has proven—they couldn't have been more right.

So if you want to be like Rich, if you want to experience success and assert a positive influence over the people around you, then *be bold!* Take risks! Live the adventure!

Chapter Four

Speak Up!

KIM BRUYN HAS KNOWN Rich DeVos for more than twenty years. "I met Rich DeVos in 1982," she says, "when I joined Amway Corporation in the public relations division. Rich was president of Amway at the time, and I had the privilege of being part of the team that traveled with him across the country as he spoke to thousands of independent business owners. I also worked with Rich in various other PR capacities, and I learned a lot from him about the art of communicating vision, energy and enthusiasm to other people."

Rich DeVos's entrepreneurial spirit—always evident in his inspirational and motivational approach with people—was contagious. After a sixteen-year career at Amway, Kim left and soon started her own marketing communications and public relations firm. Today she heads a successful Grand Rapids PR firm, and continues to work with Rich and Helen DeVos on their many projects as well as with other clients. One of the most lasting impressions she has of Rich DeVos is his ability as a public speaker. Kim shared with me one memory of Rich DeVos that particularly stands out in her mind.

> *"Rich DeVos is the best public speaker I've ever heard—even better than Ronald Reagan. When he speaks, people get excited about life, excited about America."*
>
> John C. Gartland
> Former Amway Corp. Executive

"Rich DeVos was the keynote speaker at a Chamber of Commerce luncheon," she recalled. "The luncheon was held in a hotel. Hundreds of businesspeople were on hand to hear the success secrets of the self-made billionaire. I was one of several longtime Amway Corp. executives who rode with him by helicopter to the event. As we cruised above the treetops on our approach, I noticed that Rich DeVos seemed totally relaxed. He wasn't a bit fazed or nervous about speaking before a crowd of people.

"Before the helicopter set down, he took his notes from his coat pocket. Those notes consisted of nothing more than a few talking points jotted on the back of an envelope. He gave them a quick glance, then slipped them back into his pocket.

"Rich DeVos never spoke from a text or a typed outline. An envelope or single folded sheet of paper with a few handwritten talking points was all I ever saw him use when he gave a speech. He had been giving speeches that way since he first began motivating crowds of Nutrilite vitamin distributors in the 1950s. His ability to motivate people through public speaking undoubtedly goes back even further, to the days when his rousing speeches got him elected president of his high school class.

"The structure of his speeches was simple: three main points, a number of powerful stories, and a conclusion. The titles of his speeches were also simple, such as 'Try or Cry' and 'The Three A's: Attitude, Action and Atmosphere.' He joked that all of his speeches were really the same speech with different titles, because whenever he spoke, his theme was always the same: encouraging and motivating people to be their best.

"As Rich DeVos got up before the crowd, he was introduced with a long list of impressive achievements and titles. But as he stood up before the crowd and waited for the applause to fade, I didn't see a man who basked in the glory of his own achievements. Instead, I saw a man who seemed remarkably humble. 'Thank you for that generous introduction,' he said. 'But before I begin, you should know who I really am. I'm a sinner saved by grace.'

"Rich was the senior class president in high school. I remember him preparing his graduation speech entitled 'What Does the Future Hold?' He rehearsed it over and over, and Dad was there, giving him pointers on his posture, movements and voice."

JAN COURTS
RICH'S SISTER

"Then he turned his head to the right and to the left, taking in the whole expanse of the dining room. Then he joked, 'I've given a lot of speeches on the rubber chicken circuit, but this is my first speech on the rubber *neck* circuit!'

"Within thirty seconds, Rich DeVos had made a personal connection with everyone in that room. Those businesspeople knew that this was a man of genuine humility with a down-to-earth sense of humor. For the next half hour, the audience forgot that they were listening to one of the most successful men on the planet and a member of the *Forbes* list of 400 richest Americans. In those moments, he was just plain Rich, as modest and unassuming as any next-door neighbor.

"The theme for his talk was 'Life Enrichers,' about how each of us can enrich the lives of other people. He told stories about the impact of our words and actions on other people. He talked about people who steal the dreams of others and people who encourage others to follow their dreams. He shared stories about his own successes and setbacks. He closed with a story by Charles Swindoll about a schoolteacher who encouraged a troubled student from a broken home to succeed and become a doctor.

"After the speech, I stood by the door as people filed out. I overheard many animated conversations of people who were fired up about making a difference in the lives of their employees and colleagues. I saw a number of people dabbing at their eyes with handkerchiefs, clearly moved by Rich DeVos's powerful stories. Many of those people had come to learn how to make more money. They left with a burning desire to make a difference in people's lives."

> *"Dad uses his speaking skills to improve the lives of others. When he speaks, he transfers hope to people."*
>
> Doug DeVos, Rich's Youngest Son and President of Alticor

How to Talk Like Rich DeVos

Like Kim Bruyn, I've had the privilege of hearing Rich DeVos give many speeches. Without a doubt, he is the best communicator I have ever heard. In one-on-one communication settings, he's a wise counselor and a good listener. In small group settings, such as an NBA All-Star chapel, he is warm, engaging and inspiring. In front of a huge Amway rally, he commands respect and rivets the attention of a crowd of forty thousand people.

The success and influence of Rich DeVos is due, in no small part, to his extraordinary ability as a public speaker and a storyteller. No one can reach Rich's level of success by his own efforts alone. To get billion-dollar results, you must be able to work through people, inspire people and motivate people to make your dream a reality. Your personal and professional success is determined largely by your ability to speak before an audience.

Tom Michmershuizen, a longtime employee, now retired, who started in Amway's early years, told me, "I have never heard a better speaker than Rich DeVos. During the first decade of Amway's existence, people in the order department could tell when Rich was on a speaking tour because there was always a bump in sales volume in every city he visited. Jan Mangnuson, who was in charge of sales forecasting at Amway, always wanted to know where Rich was going to speak so he could load up the warehouse in that area. As an area coordinator, I often traveled with Rich and I always came back happy because our sales volume reached a new high every time he spoke."

Down through the years, the spoken word has not only moved sales. It has moved nations, changed history and reshaped the world. America's greatest presidents and statesmen have always been great communicators. L. William Seidman, a former accountant for Amway and economist in President Ford's administration, told me, "I wanted Rich to run for president back in the early 1980s, but he declined because of the health problems he was undergoing at the time. I'm sure he made the right decision, but he would have been a credible candidate and a real factor in the race—and he would have made a great president. I have never seen anyone communicate like Rich DeVos, Ronald Reagan included. Rich communicates with people and inspires them. And he can really sell."

I've had the opportunity to watch Rich speak many times. I consider myself an accomplished speaker—I average 150 public appearances per year, and I'm listed with the top 100 speaking agencies in America. But when I hear Rich speak, I realize how much I have to learn! Rich's speaking skills

"Rich has an infectious sense of humor. He always opens a meeting with a funny story that breaks the ice and lets people know they can relax and enjoy what he has come to share with them."

EDWIN MEESE III
FORMER U.S. ATTORNEY GENERAL

have given an incalculable boost to the Orlando Magic, as both a sports organization and as a basketball team.

Mick Smith, the strength coach of the Orlando Magic, recalls, "Before my first game with the Magic, Rich DeVos came into the locker room. I looked at him and thought, *Average looking guy, nice suit, shaking hands all around, seems like an okay guy.* Then he got up in front of the team and began to speak. I thought, *Wow! This guy really connects!* He said, 'We're all family. I love you guys, and if there's anything you need, I'm here for you.' When he got through talking, I felt like I'd been in church."

Bob Hill, former Orlando Magic assistant coach, told me, "I coached with head coach Brian Hill for a year in Orlando. Bob Vander Weide hosted a dinner for the team at his house before the season opener in Miami. Near the end of the evening, Rich DeVos asked if we would all go into the living room so we could talk for a while. He spoke to the team about what it takes to be successful. You could look around the room at those players and see their imaginations catch fire. What a send-off! We went to Miami and just killed the Heat! Shaquille O'Neal scored thirty-six points alone! I can't help thinking that Rich's speech had a lot to do with it."

> *"It amazes me to watch Rich speak. He'll jot six words down on a small piece of paper, then give a forty-five-minute speech on those six words. He's so effective at moving people, inspiring people and challenging them to do their best. And he's equally effective speaking before any age group."*
>
> Betsy DeVos
> Rich's Daughter-in-Law (Dick's Wife)

Former assistant coach Tom Sterner remembers 1995, when our young ballclub got to the NBA finals. "At the start of the playoffs," he says, "Rich came in to speak to the team. The club was nervous and anxious because of the pressure, but when the players saw how calm and confident Rich was, they really settled down. Rich focused his talk on playing hard and enjoying the experience, not on winning. He said, 'I respect you guys, and I love you.' Then he paused and said, 'Why not us? Why not now?' Well, that riveted their attention. They all jumped up and picked up the refrain, 'Yeah! Why not us? Why not now?'"

Richie Adubato, former coach of the Magic, remembers that meeting. "'Why not us? Why not now?' That phrase really fired up the team. Rich understood that when you get a shot at a championship, you go for it *now,* because you may not get another shot at it. Rich really inspired us and motivated us with that talk. Even though we lost to Houston in the finals, we had a great run and we played hard. Rich's speech was the jump-start that fired us up to play at a very high level for such a young team."

> *"Rich is captivating because he is knowledgeable on so many subjects. I could sit and listen to him endlessly."*
>
> BRUCE HEYS, RICH'S NEPHEW

Rich loves to inspire and motivate at all levels. Jill Grzesiak, Rich's executive assistant, shared this story with me: "Rich's ten-year-old grandson, Dalton, was playing in a football game. His team lost and all the kids were standing around, depressed and dejected. Some were crying. Rich gathered the team around himself and said, 'Look, guys, failure is nothing to be ashamed of as long as you learn from it.' He gave them quite a pep talk, and when he was finished, the kids got right back on top of things. The transformation was amazing."

How to Speak Effectively

If you want to inspire and motivate like Rich, then you need to learn to talk like Rich. The ability to speak effectively before an audience can transform your life. Here are ten powerful principles of effective public speaking that I have learned from observing my friend, Rich DeVos.

Public-speaking principle no. 1: be prepared!

As you prepare your speech, be aware of the difference between written communication and spoken communication. If you want to convey details, statistics and data, it is better to put that information into a written form, such as a handout or flyer. But if you want to inspire, persuade and motivate people, you've got to give a powerful speech. So when you prepare your speech, avoid a lot of mind-numbing facts and statistics that your listeners will never absorb. Instead, focus on broad, visionary ideas, persuasive concepts and riveting stories.

Above all, never be boring! Make sure that every concept in your speech crackles with energy. Never plan to start out slow and gain momentum. Instead, grab your listeners by the throat from the very first word and don't let go! Wow them, dazzle them, knock 'em dead in the first thirty seconds—and keep knocking 'em dead until your big finish!

> *"There is no more important skill in life than the ability to communicate well—and Rich DeVos is a great communicator."*
>
> Gerald R. Ford
> Thirty-Eighth President
> of the United States

As you prepare your speech, think about who your audience is and what they want to learn or gain from your talk. Avoid overloading your audience with too much information. Focus your talk on three memorable principles that you want your listeners to remember long after your talk is over.

Rehearse your speech until you feel comfortable with it. On the day of your speech, arrive early, walk around the room, sit in the seats and get a feel for the room from the audience's perspective. Before you go on stage, take a few minutes to compose your thoughts, concentrate on your notes and exercise the deeper ranges of your voice (the deeper your voice, the more authoritative you'll sound). Concentrate on positive, confident thoughts.

When you rehearse, time your speech. Make sure you can start on time and end on time. Never overstay your welcome—always leave 'em wanting more.

Public-speaking principle no. 2: speak in a relaxed, conversational style

Never read your speech; have a spontaneous dialogue with your audience, as if you are speaking friend-to-friend. The more spontaneous you sound, the more the audience will like and trust you. Instead of writing out your speech word-for-word, use brief phrases or symbols as notes to jog your memory. Your notes should only give you an outline, not a script.

Retired Amway executive Bob Kerkstra says, "I have never heard any speaker who could capture an audience like Rich DeVos. Several years ago, he spoke at nearly two hundred meetings in a twelve-month period, and each speech was unique and different from the rest. He does not write his speeches. Instead, he speaks on a theme or subject from a single piece of notepaper with no more than a half dozen cue words on it. The only part of a speech he will ever write down verbatim is a list of people he wants to acknowledge—it's important to Rich that he gets people's names correct when he speaks. Other than that, his speeches all look and sound very informal and spontaneous, more of a conversation than an oratory."

> *"Rich's speaking skills built Amway."*
>
> Dexter Yager
> Independent Business Owner

Here are a few pointers to help you feel and look at ease in front of an audience: Speak naturally and conversationally. Put your hands at your side, not clasped in front of you in the "fig leaf" position (a posture that communicates insecurity and fear of the audience). Relax, be yourself—and you'll put your audience at ease.

Paul Conn is president of Lee University in Cleveland, Tennessee. He is also a writer who has worked with Rich DeVos, so he knows him well. "As a speaker," says Dr. Conn, "Rich is prepared, but the crowd feels his talk is spontaneous and original just for them. Rich is loose enough and confident enough in front of an audience to speak extemporaneously, and to lay in those little rim shots. When a speaker is that relaxed and confident in front of an audience, the audience can relax and enjoy the message."

John Brown, a former Amway executive, agrees. "Rich DeVos is a mesmerizing, spellbinding speaker," he says, "because he's so confident and comfortable on his feet in front of an audience. His speaking ability is a significant part of the company's success. He has an incredible capacity for putting people at ease and enabling people to see qualities and abilities in themselves that they never knew they had."

Public-speaking principle no. 3: practice good "eye communication" habits

Don't just glance hurriedly over your audience. Let your eyes make a two- or three-second connection with various people around the room as you speak. Let people know that you are speaking directly to them.

Grand Rapids physician Dr. Oliver Grin has listened to Rich speak many times. "If there is one thing about Rich DeVos that is more remarkable than his *verbal* skills," he says, "it is his *nonverbal* skills—especially his eye communication. Even when speaking to an audience of thousands, Rich makes eye contact in a way that makes you feel he is talking only to you. When he speaks, it doesn't seem like a speech. It seems like a conversation."

> *"Rich DeVos is a visionary. He sees things that are invisible to most of us. When he speaks, whether to groups or individuals, he lifts people up to see his vision."*
>
> JACK KEMP
> FORMER U.S. CONGRESSMAN

Public-speaking principle no. 4: move around!

Motion gets attention. Motion conveys energy and enthusiasm. Though you speak with your mouth, you should communicate with your entire body. Use big, expressive gestures to make a point. Use your hands, your facial expressions and your body to underscore, italicize and headline your message. The larger the room, the more expansive your gestures should be.

Get out from behind the lectern and move around the stage as you speak—or even out into the audience. Don't just talk *at* people—engage them in conversation. Invite questions, interaction and dialogue, even in the middle of your talk. When you invite audience participation, you increase their emotional involvement in your message.

"Dad hates lecterns," says Rich's son, Dick DeVos. "He refuses to stay rooted to one spot when he speaks. He has to move around and gesture with his hands. He loves to come down from the stage and get right on the same level with his audience. He doesn't like open space between himself and the first row. Dad has to have that personal connection."

"The first time I heard Rich speak," Paul Conn recalls, "I was twenty-nine years old, and he was addressing a company rally in

Minneapolis. It was a typical enthusiastic, high-energy crowd, with four or five thousand people present. While Rich was on stage speaking, a little old lady yelled out some word of encouragement to him. The crowd reacted enthusiastically.

"At that point, Rich came down from the stage, walked into the audience, pulled that lady to her feet and kissed her lightly on the cheek! Then he leaped back up onto the stage. Pandemonium reigned. Rich's timing was perfect. He did it just right, rewarding the lady for her exuberance—very smooth and classy. It was a great showbiz moment because Rich has a spontaneous touch. That was almost thirty years ago, and I don't remember much of what Rich said that night, but I do remember what he did."

Public-speaking principle no. 5: communicate with energy!

When you speak, your face—and, in fact, your whole personality—should radiate energy, enthusiasm and conviction. Your voice should resonate with energy. Your eyes should gleam with energy. Your smile should dazzle with energy. While it's true that some people have naturally energetic personalities, we can all learn to be more energetic and dynamic when we speak. Speaking skills can be taught, coached and learned, and one of the most important skills of all is the skill of communicating with energy.

> *"Rich DeVos is a marvelous speaker. He has an amazing ability to move and inspire people with words alone."*
>
> Gen. Alexander M. Haig Jr.
> Former U.S. Secretary of State

Mike Jandernoa is chairman of a Michigan-based pharmaceutical company and a Grand Rapids business leader. He says, "Rich DeVos's greatest strength as a speaker is his ability to emotionally connect with an audience. He touches people emotionally, transmits his own energy to them. He gets them enthused and motivated to take action and do something with their lives. Rich has an amazing communicating gift."

Public-speaking principle no. 6: become a storyteller

Stories create a powerful emotional connection with your audience. Use funny stories to loosen up your audience and put your listeners at ease. Use dramatic stories to generate strong emotions and empathy. Good stories ignite the hearer's imagination and make your point memorable, even unforgettable. Stories imprint images on the listener's mind and trigger strong emotions. All the great communicators of history have been great storytellers—from Jesus to Lincoln to Disney to JFK to Reagan to Rich DeVos.

Wayne Huizenga, owner of the Miami Dolphins, recalls, "I had always heard of Rich DeVos, but had never met him until he spoke at the Mayor's Prayer Breakfast in Fort Lauderdale. I took my office staff with me and we sat in the front row. When I heard Rich speak, I thought, *Wow! He's fantastic!* He shared his faith, and he was very inspirational and motivating. The most powerful thing about his talk was the stories he told. One of his stories brought tears to my eyes."

"Rich is an excellent speaker and an excellent storyteller," says U.S. Congressman Vern Ehlers. "He can make you laugh one moment and cry the next. He is so persuasive because he is such a great storyteller." Alticor employee Josie Luster-McGlamory agrees: "I've learned from Rich DeVos that it is powerful to use stories and parables in public speaking. Stories make it easier to hold people's interest and get your point across with emotion and power." It's true. If you want to be successful, influential and persuasive like Rich, then become a storyteller.

Public-speaking principle no. 7: vary your voice pattern

A monotone voice is boring and puts audiences to sleep. Your voice should rise and fall with the rhythms of your speech. The air in the room should tingle with the energy and enthusiasm in your voice.

Speak in a firm, clear voice that says you mean what you say. Eliminate words from your speaking vocabulary that make you seem tentative and uncertain, such as "uhhh," "ummm," "well" and "you know."

Put the "power of the pause" to work for you. Mark Twain once said, "The right word may be effective, but no word was ever as effective as a rightly timed pause." You can use a pause to quiet a restless room, to underscore an important point or to allow the audience to enjoy a comedic moment. A dramatic pause creates a moment of anticipation, adding a powerful punch to the next words you speak.

> *"Rich DeVos does many things well, but he is probably at his best as a public speaker. He crisscrosses the country by private jet, speaking at occasions ranging from small high-school graduations to gigantic sales rallies which fill massive auditoriums."*
>
> Paul Conn
> President, Lee University

Public-speaking principle no. 8: demonstrate genuine caring

Show your audience that you genuinely care about them and their needs. If your "caring" is just an act, it will show. But if you truly enjoy serving and helping people, if you take the time to truly address their needs in your speech, you will win them over and they will love you.

One thing that audiences always sense in Rich DeVos is the genuineness of his love for people. He truly wants the people in his audience to experience a full, rich quality of life. Inner-city pastor

Orlando Rivera put it this way: "I once attended an Urban Leadership Conference at Hope College in Holland, Michigan. Rich DeVos spoke to us as a group—but when his speech was over, he stayed around and talked to us individually. He took the time to learn all of our names. He didn't come just to give a speech. He actually sat down with us and shared his life with us. We came away knowing that he hadn't come just to write a check to start a project and give everyone a pep talk. He was deeply committed to improving lives. This was genuine caring—not a gimmick."

Longtime Amway employee Joan Williamson recalls, "Rich DeVos always read the Christmas story from the Bible at the Christmas employee meeting—it was a tradition. Rich continued that tradition even after his heart transplant. At the Christmas party after his surgery, Rich walked into a packed auditorium to do his annual reading—and everyone got up and gave him a standing ovation that went on and on. It was very emotional, and there were lots of tears. It was an outpouring of love. We all wanted to show our love for Rich, because we all knew that he genuinely loved and cared about all of us. How many executives ever get to experience that kind of love from their employees?"

> *"Some speakers communicate to the mind. Rich reaches the heart. Though he speaks with emotion, his speeches are logically constructed and easy to follow, point by point. Rich's sincerity rings through because his belief is so strong."*
>
> Jerry Meadows
> Independent Business Owner

Public-speaking principle no. 9: train yourself to be a more effective speaker

We can all sharpen our speaking skills; we all have room for improvement. After giving literally thousands of speeches over the years, I still ask for coaching and feedback from professional speech trainers. There are many training programs for speakers available, from weekly Toastmasters meetings to intensive executive training programs. As you train, make sure you get feedback from a speaking coach on both your strong points (natural abilities you can highlight and strengthen) and your weak points (problem areas you can work on and change). Be teachable and receptive because feedback and coaching enable you to achieve peak performance.

Rich DeVos gives credit to his first speaking coach for pointing his career in the right direction. "When I was in my twenties," Rich recalls, "I took the Dale Carnegie speaking course from a man named Walt Bass. Everyone should take a Dale Carnegie course. My entire family has taken it.

"My 'Eureka!' moment as a speaker came just days after I took that Carnegie seminar. We had a Nutrilite convention in Chicago with about three thousand people there—including Mr. Bass himself. I used all the pointers Walt Bass taught me, and I closed my speech by asking everyone to stand for prayer. After I prayed, the audience stayed on their feet and cheered. I was stunned by that response. Mr. Bass came up afterwards and said, 'You have a great gift and a great future as a speaker.' And that's how it all started."

> *"Rich is a rare communicator in that he is comfortable in the limelight, yet he is also very humble. The limelight doesn't control Rich. He controls the limelight."*
>
> PAUL GORDON
> GRAND RAPIDS BUSINESS LEADER

Another valuable tool for sharpening your speaking skills is video feedback. Rehearse your speech in front of a video camera. When you watch the playback, you'll be able to see yourself as others see you. You'll identify both communicating strengths and bad habits you never knew you had. At first, you'll wince at your flaws and flubs, but stick with it and you are guaranteed to see improvement in your performance. Video feedback will make you aware of your own communicating behavior. As you improve, your confidence level will shoot skyward.

Public-speaking principle no. 10: never pass up an opportunity to speak

If you want to be successful and influential, then grab every speaking opportunity that comes your way. If no opportunities come to you, then make your own opportunities. No speaking opportunity is too small or too large. Whether you are offered a chance to talk to a dozen Rotarians in West Overshoe or an audience of millions on network TV, seize it! Make the most of it! That's what I do, that's what Rich DeVos does, and that's what you should do, too.

Construction sales executive Ken Koldenhoven says, "I heard Rich DeVos speak at a community fund-raising event in Grand Rapids some twenty years ago. I still remember all the main points in his speech—it was that memorable. I saw Rich recently in Orlando and I asked if he could give a talk in honor of several faith-based ministries in central Florida. I thought he would probably give me a polite turndown. To my surprise, he readily accepted. I realize now that I shouldn't have been surprised, because that's the kind of generous leader Rich DeVos is."

Conquer Your Number-One Fear

You may say, "I've tried public speaking, and I can't do it! My knees knocked and my teeth chattered all through my high-school speech classes! I have stage fright and microphone fright like you can't believe! It's hopeless!"

Well, if that expresses your emotions about public speaking, you're not alone. According to *The Book of Lists* by David Wallechinsky and Amy Wallace, the number-one fear that people face is the fear of public speaking. Amazingly, the fear of death is way down the list at number seven! This astounding statistic prompted comedian Jerry Seinfeld to remark, "Studies show that fear of public speaking ranks higher than the fear of dying. I guess this means that most people at a funeral would rather be in the coffin than delivering the eulogy."

"I had just started my pizza business when I heard Rich DeVos speak at a Jaycee event in Michigan. I have never heard a greater speech before or since. I didn't consider myself a public speaker—I was very shy. But I decided I wanted to be as successful with Domino's as Rich was with Amway. So I became a public speaker, and I've given hundreds of speeches since."

Tom Monaghan
Founder, Domino's Pizza

I can certainly identify with such fears. I vividly remember my early classroom experiences with public speaking in Miss Barbara Bullard's ninth-grade English class. She had us prepare our speeches on a single 3"x 5" card. Her intention was to force us to speak from brief notes, not a word-for-word script. But I was so afraid of forgetting my speech that I wrote my entire speech on that card in microscopic lettering. When I got up in front of the class, I couldn't even read what I had written—and I froze in front of the class like the proverbial deer in the headlights. It was one of the most disastrous, embarrassing experiences of my entire adolescence. Looking back, I'm amazed that I ever got up to give a speech again!

But in my junior year at Wake Forest University, I took two crucial classes—Introduction to Speech and Oral Interpretation of Literature. In those classes, I began to realize that getting up and talking in front of an audience could actually be *fun!* Soon I was giving speeches at every opportunity, and I even had my own live interview show on the campus radio station. Since college, public speaking has been a huge part of my life, and I have given thousands of speeches in venues both large and small. Conquering my fears and learning to communicate before groups was a dramatic turning point in my life.

I have found that there are two sure-fire ways to conquer the fear of public speaking:

First, *know your material.* Rehearse your speech until you can give it confidently and convincingly in your sleep. If possible, come up with a number of "stump speeches" that you can deliver again and again to different audiences with only slight variations. Much of the fear of public speaking is due to the fear of forgetting your message and losing your place, of stammering and sweating while you grope for words. When you have your talk down pat, this fear disappears.

Second, *perform with an air of utter confidence.* If you don't *feel* confident, don't worry about it. Just *fake* it. No matter how nervous you feel inside, put your shoulders back and stand tall—a posture that communicates confidence and conviction. *Act* as if you have all the confidence in the world, and soon you will *feel* confident and at ease. Psychologists tell us that *feelings follow behavior.* So behave confidently, and the feelings of confidence will follow.

Speaking coach Ty Boyd, founder of Ty Boyd Executive Learning Systems in Charlotte, North Carolina, offers a fascinating

> *"Rich is reluctant to discuss his obvious charisma as an on-stage speaker. 'Aw, most of what I say I've borrowed from other people anyway,' he declares. Maybe so. But whether he is explaining the Amway sales plan or preaching free enterprise to the National Association of Manufacturers, he leaves those who hear him with an experience they won't soon forget."*
>
> PAUL CONN
> PRESIDENT, LEE UNIVERSITY

insight into one of the legendary public speakers of our time. "Let's talk about President John Kennedy," he says. "When JFK spoke, his voice rang with authority. He connected with his audience, the American people, so powerfully that he is still quoted, decades later. But did you know that when he spoke, his knees were shaking? A friend of mine was a Secret Service agent during the Kennedy presidency. Every time JFK got behind the lectern, my friend was standing right behind him and, as the young president juggled tough questions with apparent ease and won us over with his confident smile and self-assured words, his knees were shaking—every single time. Did his fear make him less effective in communicating with us? History has already judged that one for us, wouldn't you say?"

So if you want to have success and influence like Rich DeVos, then speak up! Conquer your fears! Communicate your vision! Motivate and energize the people around you! Learn to talk like Rich, and there is no limit to how far you can go.

Chapter Five

Be Wise!

THE YEAR 1995 WAS the worst year of my life. That was the year my first wife told me she was leaving me. In December of that year, we decided to handle the divorce quietly and amicably, without the mess and publicity of a court hearing. But just a week after we had made that decision, I received a phone call from my attorney. "Pat," he said, "we've been filed on." Once the divorce papers were filed with the court, the case of *Williams v. Williams* became a matter of public record.

I was devastated. One of my biggest fears was what the media would say about the divorce once the matter became public. I decided to get a preemptive statement out to the press instead of waiting for the reporters to come to me. I spent the entire Friday after Christmas working out a statement. I wrote up several drafts, showing each draft to various friends to get their input.

By the end of that day, I had structured a beautifully written press release. There was just one more person I wanted to show it to: my good friend and advisor, Rich DeVos. As it turned out, I could have saved myself hours of work if I had just gone to Rich first.

"It's a wise man who knows he can't do everything by himself. Rich DeVos never thought he knew everything in all areas. Instead, he would always get the right people to work for him, and then he would let them do their jobs."

Boyd Hoffman
Longtime Friend of Rich DeVos

After reading my written statement, he looked at me and said, "You don't need to say all of that. You only need three sentences: 'My wife has filed for divorce today. I regret this deeply. The children are with me and know they are loved and cared for.' That's all you have to say."

That was some of the wisest advice I have ever received.

To See Life from God's Perspective

What is wisdom?

Many people mistake *intelligence* for wisdom. But being smart doesn't make you wise. There are many people in this world with Mensa-level IQs, but with little or no wisdom. They may understand all the complexities of quantum physics or Keynesian economics, but when it comes to making wise decisions about relationships or morality, they are utterly clueless.

Many people mistake *cleverness* for wisdom. But being clever doesn't make you wise. A clever politician can fool enough people to get elected and reelected, but only a wise politician makes decisions that improve the lives of this generation and generations to come. A clever author can write a sleazy potboiler that sells a million copies, but a wise writer creates literature that touches hearts and changes lives. A clever investor can make a fortune in the commodities market, but a wise business leader builds a company that benefits society and provides meaningful employment for his workforce.

Many people mistake *knowledge* for wisdom. But being knowledgeable doesn't make one wise. So if wisdom is not intelligence or cleverness or knowledge, what is it?

The Jewish philosopher Baruch Spinoza defined wisdom as the ability to see all things from the viewpoint of eternity. In other words, it is *the ability to see life from God's perspective.* Obviously, only God can truly see *all* of life from the eternal perspective. As Isaiah 40:28 (NIV) tells us, "Don't you know? Haven't you heard? The Lord is the eternal God, Creator of the Earth. He never gets weary or tired; his wisdom cannot be measured." That is why we cannot truly become wise without immersing ourselves in the thoughts of God, as found in his Word, the Bible. "The Law of the Lord is perfect," says Psalm 19:7 (NIV). "It gives us new life. His teachings last forever, and they give wisdom to ordinary people."

> *"Read the book of Proverbs. That's where real wisdom is. You can only have wisdom when you know the Lord."*
>
> RICH DEVOS

"Read the book of Proverbs," Rich himself once said. "That's where real wisdom is. You can only have wisdom when you know the Lord."

Rich DeVos is a man of great wisdom. He is blessed with an amazing ability to understand problems and arrive at sound, fair solutions. He can sit in a meeting, sort through all the flying verbiage and conflicting ideas, then quickly and wisely move the entire group to a course of action. I believe that one of the reasons Rich DeVos is so wise is that he has devoted his life to discovering the thoughts of God, as found in the Word of God. Again and again, when we face a critical situation in the Magic organization, Rich will quote a Scripture verse from memory—and that Bible passage invariably contains the solution to the very problem we are wrestling with.

A wise person who can see life from an eternal perspective is able to live a more effective and successful life. Why? Because he sees life with clarity; he sees reality as it truly is rather than filtering reality through a haze of wishful thinking. A wise person is able to anticipate and avoid life's pitfalls. He is better equipped to manage crises and solve problems.

Wisdom is demonstrated by the way a person responds to times of trial and suffering. Rich DeVos has lived with severe health problems for many years, having suffered with diabetes, congestive heart failure and two strokes. Many people go through far less and end up full of bitterness and self-pity. "Why do all of these things happen to me?" they ask.

But Rich went through these trials without complaint or self-pity. Why? Because he is a man of wisdom. He is able to look at his problems, as Spinoza said, from the viewpoint of eternity. He is able to see his life from God's perspective, so he knows that the trials he is going through now are of little importance compared with the fact that he is going to know God and be with God throughout eternity.

"If you have faith, you learn to die," Rich says, reflecting on his health crisis and his heart transplant. "And once you have learned to die, you are ready to live. If you know God, if you have accepted Christ and you know that he has accepted you for all eternity, then the fear disappears. At that moment, you are free to live. It is fear that keeps people from truly living. Faith liberates you from fear so that you can live the life God intended you to live."

Those are wise words, expressing the eternal view—God's perspective on life. The wisdom of Rich DeVos enabled him to make firm, effective, clear-headed decisions about his life and health. "When Rich was confronted with a major decision concerning his health," recalls one of his physicians, Dr. Larry Feenstra, "he didn't hesitate. He was decisive in what to do and then didn't back down. He remained firm in his conviction, which is pretty true of his entire life."

A person with true wisdom—the eternal view of life—has a

different view of time and the flow of life. Rich's friend, Paul Conn, recalls, "One time I was vacationing with Rich and some other friends in the Caribbean. The service in the restaurant was slow, because all the businesses there run on 'island time.' Rich heard a few of us complaining and he said, 'Sure, the service is slow here—but that's the pace of the islands. Isn't that why we came down here? Don't we want to relax and not be so uptight? We all need to slow down and gear down our lives for while.' He was right, of course. And that has given me a whole new view of life and what it means to enjoy each moment as it comes. If we all could borrow Rich's 'life goggles' and see life the way he sees it, we would be much wiser people."

> *"Rich DeVos gives good advice because he has wisdom. It's not book wisdom from psychology books or Dr. Phil on TV. It's godly wisdom that comes from experience and faith. That wisdom allows Rich to see into the heart of a situation. Most of the time, he simply goes with his gut and with his faith—and his decisions and advice are 99 percent accurate."*
>
> CAROL CUNNINGHAM
> LONGTIME EMPLOYEE OF
> RICH AND HELEN DEVOS

Rich applies the same wisdom to his businesses, including his sports franchise, the Orlando Magic. "I brought a friend to a Magic game one night," Rich recalls. "It was the first time he had ever been to an NBA game. He saw one of our players miss two free throws and he said to me, 'How can you pay a player 10 million dollars and he can't even make his free throws?' Well, that made a lot of sense. So I told that story to the players one night and I challenged them to take their time and focus on their shots. I said, 'If you make your free throws, we'll win our division. So don't feel rushed, just take your time. It's all a matter of focus.' After that, we started making more free throws."

How to Be Wise

How can you become wise? While it is true that you can find a great deal of wisdom tucked away in books, you will never become wise merely by reading about wisdom. And though the word *philosophy* literally means "love of wisdom," a university degree in philosophy is not enough to make you wise. I am fairly certain that no one ever became wise by watching television, going to the movies or surfing the Internet.

Some people say that wisdom comes with experience. Yet I know many people who are very experienced yet also very foolish. Clearly, experience alone doesn't make a person wise.

I am convinced that true wisdom is the result of deliberate choices we make. No one acquires wisdom by accident. Wisdom must be desired, sought out and pursued. Wisdom is not a gift. It is a prize that must be won by hard effort.

Some people say that wisdom comes from making mistakes, but that's only partly true. Many people foolishly make mistake after mistake and never acquire wisdom. If we want to become wise, we must make a deliberate, conscious decision to *learn* from our mistakes and to never repeat them. We must also learn from our *successes,* building on the things we have done *right,* learning principles of wisdom and achievement that will serve us well in the future.

Equally important, we must learn from the mistakes and successes of others. That means we must learn from the lives of others, reading the books of wise people, sitting under the teaching of wise people, seeking out wise people to be our mentors and coaches. If we want to be wise, then we must associate with people who can share their experience, sound judgment and wisdom with us. As we read in Proverbs, the book of Old Testament wisdom, "He who walks with the wise grows wise, but a companion of fools suffers harm" (Proverbs 13:20, NIV).

If we want to be wise, we must learn to be good listeners. Dave Van Andel, Jay's youngest son, told me, "Rich DeVos is a great listener, and that has made him smart and it's made him wise. He has the ability to listen to other people and learn from them. His great listening skills are both a source of wisdom and a sign of wisdom." Neil Offen, president of the Direct Selling Association, agrees. "Rich DeVos is one of the wisest people I know, and he's a great listener. He's always open to new ideas and new insights. He keeps his antenna up all the time. When he listens, he gives you his full attention, and he genuinely considers your viewpoint."

Finally and most importantly, if we want to become wise, we must go to the source of all wisdom, God himself. Knowing Rich DeVos as I do, I can testify that he goes to that source every day, drawing wisdom directly from God through Bible study and prayer. I am convinced that the wisdom of Rich DeVos comes in no small part from the fact that he lives by the wise truths of God's Word—truths such as this one: "For the Lord gives wisdom, and from his mouth come knowledge and understanding" (Proverbs 2:6, NIV).

If you want to be wise like Rich DeVos, then do as Rich does: Desire wisdom, seek wisdom, pursue wisdom, and go to God in prayer, asking for the wisdom to live an effective, successful, godly life. "If any of you lacks wisdom," says James 1:5 (NIV), "he should ask God, who gives generously to all without finding fault, and it will be given to him."

So be like Rich. Be wise! Go to the source and ask for wisdom, and God will supply your need.

"Rich DeVos is one of the wisest, most godly men I know. There is a Rich DeVos quotation that I use all the time in my preaching: 'Friends may come and go, but enemies accumulate.' In other words, it's a wise person who avoids making enemies in the first place."

Dr. Robert A. Schuller, Vice President
Crystal Cathedral Ministries

Chapter Six

Be a People Person!

SHORTLY AFTER RETURNING HOME from their trip to South America, Rich DeVos and Jay Van Andel became distributors of Nutrilite food supplements. They learned the principles of multilevel marketing. The started their own direct-sales company, naming it after themselves—the Ja-Ri Company. They recruited other people to sell Nutrilite products as independent distributors, and they built a sales organization of over 5,000 people.

In their early days selling Nutrilite, Rich and Jay had one product, a food supplement called Double X, which retailed for $19.50 per box. In those days, when the average breadwinner earned around $100 a week, it took a lot of confidence and salesmanship to sell such a product. But Rich and Jay were good at selling and motivating others to sell, and their distributorships were generating good revenues.

In the late 1950s, internal squabbles threatened the existence of Nutrilite. Rich and Jay watched as Nutrilite's sales slipped and saw their own profits disappearing as a result. To protect themselves, they founded Amway as a means of expanding their product line and reducing their dependence upon Nutrilite.

> *"To be like Rich, you must have a genuine love and interest in people and then take the time to be with them. So many times with wealthy, powerful men, you feel as if you're a pawn in their game. You never get that feeling with Rich."*
>
> JOHN VARINEAU, ASSOCIATE CONDUCTOR, GRAND RAPIDS SYMPHONY

When Rich and Jay founded Amway in 1959, Rich's father, Simon, gave him some advice: "Always do right by the people who work with you. They have placed their trust in you. Don't ever do anything to hurt them."

Simon DeVos knew what it felt like to be hurt by an employer. He had spent years working for a large electrical firm—only to be let go as he approached retirement age. Rich had seen the hurt in his father's eyes when that happened, and he vowed never to do harm to any of his employees.

Tom Michmershuizen, who was hired by Rich in 1962, recalls, "Rich honored the advice his father gave him. There was never a layoff at Amway until the early 1980s—and the workers in that layoff were treated with dignity and kindness." People always come first with Rich DeVos and Jay Van Andel.

"Tell Me About *You*!"

To Rich, there is no such thing as a stranger. The person you or I would call a "stranger" is merely a friend Rich hasn't met yet. "When Dad sees someone new," Rich's son Doug told me, "he doesn't hesitate to walk right up, introduce himself and strike up a conversation. When we had a place in Holland, Michigan, a home was being built next to ours. Dad said, 'We've got new neighbors. Let's go get to know them.' So we all went over and introduced ourselves. As it turned out, they were from Grand Rapids. We've seen them every summer since and we've become friends."

One of Rich's physicians, Dr. Luis Tomatis, recalls watching Rich interact with people a year after his heart-transplant surgery. "Rich was back at Harefield Hospital in London, sitting in a crowded little waiting room before his checkup. The waiting room was jammed with people, most of them common laborers. Rich engaged all of them in conversation: 'Hi, my name is Rich. What do you do? Oh, you're in farming? Well, how is it going on the farm? How are the crops this year?' When he saw the nurses, he'd ask them, 'Are you married? Do you have children? What are their ages?' Rich shared his goodwill with people, and nobody thought Rich was intimidating or intrusive or too forward. They were pleased that he was interested in them, and they wanted to talk to him."

> *"When Rich DeVos asks, 'How are you doing?' he always waits for an answer. He sincerely wants to know. Even when you meet him for the first time, you can tell that he genuinely cares about you. I call him 'Uncle Rich,' and I love him because he's the real deal!"*
>
> CYNTHIA SMITH
> FORMER ORLANDO MAGIC EMPLOYEE

"I travel with Rich a lot," says Joe Elliott, one of Rich's aides, "so I see how he interacts with people all the time. Once Rich went to the Amway Grand Plaza Hotel, entering through the back way. It took him an hour to walk through the employees' cafeteria because he paused and talked to every worker he saw. These were all minimum-wage people, but he greeted them like royalty. He praised them and asked them questions. 'This looks great! It must be hard to keep this so clean. How do you do it?' Rich would rather talk to maids and busboys than to so-called celebrities. People were buzzing for days about that. Rich loves to spend time talking to people who usually don't get the recognition."

Swiss Infeld, longtime chef at the Amway Grand Plaza Hotel, told me, "Rich comes into the kitchen, puts his arm around my shoulder and says, 'How are things going? I appreciate what you do for us.' On several occasions, we have catered parties at the DeVos home. Rich always comes out to the catering truck and talks to our staff. He praises the food and the service, and he tells us how much he appreciates what we do. He treats us as if we were as important as his guests."

Vicki Weaver, president of a Grand Rapids hospital foundation, told me, "Rich is always focused on others. He makes everyone feel important, from presidents to cooks. He walks into a room and gives you a big hug. He makes sure everyone hears, 'You're an important part of my team. I appreciate everything you do.'"

> *"The moment you see Rich, you want to go over to him and shake his hand—but you're too late! He's already coming over to shake your hand."*
>
> Max DePree
> Bestselling Author and Former CEO of Herman Miller, Inc.

Former Michigan State Senator and Grand Rapids businessman Glenn Steil told me, "Back in the early 1980s, my wife Barbara and I went on a business trip to Europe with a group of other people. One day, we were having lunch at a little restaurant in Italy. We were sitting alone when Rich came over and invited us to sit with him and his family. I was acquainted with Rich at the time, but didn't know him well. When the meal was served, Rich said, 'Let's hold hands.' He asked God's blessing on the food and thanked the Lord that we were all together sharing a meal. Barb and I have never forgotten being invited into his family circle. After that day, I have always felt close to Rich."

Rich's niece, Jayne Hodgson, says, "People are drawn to Rich because he genuinely cares about other people. He is sincerely interested in what is going on in your life. He is fascinated by every person he meets. You give a person a wonderful gift when you just give them your complete attention, your caring and willingness to listen—and that's the gift Rich gives to people."

One of Rich's pilots, Danny Hamby, told me, "I remember one incident that shows you exactly the kind of person Rich DeVos is. I was part of the flight crew that had flown Mr. and Mrs. DeVos home after their fiftieth anniversary party. After everyone else had left the tarmac, Rich remained behind, even though his car was waiting for him. I walked over to him and said, 'Is there anything I can do for you, Mr. DeVos?' He said, 'I just wanted to thank the captain for a good flight home.' He was patiently waiting on the tarmac so that he could express his gratitude to the crew. It may seem like a small thing, but it's the sort of courtesy you rarely see from people of his importance. Little gestures like that are an inspiration to me and others who come in contact with Mr. DeVos."

Former associate Dan Smith recalls, "Rich tells about getting up early one day to meet the garbage man and tell him what a great job he was doing and how valuable he was. The garbage man thought Rich was putting him on. Rich said, 'No, I mean it. You're not "just a garbage man." You make life better for everyone. Think what would happen to this neighborhood, to this city, if you didn't do your job!' Rich believes that everyone is important, that everyone's job is significant and that people should be told that they are appreciated for what they contribute."

Again and again, as I interviewed people who know Rich DeVos, I heard them say, "Rich sat across from me, looked me in the eye and said, 'Tell me about *you*.'" I must have heard that from two or three dozen people. It's Rich's patented approach to connecting with people and getting to know them, getting them to open up and talk about themselves. I asked Rich's sons about this, and Dick DeVos said, "Dad loves to hear people's stories. He says, 'Tell me about you,' and this draws people out so that he can get to know them. We sometimes warn people not to get nervous when Dad starts his questions."

"Dad develops instant relationships with people," adds Rich's son Dan. "He is fascinated by people, and that question is a shortcut to getting to know people. When you say, 'Tell me about you,' you invite people to talk about whatever is most important to them—what they care about, what they dream about, what they hope for, what they fear. It's a brilliant question. It's the key that unlocks another soul."

"The idea for that question," Doug DeVos says, "came from sailing. We had just gotten a big new boat, and Dad would talk about that boat to anyone who would listen. One of our neighbors at the marina had a new boat, but it was much smaller. It occurred to Dad that this man wanted to talk about his new boat, too. So Dad went to the guy and asked him about his boat, and they had a long talk about sailing.

"From that experience, Dad figured out that everybody enjoys talking about themselves, and he also realized that he enjoys listening and learning about people. That's why he asks people, 'Tell me about you.' It's his way of getting the conversation going. Dad says, 'It's not hard to get people to talk about themselves. You just have to ask them. I'd much rather hear new stories from people I've just met than to tell my old stories again and again.'"

> *"In restaurants, Rich always greets the servers and asks for their story. If they are immigrants, he asks how they came to America and how life is working out for them. He always talks to the people who are usually ignored—the janitors, the busboys, the bellhops, the cleaning ladies—and he gives them a word of encouragement."*
>
> P. J. and Ann Shooks
> Friends of Rich DeVos

One person who has received the "tell-me-about-you" treatment is *Grand Rapids Press* reporter Greg Johnson. "When Rich DeVos purchased the Magic in 1991, he flew the Grand Rapids media down to Orlando for the press conference. When I sat down across from Rich on the plane, I thought, *I'm going to get a great interview!* So we talked, and Rich asked all the questions. When the day ended, it hit me: *Hey! Rich spent the whole trip interviewing me! It was supposed to be the other way around!*"

Eric Musselman, former Magic assistant coach and now head coach of the Golden State Warriors, recalls, "Mr. DeVos made a big impression on me during my three years with the Orlando Magic. He would walk around the arena an hour before tip-off, and he would greet everybody in the place with a big smile—arena workers, ballboys, fans, everybody. 'Hi! I'm Rich! What's your name? I'm so glad you're here tonight!'

"Then he'd go to the locker room and speak to the team, always with passion and enthusiasm. The players were totally focused the whole time he spoke, and you could feel the emotional lift his presence brings. He would always end with, 'I'm so proud of you guys!' And the team would go out on the floor, ready to slay giants for Rich DeVos."

David Nicholas, senior pastor of Spanish River Church in Boca Raton, Florida, told me, "One night, I went to a Magic home game with Rich. He had invited some of his home staff and one of the women's sons, two handymen and their wives, and his Haitian gardener, Ernest. Before the game, we went to a restaurant for dinner. Rich sat between me and Ernest. When it was time for dessert, Rich got up and got a big piece of carrot cake and two forks. He said, 'Ernest, you didn't eat much tonight. Let's do this together.' And he put the carrot cake between them. So there were Rich and the gardener, eating dessert together off the same plate. When I think of Rich, that picture always comes to mind."

Reaching out and getting to know people is the way Rich lives the adventure of life. When people share their lives with him, Rich feels that the whole world opens up to him. Elissa DeVos, Rich's granddaughter and the daughter of Dick and Betsy DeVos, told me a story that illustrates Rich's fascination with people and their worlds. "Our family was on the boat in the Marquesas Islands near Tahiti," she recalls. "Grandpa Rich befriended this old man who lived in a hut on the beach. This man had a big smile, but only two teeth. He knew the island like the back of his hand, so Grandpa hired him to be our guide to a waterfall in the middle of the island. The rest of us didn't really want to go tramping over the island in search of a waterfall, but Grandpa talked us into it.

"So this old man led us to the waterfall, and it was the most beautiful spot. We all have memories of that day to last us a lifetime—and it's all because Grandpa loves to meet people and find out about them. Most people would never bother to make friends with a toothless man on the beach, but Grandpa Rich makes friends with everyone he sees. The people he meets always lead him to exciting discoveries, like that perfect day at the waterfall."

"Rich is a student of people," says son-in-law and Orlando Magic CEO Bob Vander Weide, "and he studies people by talking to them. At one time, the corporation had a private island in the Caribbean called Peter Island. There was a staff of two hundred people who worked at the hotel and resort there. They were island people. Whenever Rich went to Peter Island, he would walk the island and talk to all of them. He was like a magnet—the people of the island were attracted to him and flocked around him. He would say, 'How are you doing? How is your family? Are there any problems you want to talk to me about?' They adored Rich and couldn't wait for his visits."

"If you go shopping with Rich, you'd better allow plenty of time. When he shops, he stops and talks to all the clerks. He makes friends wherever he goes."

PAM DEVOS
RICH'S DAUGHTER-IN-LAW (DAN'S WIFE)

Dr. Rick McNamara, one of Rich's Grand Rapids physicians, offered a similar memory of Peter Island. "One time my wife and I were vacationing on Peter Island," he said. "Rich wasn't with us, but he invited us down for a vacation. We took a walk and passed an islander who was tending the flowerbeds. We stopped to admire his work, and he started talking to us about the island. Smiling broadly, speaking in broken English, he said, 'The man who owns this island has a very big heart. He makes you feel warm from the inside.' The gardener didn't know who we were, but he wanted us to know about his employer."

Rich is truly a people person. Everywhere he goes, he makes new friends and builds instant relationships. He makes people feel warm from the inside.

Is the ability to relate to people a talent, something you're born with? Or is it a skill, an ability that you can learn, practice and improve? In Rich's case, it was probably a bit of both. As his sons pointed out, the ability to talk to people and get to know them was a skill he consciously worked on. He taught himself to become aware of people, to seek them out and greet them, to ask them about themselves. It started as a learned skill, and with practice Rich raised it to an art form.

"I've learned to be a pretty good listener," Rich told me. "I start my conversations with the question, 'Tell me about yourself.' That takes care of the next hour. People love to talk about themselves. I just listen. I may toss out a few more questions, but people will go home and say how brilliant I am. I'm not brilliant. All I did was listen.

"When we have family or friends over, we'll play a game we call 'Your Turn in the Box Tonight.' We'll be on the boat and we'll pick one person to be in the box. If it's your turn in the box, you tell us your life story. It's amazing to discover how little we really know about each other, even our best friends. We can learn so much just by listening."

"How Can I Help You?"

"Rich DeVos is the greatest man I've ever met. He cares so much about others, about all of mankind. Many people will greet you and say, 'How are you doing?' But when Rich asks, he really wants to know."

MARIA DEVOS
RICH'S DAUGHTER-IN-LAW (DOUG'S WIFE)

These days, everybody communicates by e-mail. Like most people, Rich has a computer and an e-mail address, and he checks his e-mail on a daily basis. But if you send Rich a message by computer, don't expect a computerized reply. More likely, you'll get a phone call and hear his cheery voice say, "Hi! I'm answering your e-mail!" At the very least, he'll send you a handwritten note and sign it, "Love ya!—Rich." All around the country, hundreds of people have Rich's "Love ya!" notes posted on their office walls or refrigerator doors.

It's not that Rich is a technophobe who resists modern technology. Rich has always been fascinated by new technologies and new ways of doing things. But to Rich, it seems cold and impersonal to just tap-tap-tap on a keyboard and press "SEND." He's a people person, and he'd much rather make that personal connection and hear your voice on the phone.

If you want to be like Rich, then you've got to be a people person, too. Rich DeVos has a genuine love for people. He enjoys being around people, and he treats everyone with equal attention and respect. Rich's love for people is yet another key to his enormous success and influence. People sense that his caring is genuine, not an act. And when people know that a leader genuinely cares about them, they respond with respect, enthusiasm and extra effort. Rich's love for people builds teamwork and a shared sense of mission and purpose—and that translates into success.

I once spoke to an organization in Newport News, Virginia, the naval base area. After my speech, I was approached by a young man in a navy uniform. Grinning broadly, he shook my hand and said, "Pat Williams, I'm in business with Rich DeVos. We're teammates." I knew exactly what he meant. He was an independent business owner, and he was out there building his business from the boondocks to the boat docks of Newport News.

The next time I saw Rich DeVos, I told him that story. "Wow!" Rich said. "That's the Alticor story in a nutshell. We're all teammates!" Nothing makes Rich DeVos happier than to help other people succeed in life.

> *"Rich DeVos is a humble, down-to-earth man. He talks to you like a friend. He never dominates or intimidates people. He knows how to fit in with all types of people."*
>
> Rodney Powell, Orlando Magic Equipment Manager

Paul Conn told me, "Once I was with Rich in Libreville, Gabon, on the west coast of Africa. We had landed at a small airfield, and a young African man in his early twenties came to refuel the plane. Rich got out to stretch his legs, and he began chatting with the young man. 'Mr. DeVos,' the young African said, 'my dream is to go to the United States and get an education. I want to become a pilot. Could you please help me?' Rich told him to get his travel papers ready, then contact him by mail.

"Weeks after we returned to the States, I remembered the incident and asked Rich if the young African had ever contacted him. 'Oh, yes,' Rich said. 'I linked him up with the right people and he's in the States right now, going to school.' In time, the young man achieved his dream and became a pilot. It was a chance encounter at a remote airport, but that young man's life was forever changed. Rich loves to help people who want to succeed."

Karen DeBlaay recalls, "My mother, Bernice Hansen, was one of the first independent business owners and has known Rich and Jay almost since the beginning. In 1995, my mother and her second husband Ralph were vacationing in a condo in Fort Lauderdale. They had enjoyed a wonderful day together—then that night, Ralph suddenly died. As you can imagine, my mother was in shock. She was hundreds of miles from home, facing dozens of decisions while her mind was numb with grief.

"She called Rich and told him what had happened. He immediately set everything in motion. He sent me and my two sisters to Florida on the company's largest plane so we could all be together, and he flew us all back to Michigan along with the casket. In a time of loss, people don't know what to do or where to turn. Rich really cares about people, and he made sure that all the details were taken care of."

> *"In 1976, I was severely injured in an auto accident. The first call I received in the hospital was from Rich DeVos."*
>
> TONY RENARD
> INDEPENDENT BUSINESS OWNER

Rev. Dr. David Kool is director of Jubilee Ministries, a Christian community development organization in Holland, Michigan. He recently shared this story with me: "Rich DeVos was the keynote speaker at a Partners for Christian Development dinner. One of the entrepreneurs our organization helped was an African-American business owner, Doug Wolverton. Doug had taken a few wrong turns in his life and had come out of prison, but he had opened a cleaning business in Holland, Michigan, and was making a new start. Doug had won a copy of Rich's book, *Hope From My Heart,* and at the end of the evening, he asked Rich to autograph it for him. That night, they struck up a friendship.

"It turned out that Doug's business was just down the road from Rich's house in Holland, so Rich would stop by every so often to see how Doug was doing and to offer him encouragement and support. It was great to see Rich taking the time to connect with Doug and help him along the path to success. Rich has been a blessing to the work Jubilee Ministries is doing, just as he has been a blessing to all the people he has helped to pursue their dreams of success in the business world."

L. William Seidman has known Rich for many years, and he can testify that Rich has a big place in his heart for people who are working hard to succeed in business. "Rich's essential message," he says, "is this: 'We can all go further and achieve more than we think.' He spreads this message wherever he goes. What's more, he lets people know that he's in their corner, rooting them on, encouraging them and motivating them. The theme of Rich DeVos's life is, 'How can I help you?'"

Rich DeVos reminds me of a man in the New Testament, a biblical "people person" named Barnabas. We meet Barnabas in Acts 4:36–37 (NIV), which tells us: "Joseph, a Levite from Cyprus, whom the apostles called Barnabas (which means Son of Encouragement), sold a field he owned and brought the money and put it at the apostles' feet." From this one sentence, we learn a lot about Barnabas, including these facts: (1) He was a man of influence, because he was a Levite, a member of the priestly tribe of Israel; (2) he was a wealthy man, because he was a landowner; (3) he was a generous man, because he sold a piece of land and gave the proceeds to the church; and (4) he was well-known for the way he encouraged and helped the people around him, because the church leaders changed his name to Son of Encouragement. Wherever Barnabas went, he left a trail of people who had been encouraged, empowered, energized, motivated and inspired.

If ever there was a modern-day Barnabas, it is Rich DeVos—a man of influence, wealth and generosity, and one of the most encouraging and inspirational human beings I have ever known. Everywhere Rich goes, people are encouraged and inspired to reach for their dreams and to experience the abundant life that comes from faith in Jesus Christ. "You need to tell people how you feel about them," he says. "You need to say, 'I believe in you,' 'I respect you,' 'I trust you.' Put those words in your vocabulary and incorporate them in your daily conversation. I tell my children and staff, 'You can do it better than I ever did it,' and I mean it! When people receive that kind of encouragement, they can do anything."

> *"Rich's love for people and his vision to help them be the best that they can be has deeply affected me and my personal outlook."*
>
> C. Everett Koop
> Former U.S. Surgeon General

Longtime Amway employee Joan Williamson affirms this picture of Rich DeVos. "We have been living with a family crisis," she told me. "Our granddaughter has been very sick for the first year of her life and has spent most of that year in the hospital. Whenever Rich sees me he asks, 'How is the baby? We're praying for her.' He has encouraged and uplifted our entire family through this ordeal."

One way Rich encourages people is by empowering them, trusting them to make decisions and being patient with them when they make mistakes. He knows that mistakes can be powerful tools for learning and growth, and he wants to make sure that people learn and benefit from their experiences. Here's an example of how Rich is an encourager even to people who make expensive mistakes:

When Rich was president of Amway Corp., he had an employee who had numerous duties, including managing the annual renewal of Amway distributorships. Under the standing policy, distributors had to renew their Amway business affiliation every January. At the beginning of every year, the office was flooded with thousands of renewals. So this employee came up with an idea that allowed distributors to send in their renewals several months early, which relieved a lot of pressure in January.

When Rich learned of this change in the renewal policy, he went to this lady and asked her if she knew what this policy change would cost. "Oh, it won't cost the company any extra money," she said.

> *"Rich reads people well. He has a feel for them. He sizes them up and trusts them. He trusts his gut, and he's rarely wrong."*
>
> PAUL CONN
> PRESIDENT , LEE UNIVERSITY

"Oh?" said Rich. "By my calculation, it's going to cost the company about $75,000 a year."

The woman's heart sank. "But how can that be?" she asked.

Rich took pencil and paper and showed her that the new policy created a loophole that enabled distributors to get eighteen months' worth of membership at a twelve-month price every other year. Projected cost: $75,000 a year.

"I can see what you were trying to accomplish," Rich said, "and we really do need to do something about that paperwork blizzard every January, but we need a less expensive solution."

Rich handled the situation gently—yet the employee still felt terrible, knowing that her decision had cost the company such a huge sum of money. After Rich left the room, she cried and felt so depressed that she went home early.

The next morning, when she returned for work, she found a vase with a dozen red roses on her desk—a gift from Rich DeVos. Along with the roses was a card of encouragement signed by Rich. The lesson for you and me? If you want to be like Rich, then be an encourager—especially when people make mistakes.

True Generosity

It is easy for a rich man to write a check and pass himself off as a generous man. But the real test of a person's generosity is this: Is he willing to share his *time?* Is he willing to share *himself?* Rich DeVos is not only generous with his money. He is generous with

"I have been with the DeVos family for forty-five years. Rich DeVos cares for people, and it doesn't matter whether you are the top dog or the underdog. He cares about everyone."

HELEN VERBURG
EMPLOYEE OF RICH AND HELEN DEVOS

his time. Why? Because he genuinely cares about people.

Paul Conn, the president of Lee University, recalls, "Rich and Helen DeVos once came to our campus for a luncheon event. We met their plane at the Chattanooga airport and drove them back to the campus in Cleveland, Tennessee. As we drove, I said, 'Rich, our daughter Vanessa attends Lee, and she's going to be at the luncheon. But our younger daughter Heather is in high school, and she's upset that she can't get out of school to hear you speak.' Rich said, 'Well, it's only eleven A.M. now, and the luncheon isn't until noon. Why don't we swing by the high school so I can visit with Heather?'

"So we drove to the high school, and we trooped into the office. Rich walked up to the secretary and said, 'Hi, I'm Rich, and we're here to see Heather Conn.' The next thing we heard was, 'Heather Conn, please report to the office.' Minutes later, Heather arrived, and Rich greeted her with a big hug and chatted with her for a while. Then we headed on to the event.

"That was almost fifteen years ago, and Heather is grown up now, but she still talks glowingly of the time Rich DeVos went out of his way to visit her at her school. Rich does things like that all day long for people—encouraging people, investing in people, making them feel special. He cares especially about future generations, and he gives generously of his time to build up young people."

Longtime sailing friend John Bertrand tells a similar story. "I was out on Annapolis Harbor in a small runabout, watching my twelve-year-old son, Alex, during his after-school sailing practice. We went past a 175-foot yacht that was anchored there, and I realized it was Rich's boat, the *Independence.* Rich and Helen were onboard. I motored up to say hello, and Rich invited me aboard. I told him I was watching Alex go through his sailing program, and he said to bring Alex aboard when he was finished.

"So Alex and I went aboard and visited with Rich and Helen. Then Rich gave Alex the tour of his yacht. It was my first time aboard the *Independence,* so I tagged along. Rich treated my son like royalty. It was a forty-minute tour, and he showed Alex everything. Alex is fascinated with sailing, so he drank it all in. Rich treated him like the most important person in the world, and my son will never forget it. Nor will I."

There Are No "Little People"

Advice columnist Abigail Van Buren ("Dear Abby") once observed, "The best index to a person's character is how he treats people who can't do him any good." In other words, a person of character treats everyone the same, whether they are rich or poor, powerful or powerless, famous or anonymous. Rich DeVos lives by the biblical adage found in James 2:1–4 (NIV):

"My brothers, as believers in our glorious Lord Jesus Christ, don't show favoritism. Suppose a man comes into your meeting wearing a gold ring and fine clothes, and a poor man in shabby clothes also comes in. If you show special attention to the man wearing fine clothes and say, 'Here's a good seat for you,' but say to the poor man, 'You stand there' or 'Sit on the floor by my feet,' have you not discriminated among yourselves and become judges with evil thoughts?"

If you want to be like Rich, then you've got to be a "people person," the kind of person who loves all people, not because of what they can do for you, but simply because all people are made in God's image and deserve your respect and caring. Here is what people say about the way Rich DeVos treats people:

Gary Vos, Grand Rapids Construction Executive:

"There are no 'little people' in Rich DeVos's world. Rich works through people, and he values everyone, including those whom others would call 'little people.' Rich won't forget them because they are important to him."

Jim Payne, Amway Executive:

"Rich has the ability to walk into a room filled with kings or paupers and make all of them feel special. He treats everybody with dignity and respect."

Gordon Loux, Corporate Fundraiser:

"Rich DeVos treats all people equally. He makes everyone he meets feel important. He looks you in the eye and tells you how much he appreciates you and what you have done. Rich treats each person he meets like a child of God."

Joan Williamson, Longtime Amway Employee:

"Rich DeVos is the ultimate 'people person.' He always makes everyone feel special. Whether he's talking to an executive or the janitor or gardener, he says, 'The job you do is important to Alticor's success. Keep up the good work!' He makes everyone feel special and valued, and that motivates us to keep doing what we're doing, and to do it well."

Carol Cunningham, Longtime Employee of Rich and Helen DeVos:

"Rich takes time to validate people by cheering them on. We all need that. People need to know they have worth and value. Wherever he goes, Rich is always affirming someone, whether it's the maid at the hotel or a top executive. He tells people, 'You're doing a great job! Keep it up!' That makes their day."

Arie Goudswaard, Amway Employee:

"Rich DeVos doesn't care about your station in life. To him, everyone is a human being, entitled to dignity, respect and a kind word. If you perform

well, he'll praise you. If you don't perform to the level you are capable of, he will hold you accountable for doing better next time. We sometimes forget that holding people accountable is a caring thing to do. Rich doesn't care about your wealth, race, religion, appearance, intelligence or talent. He cares about you as a person."

A Genuine Love for People

Has success changed Rich and Helen DeVos? Ask Bud Berends or any other longtime DeVos friends. "There are ten of us couples," says Bud, "and we're all friends since high school. We have been getting together for monthly potluck dinners, year after year, for more than fifty years. Rich and Helen rarely miss. They are the same people they were when Rich was just out of the service, selling Nutrilite. Success hasn't changed them a bit. Their old friends are still an important part of their lives."

Rich's son Dick confirms Bud Berends's observation. "That potluck is important to Mom and Dad because their friends are important to them," he says. "Mom and Dad bring their casserole dish like anyone else, and they can't wait to get together with the people they love. Dad never forgot where he came from or who his real friends are. He's a true 'people person.'"

One of the attitudes that makes Rich DeVos such a "people person" is that he does not let barriers come between him and other people. To him there is no such thing as an age barrier or generational barrier; he is equally at ease talking to teenagers and golden agers. There are no racial or ethnic barriers in his mind; he sees every human being as a person made in the image of God. There are no economic or class barriers; he relates equally well to both rich and poor—and perhaps that is because he has

> *"Rarely do you find such generosity of spirit and singleness of purpose in one man. People are usually either generous or they are ambitious. Amazingly, Rich DeVos is both. His goal is to share his spirit with you, not to impress you with his success, wealth and power."*
>
> Rick Breon
> Grand Rapids Health-Care CEO

been rich and he has known poverty.

There are not even any barriers of ideology and politics in Rich's mind, despite the fact that he has very strong ideological and political opinions himself. As Paul Conn notes, "There's only one thing Rich can't do and that's get in the head of a liberal Democrat. That's the one thing he doesn't understand, or want to." Even so, Rich understands people, and people are really all the same, no matter how they vote or where they can be found on the political spectrum. Though a confirmed conservative Republican, Rich manages to get along just fine with liberals and Democrats. He doesn't let politics come between himself and other people.

Neil Offen, president of the Direct Selling Association, told me, "I'm very active in the Democratic Party. One year, Rich DeVos was the chairman of the Direct Selling Association Board and I had lunch with him. Rich said to me, 'I don't understand how a man as smart as you could be a Democrat.' I responded by giving him five key reasons why I'm a Democrat and how the federal government helps me. Rich didn't argue with me or disagree. He simply said, 'Neil, you would have made it anyway. It wasn't the government, but talent and hard work that made you successful.'"

Former Amway Corp. executive John Brown recalls, "I worked on government relations for the corporation for over seventeen years. On one occasion, we brought a dozen Michigan state legislators to the Amway Grand Plaza Hotel to meet with the corporate officers. Over lunch, Rich, the staunch Republican, sat between two state legislators—both women and liberal Democrats. Rich was wonderful with them, very charming throughout their conversation.

"The desserts served at the Grand Plaza are opulent thousand-calorie masterpieces—wonderful to taste but not the best thing for a person with heart problems. So they served Rich a 'heart-smart' dessert. As Rich was about to taste his dessert, he noticed that the two lady legislators on either side of him were not eating their desserts. So Rich said to them, 'Ladies, you'll have to try mine!' They both politely declined, but Rich insisted, taking his spoon and actually spoon-feeding each of them! So the three of them finished Rich's dessert—and Rich *literally* had these two liberal Democrats eating out of his hand. That is so symbolic of the way Rich is able to reach across ideological barriers to charm and befriend other people."

How do you become a true "people person" like Rich DeVos? It all begins with a thing called *love*. You must have a genuine love for people—and that means individual people, not just some abstract concept of "humanity." Everyone Rich meets is a friend and a neighbor. His love for people is genuine, not an act. "Rich is captivating but not contrived," observes Diana Sieger, president of the Grand Rapids Community Foundation. "There's not an artificial or manipulative bone in his body."

> *"I think you can credit much of Rich DeVos's business success to the fact he is a 'people person.' If people like you, they are willing to do business with you. Rich has often said, 'The secret of Amway's success is that it's a people-to-people thing.'"*
>
> JOHN VARINEAU
> ASSOCIATE CONDUCTOR,
> GRAND RAPIDS SYMPHONY

Next, if you want to become a "people person" like Rich DeVos, you must *be a student of humanity*. You must study human nature, human behavior and human motivation. Quixtar executive Ken McDonald says,

> *"Rich DeVos has a heart for God and a heart for people. When you meet him, he says, 'I'm a sinner saved by grace.'"*
>
> Gordon Loux
> Corporate Fundraiser

"There are two kinds of people in the world: those who 'get it' and those who don't. Rich gets it. He understands human nature. His secret is that he studies what makes people tick. He listens to people intently, so he understands what motivates and inspires people. He understands human dreams and aspirations—and he does what it takes to help people achieve those dreams and aspirations.

"Rich DeVos has a mission in life, and his mission is to help people help themselves. Rich has focused his entire life on helping other people, and that is why he always puts other people first. He has impacted millions of lives over the years by his approach to life."

Rich DeVos is successful and influential because he works through people. He delegates authority to people. He motivates and inspires people. He builds on the strengths and abilities of people. He taps into the knowledge and skills of people. He communicates with people, both as a talker and a listener. He leads people and builds teams of people. His business is people, people, people.

If you want to be successful and influential, then be like Rich—be a "people person."

Chapter Seven

Be a Life Enricher!

IN HIS SPEECHES, RICH DEVOS often quotes a statement originally made by Walt Disney. "There are three kinds of people in the world today," Disney said. "There are 'well poisoners,' who discourage you and stomp on your creativity and tell you what you can't do. There are 'lawn mowers'—people who are well-intentioned but self-absorbed; they tend to their own needs, mow their own lawns and never leave their yards to help another person. Finally, there are 'life enrichers'—people who reach out to enrich the lives of others, to lift them up and inspire them. We need to be life enrichers, and we need to surround ourselves with life enrichers."

Well, that's exactly the kind of person Rich DeVos is. He encourages people to be what he calls "life enrichers." Ask him what his role is with Alticor or the Orlando Magic or any other organization he's involved with, and he'll say, "I'm the head cheerleader!" Boy, is he ever! That's his job description in a nutshell.

Rich has a wonderful ability to praise, encourage, inspire and motivate. Whenever he comes to visit the Orlando Magic, he'll stop by my office and spend time with me, asking me about my life, my work and my family. He'll offer sincere encouragement: "Is there anything you need? Any way I can support you and pray for you?" Then he'll close with an uplifting word: "Well, Pat, you're doing a terrific job. We couldn't do it without you!"

Whenever Rich and I are together with one other person or with thousands, he never fails to acknowledge the role I had in helping to launch the Orlando Magic. He'll always say, "Pat Williams started all this. Without him, we wouldn't be here. There wouldn't be a team without him." He has said that literally dozens of times to countless people, and whenever he does that it makes me feel ten feet tall. While many bosses steal the credit for what people around them do, Rich loves to spread the credit around and acknowledge the contributions of others. That's one reason why I always feel inspired and energized after a few minutes with Rich DeVos, the head cheerleader and chief life enricher of the Orlando Magic.

> *"I'm a cheerleader. From the time I started my own business more than fifty years ago and took on the role of leading people, I've been telling them, 'You can do it!' I've given hundreds of motivational speeches, and I'm still asked to make more because people tell me I'm a great motivator. They want to know the 'secret to success.'"*
>
> RICH DEVOS

Cartwheels and Handsprings

When Rich calls himself a cheerleader, it's not a figure of speech. "It's literally true," says his high school friend Marvin Van Dellen. "Rich was actually a cheerleader for the basketball team at Christian High—and you should have seen him! He would do handsprings and cartwheels the length of the court and get the crowd all stirred up. I guess that's why he's been a cheerleader ever since."

Rich's wife, Helen, recalls one incident from Rich's cheerleading career. "One day, in front of the whole student body," she recalls, "Rich did a cartwheel and ripped the seat of his pants out! He turned red and walked off the court backwards—but he didn't let that stop him. He loves to get the crowd worked up. He loves to get the team fired up. Cheerleading has carried over to the rest of his life. It's one of the biggest reasons for his success."

Dr. David Nicholas, senior pastor of Spanish River Church in Boca Raton, Florida, told me how much Rich's cheerleading has meant in his life. "Rich is the most encouraging man I've ever met," said Pastor Nicholas. "You'll never hear a negative word from him. He'll always put a positive spin on every situation.

"My wife left me when I was in seminary, and she took my three sons with her. As a result, my sons didn't grow up with me. That was very hard on me, and it was difficult to maintain any kind of relationship with my boys. When I was at a point of real discouragement, Rich put his arm around me and said, 'Be aggressive! Call your boys—don't wait for them to call you. Love them, pursue them and talk to them. Don't let anything come between you and your sons.' I did what Rich said, and today I have the best relationship I've ever had with them. Rich's encouragement and positive reinforcement are a big part of that."

D. James Kennedy, senior minister at Coral Ridge Presbyterian Church in Fort Lauderdale, recalls a commencement speech Rich gave at the church's Westminster Academy High School. "That year, the school had an extraordinarily high percentage of students who were on the dean's list or the honor roll, or had received honors from national academic societies. As I recall, some 60 percent of the students were mentioned, and some of them collected as many as seven or eight tasseled cords, which they hung around their necks.

"When Rich got up to give the commencement address, he said that when he graduated from high school, he won no honors at

> *"Here's the centerpiece of Rich's wisdom: We flourish only by helping others to flourish. Rich's entire life has been spent helping other people to achieve great things."*
>
> REV. NEAL PLANTINGA, PRESIDENT, CALVIN THEOLOGICAL SEMINARY

all. Then he proceeded to focus his attention on the other 40 percent of the students, those without honors, without tasseled cords. He encouraged them and told them that *every member* of that graduating class could accomplish great things for the Kingdom of God.

"The students who won no honors had probably entered that ceremony feeling like nobodies. Thanks to Rich DeVos, they went out believing that they could conquer the world. It was a marvelous demonstration of Rich's unique gifts of compassion and encouragement."

Dr. James Fahner, chief of pediatric hematology and oncology at DeVos Children's Hospital in Grand Rapids, is also grateful for the cheerleading of Rich and Helen DeVos. "They are such an inspiring and energizing couple," he told me. "They make you believe in yourself so strongly, and they make you want to be the best you can be. Let me tell you a story about the way they have been cheerleaders in my life.

"To honor Helen for her support of our children's cancer program, we established an annual lectureship—the Helen DeVos Distinguished Lectureship in Pediatric Oncology—that has become nationally recognized and applauded. Each August, that event attracts a major leader in the field of children's cancer research to speak at a formal dinner.

"One year, when our children's hospital was still fairly new, a world-renowned children's brain-tumor surgeon from New York was the guest speaker. He was chatting with Rich and Helen over dinner. I was just within earshot when he said, 'Mr. DeVos, you've got quite a facility here. Just wait—in a few more years you'll be able to attract the best and brightest young physicians from around the country to practice here.'

"Without missing a beat, Rich proudly replied, 'Just take a good look around these tables tonight! A lot of the best and brightest are already here!'

"Rich's spontaneous words of pride and confidence were like a huge pat on the back for me. I was deeply touched and encouraged. To this day, I have never told Rich that I heard his words that night or how much they meant to me—so when you read this, Rich, thanks from the bottom of my heart!"

"The highlight of the year for the hospital staff is when they meet with Rich. These people have a tough job, dealing with life-and-death issues of sick children. When Rich speaks to the staff, it's a real shot in the arm. They love to be around Rich because he inspires and motivates them."

VICKI WEAVER, PRESIDENT,
GRAND RAPIDS HOSPITAL FOUNDATION

Another person whose life has been profoundly affected by Rich's cheerleading is Alticor pilot Rick Fiddler. Rick told me a fascinating story. "On September 14, 1983," he said, "I was a young pilot in my late twenties, flying a Sikorsky S76 helicopter from Chicago to Grand Rapids with four Amway executives aboard. We had a problem with the tail rotor and ended up crashing into Lake Michigan. It was near sunset, and we were floating in life jackets in fifty-four-degree water. After about an hour, the Coast Guard picked us up and took us to the Chicago station.

"While all this was going on, Rich was in his Florida home getting ready for dinner when he got a call informing him of the crash. Rich called the Coast Guard to find out about us and insisted on staying on the line until we were safe. When we got to the station in Chicago, someone told me, 'There's a phone call for you—the man has been on hold for an hour, waiting for you.'

"I took the call, and it was Rich. He said he had been praying for us, and he was relieved that we were safe. The next day he flew back to Michigan. I was at the hangar when a call came in saying, 'Mr. DeVos wants a helicopter ride. Pick him up in front of the company headquarters.' I was still shaky from the crash, but I climbed into the company's other helicopter and took off. When I got to the headquarters, Rich was waiting for me. I let him in and said, 'Where do you want to go?' He said, 'I don't care. Let's just go for a ride.'

"He just wanted to show me—and show everyone else—that he had confidence in me. At that moment, he had a lot more confidence in me than I had in myself! But by taking that ride right away, he sent a message of encouragement, loud and clear. Later, he had me get up and tell the whole story in front of a meeting of Amway independent business owners, and he praised me for ditching the helicopter on Lake Michigan without any loss of life. Whenever I hear Rich DeVos talking about being a 'cheerleader,' I think about how he cheered and encouraged me, and got me right back into the air."

"I once visited South Africa with Rich aboard his boat. We were docked near a village, and a group of African teenagers sang and entertained the tourists. Rich invited all of them aboard his boat, and he talked with them. He encouraged them to pursue their dreams, and you could see their faces light up as he spoke. They sang for us on the boat, and it was the most beautiful, enthusiastic music I've ever heard."

Dr. Gaylen Byker
President, Calvin College

Bill Boer is Rich's senior business advisor. "It was a few days before Christmas," he recalls, "and I was driving to inspect some property we had recently purchased for the DeVos family. My cell phone rang, and it was Rich. I assumed he was calling to ask me about the property and the development plans, so I immediately began filling him in on all the details about the property. He listened for a few minutes, then he said, 'Well, that's all very nice, Bill, but I was really just calling to say, 'Merry Christmas.' He paused, then added, 'I love you, Bill.' I was at a loss for words. Never in my life had anyone I worked for told me, 'I love you.'"

Are you a life enricher and a cheerleader like Rich DeVos? If not, then you can become one. Cheerleading is a skill we can all acquire and cultivate.

Imagine how much more successful your organization would be if you would become the head cheerleader. Imagine how much happier your family would be, how much stronger and healthier your family dynamics would become, if you decided that—starting right now, today—you would become the chief life enricher for your spouse and kids.

And what about your own spiritual and emotional needs? Do you have cheerleaders and life enrichers in your own life? Do you have people around you who encourage you and root for you and motivate you to be the best you can possibly be? We all have enough well poisoners and lawn mowers in our lives. We have all too few life enrichers.

Where do you find cheerleaders and life enrichers for your own life? You'll find them in your church, at the office, in your neighborhood, at your university or on your team. The best way to find a life enricher is to *be* a life enricher. Positive, encouraging, cheerleading people tend to gravitate toward other positive people. If you go out of your way to encourage other people, then they will seek you out and encourage you.

The word "encourage" is derived from the French *cour,* meaning "heart." Life enrichers are big-hearted people who devote themselves to strengthening the hearts of others. I believe one of the reasons Rich DeVos is such a great encourager is that he has such a big heart for people—and for God. He is totally dedicated to living out his faith. His Bible tells him, "Therefore encourage one another and build each other up, just as in fact you are doing" (1 Thessalonians 5:11, NIV). If you call yourself a Christian but you are not an encourager, then you are not practicing your faith!

If you want to be like Rich, then have a heart! Be an encourager!

What Stops You from Being a Life Enricher?

Many people have mental objections that keep them from becoming life enrichers and cheerleaders. If you want to be successful, effective and influential like Rich DeVos, then you need to overcome these obstacles and objections.

Obstacle no. 1: childhood barriers

If you grew up in a home where encouragement was scarce, where criticism and sarcasm reigned, then the idea of being an encourager and a life enricher may be foreign to you. If you never had a good parental role model of a cheerleader, then you probably didn't even know that people should encourage one another. If you were subjected to judgment and criticism throughout your formative years (or worse, verbal or physical abuse), then how could you know anything else?

> *"Rich DeVos was gifted by God to help people. When I started working for him over forty years ago, I was self-conscious and afraid of a lot of things. He helped me to become more confident."*
>
> Helen Verburg
> Employee of Rich and Helen DeVos

Now that you are an adult, however, you must retrain your mind and reprogram your behavior. Encouraging others is a deliberate choice you must make. It's time to break through old childhood barriers and become the person you want to be. It's time to consciously decide to become a life enricher and a cheerleader.

Obstacle no. 2: insecurity and self-centeredness

Some people, out of a deep sense of insecurity and inferiority, find it difficult to encourage and affirm other people. Over the years, they have developed behavior patterns of building themselves up by tearing other people down. They look for faults and failings in other people in order to feel superior.

If you feel blocked from encouraging others because of your own insecurity and self-centeredness, it's time for you to grow up. It doesn't cost you anything to encourage others. You don't lose anything by affirming, praising and inspiring other people. In fact, you gain—big-time! When you become known as an encourager and a cheerleader, you are the winner. People who tear others down only diminish themselves; people who build others up build themselves up as well. Authentic greatness is demonstrated by the choice to become a life enricher and a cheerleader.

Obstacle no. 3: thoughtlessness

Some people simply don't take the time to enrich someone else's life. We all know it doesn't take much time or effort to say a kind, encouraging word or to send a note of encouragement—but we think, *I'm busy right now, and there's always tomorrow.* In our casual thoughtlessness, we fail to realize that this isn't necessarily so—sometimes, tomorrow doesn't come. That person you've been meaning to encourage may not be here tomorrow. Or you may not be here tomorrow.

So don't be thoughtless. Stop putting it off. Be an encourager *now,* while there is still time.

"Rich DeVos is one of the most thoughtful people I know," says Jill Grzesiak, Rich's executive assistant. "You can imagine the incredible volume of requests and invitations he receives. I remember one request he received from an unpublished poet in Michigan who wanted help finding a publisher. The man had written a book of poems dedicated to his late son. He wanted to sell the book locally and at his church, with some of the profits going to charity. He had been turned down by publisher after publisher. Finally, he sent the manuscript to Mr. DeVos, who read it and was very moved by the dedication the man had written to the memory of his son. Mr. DeVos sent the manuscript to his own publisher, but they weren't interested. So he helped the man get the book printed locally. Most people would have told the man, "I wish I could help you," but Mr. DeVos went out of his way to help the man honor his son's memory with a book of poems. That speaks volumes about the thoughtfulness of Rich DeVos."

Obstacle no. 4: ignorance

Another common obstacle is that some people simply don't know how to encourage other people. They don't know where to begin, what to do or what to say. Here, then, are some steps to take that will make you a life enricher to the people around you:

How to Be a Cheerleader

Step no. 1: be cheerful

How can you be a cheerleader if you have no cheer? Many people think that cheerfulness is the result of an emotional high or happy circumstances, such as winning the lottery. In reality, cheerfulness is a choice. It's an attitude that we choose. No one can be on an emotional high all day long, but anyone can choose to be cheerful. No one has cheery circumstances all the time—we all have to pay taxes; we all lock our keys in the car sometimes; we all get bad news in the mail every now and then; we all get headaches, colds and stiff backs from time to time. Yet even when our circumstances are less than cheery, we can choose a cheerful attitude.

> *"Rich DeVos treats his people well, both players and staff. He also wants to win, to be the best. He has set out to prove that you can win and treat your people well at the same time."*
>
> John Weisbrod, Chief Operating Officer, Orlando Magic

Cheerfulness comes from adopting an optimistic outlook on life. It doesn't mean that we pretend that bad days don't happen. It means that we choose to maintain a positive disposition even on days when things don't go our way.

Cheerful people energize the people around them. Cheerless people are an emotional drag. They suck the life and enthusiasm out of you. So in order to be a cheerleader, you need to be cheerful—and you need to spread that cheer around.

Step no. 2: give verbal encouragement

Visit or call the person you want to encourage. Ask how he or she is doing—not in a glib "Howzit goin?" way, but with genuine interest. Tell that person you are praying. That's the kind of encourager and cheerleader Rich has been to me and to countless other people, both in one-on-one encounters and in large groups.

Retired Amway employee Tom Michmershuizen recalls the early days of the company. "Rich's verbal encouragement was a big part of the meetings for independent distributors and the meetings for employees. He would always arrive early and stay late, talking with

> *"I had the privilege of traveling with the entourage when Rich was doing his 'Evening with Rich' events around the country. One night I was watching from backstage as he gave his talk. When he came off the stage, I said, 'Great job, Rich!' He turned, and his face lit up. 'Really?' he said. 'What point did you think was the most effective?' I had just assumed that Rich is the guy who encourages others. I was surprised to discover that Rich needs a pat on the back like everybody else."*
>
> Sherri Brewer
> Alticor Employee

people, encouraging and motivating them, signing keepsakes, patting people on the back. Everyone wanted to be around Rich because he was such a source of inspiration.

"Each month we had an employee meeting, and Rich would get up and tell us the latest on where the company was going. Then he would have each new employee get up and talk about her job and what her hopes for the future were. And Rich would always have some word of affirmation for the great job each person was doing. The meetings were fun and filled with excitement and enthusiasm. Everybody looked forward to them.

"Rich would even conduct a special meeting for the corporate truck drivers. He would show up in denim overalls, and he'd just be one of the guys—shaking hands, swapping jokes and stories, and telling the drivers how much he valued the work they did. He wanted everyone in the company to know that they were valued and appreciated, and that their work mattered."

Step no. 3: send cards and notes

Send notes of appreciation, encouragement and inspiration. Rich DeVos says, "For years, I've been sending letters of congratulations out to people for things they do in the community. I may read about it in the paper or someone may mention some good deed someone has done. I'm often inspired to just drop that person a note. It only takes a few minutes to write a note, but it can be a powerful act of inspiration and encouragement."

Step no. 4: offer your time

Would you like to be a life enricher for a friend, a neighbor, your pastor, your coworker or your boss? Then go to that person and say, "I have so many hours that I want to give you. Let me serve you. Let me wash your windows or organize your files or watch your children so you can have an evening out." The gift of your time can be a powerful encouragement and life enrichment for others.

Step no. 5: give a gift

It doesn't have to be expensive. Give something small, thoughtful and encouraging—some token of your kindness and encouragement.

Step no. 6: celebrate for no reason at all

How about inviting a friend out for dinner and a show? Or a home-cooked dinner at your house? Or a party? A round of golf or a few sets of tennis? Or a night together with no agenda except a lot of laughs and a closer friendship? One of the best ways you can be a cheerleader and a life enricher for others is to celebrate special moments, milestones and events—or celebrate for no reason at all!

> *"My parents were life enrichers. My father always told me, 'Whatever you choose to do in life, you can do it!' And he turned out to be right. So that's the message I preach wherever I go: 'You can do it!'"*
>
> RICH DEVOS

> *"I get a tremendous boost from the people around me. When I motivate someone else, it actually does as much for me as it does for the other person. I'm motivated by a sense of being appreciated and loved—it tells me I'm important, that I make a difference in this world. The ability to have a positive impact on someone else's life is a tremendous gift for your own life."*
>
> RICH DEVOS

Step no. 7: accept and affirm people when they fail

Lift people up when they fall. Allow people to be human and make mistakes. If you see someone drop the ball, encourage that person to get back into the game.

Step no. 8: defend reputations

Do everything you can to put an end to gossip, criticism and character assassination. Nothing is more discouraging than being the target of a rumor mill. If someone comes to you with gossip, say, "I'm not going to listen to this. If you have a complaint against someone, you need to go directly to that person. Don't bring it to me and don't spread it around." Life enrichers stand up for people who aren't present to defend themselves.

Step no. 9: pray

Prayer is a powerful source of encouragement. As you pray, let people know that you are praying for them. Pray specifically about that person's spiritual, emotional, health, family and financial needs.

Step no. 10: be a mentor

A mentor is an in-depth life enricher. Mentoring is a one-on-one relationship of teaching, guiding, sharing and cheerleading. (The issue of mentoring is so vitally important that we will devote the entire next chapter to it.)

Meanwhile, if you want to be a life enricher like Rich, then you'd better practice your handsprings, cartwheels and cheers. Look around you. Everywhere you turn, there are people in need of a cheerleader. Go tell them that they matter to you, that you believe in them, that you're cheering for them. Make a difference in just one life every day and see how *your* life changes!

Chapter Eight

Be a Mentor!

"I USED TO WORK in a sign-painting business," recalls Paul Collins, an African-American artist from West Michigan. "I got to know Rich DeVos because we did the lettering on Amway vehicles. I told him that I wanted to be an artist and paint for a living, and Rich told me how to go about it. He said I needed to be independent in order to succeed, and he helped me find investors so that I could launch myself as an artist. Rich was so open and generous with his time—just like a surrogate father.

"We became close friends, and his door was always open to me. The fact that I was black and he was a white Republican billionaire just never seemed to matter. I had a dream of becoming an artist, and he wanted to help me. Because he cared enough to mentor me, I have lived all over the world, doing my painting."

John Eldred, a consultant to the DeVos family, told me, "What Rich did for Paul Collins is typical of what he does in all of his mentoring relationships: He takes a dependent relationship and turns it into an independent relationship. He shows people how to stand on their own feet and achieve their own dreams."

Rich DeVos is one of the greatest mentors I know. He has mentored scores of people in the principles of business and success, including Steve Van Andel, the son of Rich's partner, Jay Van Andel. "When I got out of school," Steve told me, "I started working at Amway Corporation. Rich took me on a five-city tour with him that was called 'An Evening with Rich.' We did leadership-training sessions each day and held a rally each night.

> *"Dad never took a 'Mentoring 101' course. His commitment to mentoring comes from his interest in people and from being in the people business. He never stops mentoring, but he's a student, too. He wants to read, learn and be challenged himself."*
>
> Doug DeVos
> Rich's Youngest Son
> and President of Alticor

"I remember I was going through some personal issues at the time, and I really wanted to talk to Rich about it, but I was nervous about approaching him. Billy Zeoli was traveling with us, and he could see that something was bothering me, so he said something to Rich while Rich was in a meeting.

"Wouldn't you know it? Rich dropped what he was doing, left the meeting, sought me out and took me to his room for a talk. It was such a relief to be able to talk to him about that issue, and he gave me some very good, wise counsel. That's what a mentor does: stop and help. Rich cares more about people and their needs than he cares about a meeting or an agenda or a schedule. I admire that, and I try to do the same thing. I want to be the kind of person who will drop everything in order to give people my time and help when they need it."

Steve's younger brother, Dave Van Andel, says, "I had *two* fathers growing up—Dad and Rich DeVos. Our families lived next door, and we spent a lot of time in each other's homes. Rich mentored by example as much as by word, and a teacher who is a great example is the most effective mentor you can have."

Marc Lovett is an event producer who has produced many theatrical shows. "Alticor is a client of ours," he told me. "We produced a series of major events in Japan a number of years ago. We took eighteen performers with us for the events, and Rich DeVos spoke each night. I particularly remember one story he told of a Vietnamese refugee who had escaped from the communists in a boat, and had come to America and had succeeded in America. The way Rich told the story, you felt you were right in the boat with the man as he made his escape.

"At the last event in the series, Rich gave a toast to the performers and to us as an expression of gratitude for the work we had done. I appreciated that so much. Afterwards, Rich took me aside and gave me some tips on the ways of Japanese culture. He told me what to say and how to address the Japanese people when I spoke. Looking back, I realize that it was actually a lesson in respecting others and thinking beyond oneself. Rich cared enough to mentor me because he genuinely cared about me as a person. I continually marvel at the way he cares about people and goes out of his way to help them."

Karen DeBlaay, daughter of longtime IBO Bernice Hansen, told me, "I asked Rich to mentor me in the area of stewardship. I called his office and his secretary said that Rich would call me in an hour. Sure enough, he called and gave me the guidance I needed. He gave me an unlimited amount of his time to help me."

In these few stories, we catch yet another glimpse into the soul of Rich DeVos, and we discover one more reason for his enormous success and influence: Rich DeVos is a mentor.

Why Be a Mentor?

Helen DeVos explained to me Rich's motivation for mentoring others. "It comes from his faith," she said. "Jesus mentored the disciples. He taught them, spent time with them and laid down his life for them. Rich looks at the life of Jesus and says, 'That's my example. That's the pattern for my life.' So being a mentor to others just flows from who Rich is and what he believes.

"Rich DeVos is more than a mentor. He's like a father to me. He has impacted every area of my life. I became a Christian because of his influence. I became an entrepreneur because of his influence. He impacted my political views, my economic views, my personality, my spirituality. Rich probably has no idea that he has had such a powerful effect on my life."

JIM DORNAN
INDEPENDENT BUSINESS OWNER

"As a mentor, Rich is always encouraging and teaching, always passing along insights and experiences. He doesn't usually say, 'Here's what you should do.' More often he'll say, 'I faced a similar situation, and this is what I did, and here's what happened as a result.' He gladly shares his own experiences and the things he has learned, but he doesn't force it on anyone.

"Anyone who asks Rich for counsel and advice will receive it. He doesn't turn anyone down. And at the end of the conversation, he always says, 'Feel free to come back to me anytime.' He is so generous with his time."

Rich's son-in-law and Orlando Magic CEO, Bob Vander Weide, says, "Why is Rich a mentor to so many people? Because he can't help himself! He loves people so much and he wants to see them succeed, and he clearly has plenty of insight to share about life. He's been a mentor to all of us in the family and in his businesses. He doesn't mentor in a forceful or intimidating way. He mentors by encouraging, by cheerleading. He loves to cheer you on to do your best.

"Right now his emphasis is on mentoring the grandchildren. He feels they are his legacy—not Alticor, not the Magic, not the many charities and foundations he supports. No, his legacy is his grandchildren, and he is continually encouraging, teaching and mentoring them. In a way, his grandchildren are his gift to the world, and he believes that they will go on long after he is gone, and they will help make the world a better place."

Bob's wife, Cheri Vander Weide, also reflected on the mentoring commitment of her father, Rich DeVos. "Dad is a teacher at heart," she says, "and as he's gotten older, he has become even more of one. He has acquired wisdom and experience far beyond that of the average person, and he has a desire to impart that wisdom to others. He wants to take advantage of every teaching opportunity he has."

Former Amway chief operating officer Bill Nicholson takes us inside his mentoring relationship with Rich. "There's a big difference," he says, "between mentoring and teaching. Mentoring goes much deeper than teaching. A teacher goes over material with you, gives you an assignment and evaluates your performance on a test. There may be some one-on-one interaction in a teaching situation, but most of the process takes place in a classroom, and it's fairly impersonal.

"Dad once said, 'You have to make the most important choices in life when you're the least prepared to make them.' He meant that when you are in your late teens to early twenties, you must make choices that decide the entire course of your life: what college to attend, your college major, your career choice, your spouse—plus there are all the temptations that can destroy you, such as drugs and alcohol. You have to make all of these critical decisions while you are young and inexperienced. That's why young people need mentors."

DOUG DEVOS
RICH'S YOUNGEST SON
AND PRESIDENT OF ALTICOR

"But mentoring, as Rich does it, involves a relationship. It's a form of instruction that reaches the learner at a much deeper, more personal level. Rich is a great teacher and motivator when he stands up before an audience. But he is an even greater one-on-one mentor. I'll give you an example.

"One day, some years ago, Rich and I had been in an employee meeting. After the meeting, he took me aside and said, 'Bill, let me give you a suggestion. I watched you in that meeting. Next time, why don't you spend some time letting people get to know you? You've got a good sense of humor—you ought to let it come out more. Take time with people and show them you're interested in them as people. If they get to know you better, they'll like you and trust you. You'll find it's easier to get the results you want.' That was great advice, and he was right—and that's just one example of hundreds of moments where Rich has been a mentor to me."

My friend Rich DeVos has been a great mentor to me and to many other people in the Orlando Magic organization. John Weisbrod, chief operating officer of the Magic, told me how much he appreciates the mentoring relationship he has had with Rich.

"As a mentor," says John, "Rich teaches you in such a way that you hardly notice how much you are learning. He doesn't make you feel incompetent or inferior. He never says, 'Now, let me sit you down and impart all my knowledge to you because, boy, do you need it!' He's so casual about the way he approaches you that it's totally disarming. He suggests different approaches, he tells stories from his own experience, he

> *"Rich DeVos takes a personal interest in everyone on the team. When he comes into the locker room, he spends time talking to each of us. And he doesn't just talk. He listens."*
>
> Andrew DeClerq
> Orlando Magic Player

identifies with you, he coaches you and encourages you, he inspires you to go out and do what you never thought you could do. That's the key to great mentoring: inspiration. A teacher can impart knowledge and information, but only a real mentor can fill you with the inspiration and the belief that you are capable of more than you ever imagined."

Rich is also a mentor to the players on the team. Shaquille O'Neal, star center for the Los Angeles Lakers, started his NBA career playing for the Orlando Magic. Shaq once told Rich, "You're a mentor to me. I never forget anything you tell me." Shaq told me one of the life lessons he learned from Rich DeVos. "Soon after Rich bought the team, he met with the players and talked to us about money. He said, 'I know you guys make a lot of money. So do I. But you can't let money destroy who you are. Keep your humility. Be nice to people. Never let money change the way you treat others.' I never forgot that."

One of our former players, Shawn Kemp (who also played with the Seattle Sonics, Cleveland Cavaliers and Portland Trailblazers), told me, "Rich DeVos is unlike any NBA owner I've ever known. I've never had an owner sit down and talk with me like a real person. Most owners shy away from the players, but Rich has shown a real interest in me. Let me tell you, ball players appreciate that."

Another former Magic player Darrell Armstrong said, "Rich is always checking in with us, one-on-one. He's always telling us how proud he is of us and praising us for being well-behaved on and off the court. I always enjoy it when he comes around. After a game, he comes in and talks with us whether we've won or lost. That means a lot."

Another former Magic player Penny Hardaway recalls, "Rich cares about you on and off the floor, and there aren't many NBA owners like that. He'd pull me aside and talk about money matters and keeping God in my life. He took a personal interest in me, and he didn't have to do that. All he had to do was pay us, but he wanted to do more than that. He wanted to make a difference in our lives. That's what makes Rich DeVos unique."

John Weisbrod recalls, "I once told Rich about a player we wanted to sign—a star player with a lot of talent, but also some off-court behavior problems involving drugs and fathering children out of wedlock. I laid it out for Rich, and he said, 'You know, I want to make a difference in his life. That's what we're all about. Let's bring him here and help him get straightened out so he can go on and live a productive life after basketball. Yes sir, we can help that young man.' That's the way Rich looks at his players. They're all individuals with individual needs, and he wants to help them and mentor them."

One of the ways Rich mentors the Magic players is by counseling them to invest wisely and tithe the huge amounts of money they are making on the basketball court. "A lot of these young men," he says, "have all kinds of so-called 'experts' coming after them, claiming to have their best interests at heart. I tell them that that I'm the only fellow in town who really wants to save them money. I really want the best for these guys. A lot of players actually seek me out and ask for my advice. I meet privately with them, talk to them about life and pray with them. Being an NBA owner has given me a whole new set of opportunities to be a mentor and a cheerleader."

Rich is so eager to encourage, coach and mentor the people in his organization that it is sometimes comical. I remember an incident at one Magic home game, not long after Rich had purchased the team. I was watching the game from my usual place in the tunnel behind the visitors' bench, and Rich was sitting behind the Magic bench. It was late in the game, the Magic was behind but on a roll, making a comeback. A time-out was called and the building was rocking; the crowd was on its feet; the dance team was keeping things in a frenzy; it was a madhouse.

I was watching all of this when one of our young marketing guys ran up to me. His eyes were as big as dinner plates. "Look down there!" he shouted at me in a panicky voice. "Mr. DeVos is in the huddle!"

I looked—and sure enough, there was Rich, on the floor in front of the bench, right in the middle of his team. The coach was standing there, slackjawed, clipboard in hand. The players were listening attentively. Rich wasn't talking strategy or X's and O's. He was just doing what he always does wherever he goes: encouraging, cheerleading, mentoring. He loves his players, and he was giving them a good word—"Great job! You've got 'em where you want 'em! Keep it up!"

> *"Rich DeVos is a mentor to me because he walks the walk that he talks about."*
>
> Steve Hiaeshutter, Former Alticor Employee

What was Rich supposed to be doing? Just sitting behind the bench, watching the game, leaving the pep talks to his coaches? Was it a violation of protocol for the team owner to jump into the middle of a huddle during a time-out? Absolutely—and Rich never did it again.

But you've got to love his enthusiasm as he was caught up in the excitement of the moment. You've got to admire his mentor's heart. What Rich DeVos did that night is what he does all the time with his young players: He encourages them, he builds them up, he mentors them—and they love him for it.

"There's nothing very complicated about being a mentor to someone else," Rich told me. "If you encourage people, if you enrich people's lives and pass on some of your own experience to others, then you are a mentor. I want to do that for other people because I know what an impact my mentors have made on my life.

"My dad was my real mentor. The principles and values he taught me are the basis of Alticor and the basis of the way we run the Magic organization. Another of my mentors is Jay Van Andel—a real smart guy with a strong personal foundation of faith, principles and character.

"What does it take to be a mentor? Well, you have to pay attention to people. You have to get to know them in more than a superficial way. You have to ask them questions and find out what makes them tick. You have to build a relationship of trust so that they will feel comfortable opening up to you and sharing their problems and questions with you. If you give people your attention, if you share your experience with people, encourage them and enrich their lives, then that leads to being a mentor.

"A mentor is nothing more than a person people look up to. A person, usually younger and less experienced, sees something in your life that they like and admire. They want to be like you in that way, and they want to learn from you. That's why we need to be very careful how we live our lives. If you don't set a good example, then people will think that doing the wrong thing is acceptable, and they'll do the wrong things, too. A mentor has to be constantly aware of his or her influence on others."

What Mentors Do

The word "mentor" comes from the *Odyssey* of Homer, the story of the adventures of Odysseus during his ten-year journey following the Trojan War. While he was away from home, Odysseus entrusted his son to a friend, asking this friend to guide, educate and care for the boy. The name of this trusted friend was Mentor. Today, any person who teaches and guides others in a one-to-one relationship is called a mentor.

In his book *Compassionate Capitalism,* Rich devotes an entire chapter to the importance of having mentors and becoming a mentor. "We need to find someone," he writes, "whom we admire who has already achieved what we want to achieve and ask that person to help us reach our goals." The person, Rich says, is a mentor.

Rich goes on to describe what mentors do:

1. Mentors are the keepers of important traditions and life-shaping stories. Ancient craftsmen, from carpenters and metalsmiths to artisans and painters, employed young apprentices and mentored them in the trade. The apprentices not only learned valuable skills, but the traditions and stories that shaped their attitudes. Traditions and stories embody the intangible aspects of a calling, from craftsmanship and excellence to honesty and diligence.

> *"A mentor is not a person who can do the work better than his followers. He is a person who can get his followers to do the work better than he can."*
>
> FRED SMITH, PRESIDENT,
> FRED SMITH ASSOCIATES, DALLAS, TEXAS

2. Mentors pass on the knowledge that would be difficult for anyone to learn on his own. Without mentors, each generation of learners would have to "reinvent the wheel." Mentors transmit knowledge to learners—and learners reach new heights by standing on the shoulders of their mentors.

3. Mentors teach us what we need to know to be successful in life. Glen Early started his Harrisonburg, Virginia, construction company when he was only twenty-three years old. Within two years, his company was broke and Early was thousands of dollars in debt. He mortgaged his home to pay his debts, then he apprenticed himself to the owner of a successful construction firm.

As he was mentored by this experienced businessman, Glen Early began to realize how much he had to learn about estimating, bidding and contracting. For seven years, he worked alongside his more experienced mentor, then he left to form a new construction company. Six years later, Glen Early's company was listed by *Inc.* magazine as one of the fastest-growing entrepreneurial business in the nation.

That is why we need mentors. Their knowledge and wisdom is the key to our success.

4. Mentors teach most who love best. Paul Tournier, the Swiss Christian psychologist who has mentored hundreds of people from around the world, was once asked about his teaching, counseling and mentoring techniques. Tournier's reply: "It's a little embarrassing for me, having all these students coming from all over the world to study my 'techniques,' for they always go away disappointed. All I have learned to do is simply love and accept people right in the midst of their struggles." As Rich DeVos puts it, "People don't care how much you know until they know how much you care."

The apostle Paul expressed the heart of a mentor when he told his friends in Corinth, "For I wrote you out of great distress and anguish of heart and with many tears, not to grieve you but to let you know the depth of my love for you" (2 Corinthians 2:4, NIV). Paul mentored a young man named Timothy and once wrote to him, "I long to see you, so that I may be filled with joy. . . . Do your best to get here before winter" (2 Timothy 1:4; 4:21, NIV). Genuine love for people was at the heart of the mentoring process of the apostle Paul.

5. Mentors have the courage to confront. Sometimes, love must be tough. As David Augsburger put it in *Caring Enough to Confront,* "If you love, you level." It's a principle as old as the Bible: "As iron sharpens iron, so one man sharpens another" (Proverbs 27:17, NIV). If we are never corrected, we will never learn and grow.

True, it never feels good to be confronted about some character flaw, failure or sin. Correction and confrontation are painful to give and painful to receive. But a mentor who truly loves will care enough to confront the flaw in order to strengthen and sharpen the learner's character. As Proverbs 27:6 (NASB) tells us, "Faithful are the wounds of a friend."

There are many examples of mentoring in the Bible. Moses mentored Joshua. Naomi mentored her daughter-in-law, Ruth. Ezra mentored Nehemiah. Elijah mentored Elisha. Barnabas mentored Paul and John Mark. Paul mentored his spiritual son Timothy, as well as Priscilla and Aquila, who in turn mentored Apollos.

> *"Aside from my father, Rich has probably been my most important mentor. With his noncritical spirit, his unshakeable faith in Jesus Christ and his genuine love for people, Rich has the ideal mentor's temperament."*
>
> MARVIN DEWINTER
> ARCHITECT AND REAL ESTATE DEVELOPER

Of course, the greatest mentor and life enhancer of all time was Jesus of Nazareth, who mentored twelve men, pouring his life into them. One of those twelve men betrayed him—but the other eleven took what they had learned from him and altered the course of world history.

Ten Steps to Finding Your Mentor

Are you looking for a mentor—someone who will build a relationship with you, someone to teach and advise you and enable you to become a wise and effective human being? Here are ten steps to finding that person:

1. Look at the People You Know

Look around at the people in your personal and professional life. Is there someone you admire? Someone you would like to emulate in some way? Someone who has the wisdom you need?

2. Consider People You've Never Met

Research the top individuals in the businesses, organizations and trade associations of your chosen field. Find out as much as you can about them. Identify those individuals whose values and accomplishments you most admire.

3. Select a Mentor Who Is a Good Role Model

Look for someone who is not only famous or successful, but who has a reputation for character and solid principles. Look for someone you can admire and respect as well as emulate.

4. Select a Mentor Who Is a Good Listener

The best mentor is one who gets to know *you*—your skills and strengths and weaknesses, your individual personality and your aspirations. A good mentor should not serve as a lecturer, but as a sounding board who will help you with your struggles and help you to clarify your principles and beliefs.

5. Select a Mentor Who Levels with You

A good mentor doesn't just encourage you, but will also tell you the blunt truth when you are moving in the wrong direction. It is also a good sign if your mentor is candid and open about his or her own life. Anyone who has accomplished great things has made mistakes along the way and will share those experiences freely so that you can learn from them.

6. Look for Someone Who Is Unlike You in Some Important Way

Our tendency is to gravitate toward those with whom we have a lot in common. But in seeking out a mentor, it is wise to seek out people who have strengths that we lack. For example, if you are a shy and introverted person, seek out someone who is bold and gregarious. Instead of pairing up with someone who will reinforce your weaknesses, find someone who will challenge you to acquire new strengths.

7. Be Open to Finding a Mentor in Unlikely Places

We tend to think of a mentor or teacher as someone with gray hair and a well-lined face. Not necessarily! A mentor could be anyone who has something to teach you and could be the same age or even younger than you. A mentor could be someone of lower rank and social standing than you.

8. If the Person Doesn't Know You, Approach That Person with a Brief Letter of Introduction

You might say, "I have followed your achievements in the field of _______________, and I eagerly read your book on _______________. Like you, I am very concerned about the issue of _____________________, and I hope to make a contribution in these areas myself someday. I am looking for a mentoring relationship, and I would be grateful if you could spare thirty minutes to discuss such a possibility with me."

9. Make Personal Contact

Don't be shy. Ask, "Would you be willing to mentor me?" You may think you are imposing on that person, but I have found that most people who have achieved a place of accomplishment in life are eager to share their wisdom, experience and knowledge with others. When you ask someone to be your mentor, you are truly offering them high praise.

10. Remember, You Are Never Too Old to Be Mentored

I have reached a point where I know I have a lot of knowledge and experience to offer others—but I still have a lot to learn! That's why, despite my age and gray hair, I still seek out people to mentor me—people like Rich DeVos!

We have bought into the mistaken notion that the best way to impact the world is through mass media. We think that the best way to get our message out is to spend a bazillion dollars on print and broadcast advertising. But the problem with mass-communication techniques is that, while they may reach millions, they do not make a deep or lasting impression on a person's life.

Mentoring, by contrast, operates on the principle of exponential growth. Initially, the mentoring process impacts only a few people, but it does so at a deep and lasting level. Lives are completely transformed by the mentoring process. Mentoring yields deceptively small returns at first, but soon mushrooms as the yield in human lives compounds. An analogy will make this principle clear:

Suppose you apply for a job and your employer offers you a choice between two different salary plans. Plan A: You are paid $2,000 a week for the next twenty-five weeks. Plan B: You are paid a penny the first week, two pennies the second week, four pennies the third week and so forth, doubling your salary every week for the next twenty-five weeks. Which plan would you accept?

Well, if you are smart and do the math, you will take Plan B—the plan with the pennies. Why?

Plan A certainly *seems* attractive. At $2,000 a week for twenty-five weeks, you would make $50,000 in less than half a year—not bad. But what about Plan B? Well, if you double that penny, double it again, then again and again, week by week for twenty-five weeks, how much money will you have at the end of twenty-five weeks? *A whopping $335,544.31!* It's an eye-opener when you see how this actually works and how quickly one penny grows to over 33 million pennies.

> *"Mentors open the window and let the future in."*
>
> Howard A. Adams
> Director, GEM National Institute on Mentoring

Week	Pennies
1	1
2	2
3	4
4	8
5	16
6	32
7	64
8	128
9	256
10	512
11	1,024
12	2,048
13	4,096
14	8,192
15	16,384
16	32,768
17	65,536
18	131,072
19	262,144
20	524,288
21	1,048,576
22	2,097,152
23	4,194,304
24	8,388,608
25	16,777,216
Total	33,554,431

[Tabulations compiled by Jeff Bissey, Orlando Magic Controller]

That, my friend, is the power of exponential growth! So if I mentor you, that's two people. If you and I mentor two more people, that's four. If the four of us each find another person to mentor, that's eight. On and on and on it goes—and where it stops, nobody knows!

So what is the best way to be a life enricher? A grand mass-media marketing campaign? Or one-on-one mentoring? You be the judge.

(But maybe, just maybe, we have stumbled onto a clue as to how Amway got to be so big!)

"My Mentor, Rich DeVos"

Doug Seebeck, director of Partners for Christian Development, recently shared his story with me. "Let me tell you," he said, "about my mentor, Rich DeVos. I often say to Rich, 'I wish we had met in 1978 before I went off to Bangladesh! Or in 1982, immediately upon my return! The time I have wasted by not knowing you earlier!'

"But, of course, God does not waste anything—not even our mistakes. I didn't always know what I was doing during my eighteen years of international development work in Asia and Africa. Yet those years prepared me for my present work with Partners for Christian Development, a ministry that seeks out businesspeople for ministry, affirms their business as an outstanding calling and engages them as agents for social and spiritual change in their communities.

"Rich DeVos has been a mentor, guide, confidant and friend. I first encountered this man by reading his book, *Compassionate Capitalism.* As I read, I kept saying, 'Wow! I need to meet this man! I need to learn from this man!' When I got to chapter 10 on mentoring, I thought, *That's what I need! A mentor! I have a vision for Partners to become a worldwide movement—but I don't know how to get there! Here's a man who has already built a worldwide movement. I need to have him teach me how it's done!*

"So I arranged a meeting with Mr. DeVos, and I took that book along with me. He asked me, 'How can I help you?" And I opened the book and pointed to the chapter on mentoring. 'I need a mentor,' I said. And that

> *"To me, Rich's life is about integrity and honesty. He seeks to do the right things and he won't ever compromise. He sticks to his principles no matter what. Rich DeVos is not influenced by the crowd. People are influenced by Rich DeVos."*
>
> RON HALE
> INDEPENDENT BUSINESS OWNER

was the beginning of his commitment to mentor me and my organization toward our global vision.

"What has that mentoring process been like? It's not formal. It's not planned. It's more like a whirlwind of ideas, energy, passion and dreams. He takes his whole lifetime of experience—the places he's been, the things he's been though, his failures and successes—and he lays it all out for me to learn from. I have the rare privilege of watching his life up close, of seeing his character in action, of witnessing his commitment and his faith in God. I see how he focuses on what's important—and what's important to Rich is *people.* And through it all, I receive his continual encouragement. Rich calls himself a cheerleader—and he is!

"As I'm working and building this ministry, I often think, *I need to talk to Rich. I need to get another booster shot of Rich DeVos to carry me through the next six months.* I can always use more of his wisdom and character, and I never get enough.

"I've talked to a lot of people who know Rich, and the amazing thing is that everyone who knows him feels the same way. It doesn't matter who you talk to. Everyone loves Rich, because Rich loves everyone—he loves people, he loves life. He believes in people because he loves Jesus Christ, and Jesus is Rich's number-one mentor.

"Rich DeVos is much more than a mentor to me now. I have come to love him as a brother, as a father, as a dear friend. He's the person in my life who always says, 'You can do it, Seebeck!' And when he says it, he believes it, and he makes me believe it—and that's why it happens! Thank you, Rich, for being my mentor, my cheerleader, my friend."

There is an old proverb that captures the philosophy of a true mentor: "If you are planting for a year, plant grain. If you are planting for a decade, plant trees. If you are planting for a century, plant people." Mentors plant people. They cultivate and nurture people.

They enrich and encourage people. And the work of a mentor yields a harvest that continues to bear fruit for years, decades and even for eternity.

If you want to have the kind of influence and impact on lives that Rich has had, then be like Rich. Plant people. Be a mentor.

Chapter Nine

Get Out and Sell!

RICH DEVOS'S GRANDFATHER was a huckster.

Today, the word "huckster" sounds like an insult. It suggests someone who is sleazy, dishonest and disreputable, like a carnival barker or a guy in a checkered suit who sells "genuine" Rolex watches out of the trunk of his car.

But Rich DeVos's grandfather was an old-fashioned huckster, as honest and hardworking as the day is long. The word "huckster" originally comes from the old Dutch word *heukster,* meaning "peddler" or "salesman," and in the original sense of the word, there was nothing dishonorable about it. Rich's grandfather would drive his old truck to the farmer's market every day, buy quantities of vegetables, then drive through the neighborhood, selling his wares from door to door at a slight markup.

"I think Alticor today owes a lot of its success to that Dutch vegetable huckster," Rich says with a grin. "Most of the early lessons I learned about selling, I learned from my grandfather. As a boy, I went with my grandfather on his rounds through the neighborhood. I was always around the business of selling.

"After my granddad finished his regular route, he sometimes had some leftover vegetables, and he would let me sell them and keep the proceeds. I vividly remember my first sale, which I made under his watchful eye. He gave me a few onions to sell, and I sold them to a neighbor lady. I only made a few pennies on the transaction, but I learned a million-dollar lesson: Don't let the fear of rejection stop you. Keep knocking on doors, keep pitching until you make the sale. Be persistent and you'll be rewarded."

> *"I was fortunate enough to grow up in a home in which salesmanship was not looked down on, and I've never had to swallow my pride in order to sell something."*
>
> RICH DEVOS

I have personally watched Rich DeVos in various selling situations. There are twenty-nine teams in the NBA, and the Orlando Magic is in the second smallest market. So for our franchise to succeed, our owner, Rich DeVos, has had to sell this team to the Orlando community and to the talented players we have recruited. The most highly recruited players tend to prefer teams in the big, glitzy cities like L.A., Boston, Philly and New York. It's not easy for a town like Orlando to compete against those venues. But Orlando does compete—and successfully.

"League-wide, Orlando is known to have the best ownership in the NBA," says the Magic's general manager, John Gabriel. "That's because our owner is a consummate salesman.

"For example, when we were recruiting Horace Grant, Rich sent his son-in-law Bob Vander Weide and me in a helicopter to pick up Horace and his agent, Jimmy Sexton, in Chicago and bring them out to Rich's home in Holland, Michigan. We flew over Lake Michigan—the view was breathtaking. Then we landed in Rich's backyard. Waiting to greet us was a man in shorts, a casual shirt and bare feet—Rich DeVos himself. Rich waved hello and welcomed Grant to his home.

"We all had lunch and casual conversation, and Rich won Horace Grant over immediately. After lunch, Rich took Grant out on his boat, and they talked about life and basketball, and what it would be like to play in Orlando. Ten days later, Grant signed with the Magic and became the final player piece that would take our team all the way to the NBA Finals in 1995."

Rich has loved selling all his life—and he has always been amazed at the fact that this time-honored profession is so often looked down upon. For some reason, salesmanship in general has gotten a bad name, and person-to-person salesmanship has gotten an especially bad rap. In his first book, *Believe!* Rich relates:

> I've had people say to me before, "Oh, Amway. You guys are in that direct-selling deal." My answer: Sure we are! We are in the personal service business. We happen to think that personal service beats making the customer stand in line. We don't apologize for it. I respect the man who is in a business where the customers need not beat their way through traffic, park way out in a crowded parking lot and run through the rain or snow to get their goods. I respect the man who brings it to their doors, and if he respects the value of his own service, he is to be praised and not put down for it.

Today, as part of Alticor, Amway is an international force of some three million independent business owners. "As a leader of those people," Rich reflects in *Believe!* "my first job is to communicate the respect that I genuinely feel, and hope that my respect will rub off on them and what they are doing."

Rich's respect for salespeople extends not only to people who are selling *for* him, but also to people who are selling *to* him. He is always willing to listen to a sales pitch—and he admires a salesman who can get him to close the deal. Architect and developer Marvin DeWinter, president of Hartland Investments in Grand Rapids, says, "Rich tells a story from Amway's early years. A salesman wanted to sell a corporate jet to the company. At the time, Amway owned prop planes and Rich wasn't interested in owning a jet. A salesman asked Rich to come to the airport and examine the plane. Rich agreed—but he insisted that he was just looking, and he had no intention of buying.

> *"Selling is the most honorable of all professions. To sell is to serve. Rich DeVos has always been a salesman because he has always been a servant."*
>
> Dan and Bunny Williams
> Independent Business Owners

"Once at the airport, the salesman offered to take Rich for a ride. So they took off from Grand Rapids, circled around Detroit, then landed again. 'It's nice, all right,' Rich said, 'but we can't afford a plane like this.' The salesman offered to let him keep the plane for a month, rent-free, paying only the maintenance expenses. Rich agreed, and he used the plane for a month. 'After thirty days,' Rich recalls, 'they wanted to take my plane away from me!' And that's how Rich DeVos, the master salesman, was sold a jet airplane."

Rich DeVos is probably the greatest salesman in the world. In his career, he has sold everything from a handful of onions to nutritional supplements to patriotism to faith in God. Whatever he sells, Rich truly believes in his product, and he makes believers out of everyone within earshot. How does Rich do it? What are the character qualities, personality traits and skills it takes to sell like Rich DeVos?

Four Ingredients of Great Salespeople

I've had a chance to observe Rich in many selling situations and have observed four crucial salesmanship ingredients in his life:

Salesmanship ingredient no. 1: honesty

All great salespeople are honest. Honesty is the key to building trust, and trust is the key to building a lasting relationship with a customer. If a customer catches you in a lie, the relationship is over. You may make one sale by stretching or breaking the truth, but you won't get to make another—not with that customer. A great salesperson doesn't focus on a single sale, but a long-term relationship with the customer.

Some salespeople lie in order to avoid seeming ignorant. If a customer asks a question and a salesperson doesn't know the answer, he or she makes up an answer—and a made-up answer is a lie. Here's the honest approach: If a customer asks a question and you don't know the answer, say, "I'll find out and get back to you." Jot down the question in a notepad and make sure you get back to the client with honest information. There's no shame in not knowing the answer to a question—but there's *enormous* shame in getting caught in lie.

> *"Lots of folks think they are too good to sell. They have forgotten that every dollar that is made in America is made because somebody somewhere sold something."*
>
> Rich DeVos

I have lost count of the number of people who have told me of the absolute honesty of Rich DeVos. A typical comment came from independent business owner Ron Hale: "Rich's life is about integrity and honesty. He sticks to his values and principles no matter what. People know that Rich tells the truth."

Always tell the truth about your product. If you don't believe in it enough to be truthful, find another product to sell.

Never promise more than you can deliver. It's much better to under-promise and over-deliver than vice versa. Stand behind your promises and your products. If you are known as a person of integrity and honesty, you will have a long, successful career in sales.

Salesmanship ingredient no. 2: enthusiasm

All great salespeople are fired up and enthused about their products. Enthusiasm is the visible manifestation of your inner passion for your product—and it is contagious. When Rich begins to sell, people respond enthusiastically. It doesn't matter whether he is selling his company's products, selling America or sharing his faith in God. People catch his enthusiasm, and they want what he has. If you are enthusiastic about your product, your customer is bound to get excited about it, too.

> *"Rich DeVos is a remarkable salesman, and he knows how to move an idea in the marketplace."*
>
> GEN. ALEXANDER M. HAIG JR.
> FORMER U.S. SECRETARY OF STATE

Where does enthusiasm come from?

First, enthusiasm comes from God. The word *enthusiasm* comes from the Greek word *entheos,* meaning "filled with God" (from *en,* "within," and *theos,* "god"). Rich's enthusiasm comes from the fact that he is possessed and indwelt by God—he is truly a God-filled, enthusiastic individual. (You'll learn more about how to be a God-filled person like Rich in chapter 13.)

Second, enthusiasm comes from faith in your product. When you know that the product you are selling is something that everyone needs, then how can you help but be excited about it? If you are selling a product, you should also be using it, learning its benefits, and getting excited and enthused about it so you can promote it with energy and conviction. If you have faith in your product, then you know you are doing your customer a favor by sharing its marvelous benefits with them.

Third, enthusiasm comes from your vision of an exciting and successful future. You know that with every sale, you advance one step closer to your goals. You envision the rewards that await you. Your vision of success excites you and ignites your enthusiasm for your product.

Fourth, enthusiasm comes from the support of positive people in your life. If you want to be enthusiastic, you must have people in your life who will encourage you, affirm you and cheer you on. Pessimists are enthusiasm killers. Optimists lift your spirits and enable you to believe in yourself and your dreams.

So if you want to sell like Rich, then grab some of Rich's enthusiasm. Get fired up for success!

> *"Whenever Rich spoke to the independent business owners, he was selling them on the belief that 'You can do it!' He'd tell them success stories, and he'd fire up their enthusiasm and build their confidence. He'd challenge them to pursue their dream and make it happen. He was the ultimate pep-squad leader."*
>
> BILL NICHOLSON, FORMER AMWAY CHIEF OPERATING OFFICER

Salesmanship ingredient no. 3: confidence

All great salespeople have confidence. In his book *Believe!* Rich writes, "I believe that one of the most powerful forces in the world is the will of the man who believes in himself, who dares to aim high, to go confidently after the things that he wants from life." In sales, winning is all about attitude. An attitude of confidence wins; an attitude of self-doubt defeats you before you even begin.

Whatever you sell, you must begin with an attitude of confidence. You must believe that you can sell your product even in a down economy, even in an off season, even if you've been in a slump. You can't sell to a customer with a "you-don't-want-to-buy-my-product-do-you?" attitude. Confidence sells—but confidence isn't always easy to come by.

Sure, some people seem to be born with a natural belief in themselves, while others are naturally shy. But if the truth were known, many people who *seem* bold and confident are actually as riddled with self-doubt as you are—but they have made a decision to say "no" to their self-doubts and press on toward their dreams and goals. They may seem confident and comfortable when they sell, but the truth is that they have actually stepped far outside their own comfort zone in order to become successful in sales. If you're looking for success, you'll never find it in your comfort zone.

The Secret of Rich's Success

There are people who have amassed more wealth than Rich—but Rich would be the first to tell you that wealth is not the only measure of success. What, then, are some of his other successes?

Rich is successful as a husband; he has remained married and in love with one woman throughout his life. He is successful as a leader; few people are so universally appreciated and admired by their employees and business associates, and by people ranging from janitors and waitresses to U.S. presidents.

I have asked a number of people (including Rich himself) the secret of his astounding success, and this is what I've learned:

Bob Vander Weide, Rich's Son-in-Law and Orlando Magic CEO:

"Why did Rich and Jay have such amazing success with this idea called Amway? Rich would tell you that he and Jay were blessed by the fact that the timing was right and they took advantage of their marketing opportunities. But here's my analysis of Rich's success:

"1. Delegation. Rich and Jay hired good people, trusted them and turned them loose to do what they do best.

"2. Common sense. Rich is not a college graduate, but he has the incredible ability to cut through seemingly complex issues and get right to the core. He won't beat an issue to death. His whole mission is to find resolution and move on.

"3. The ability to inspire others. Rich has the gift of being able to move and motivate people and call them to action."

Hyrum Smith, Cofounder, The Franklin-Covey Company:

"Rich DeVos built his success on the desire to make other people successful. He gets genuinely excited about the success of his people. Most businesspeople are threatened when the people around them succeed. Not Rich. Amway is based on the principle that when others succeed, he succeeds. That's why Rich is a hero to so many people—and that's why he's so successful."

Jack Hogan, Grand Rapids: Broadcaster:

"Why is Rich so successful? I can explain it with a story:

"One night, Rich and I were celebrity waiters at a dinner to raise money to fight cystic fibrosis. We were dressed up in tuxedos, and the idea was to collect big tips from the diners for charity. We ate together before the banquet, and I asked him how much Amway was worth. Rich pulled out a paper napkin and started figuring out how much the company had made just that week. He was shocked! He couldn't believe the success of the business. He said to me, 'Wow, we're so busy building this company that I never stopped to think how well we're doing!'

"To Rich, it was never about the money. He was always on a mission to spread goodwill and help other people achieve their dreams. All he wanted was to help other people succeed, and his success was the happy byproduct."

Joe Tomaselli, Vice President and General Manager, Amway Grand Plaza Hotel:

"One day I asked Rich DeVos about his success. I said, 'Did you plan to be so successful?' He said, 'No. The money was secondary. Every day I had so much fun, and I enjoyed it immensely. I especially enjoyed watching so many other people find success in their lives—that was a thrill. And that's all I did. I didn't know what I had going. Jay and I just had this idea, we worked at it hard, and we had fun. Then it got going and going and going. And it's still going.'"

Cheri Vander Weide, Rich's Daughter:

"Dad's success was driven by his mission, not a desire to get rich. He always had a desire to help others along the way. His decisions were based on how people and their families would be impacted."

Rich DeVos:

"Success comes from having a dream and setting tangible, realizable goals that enable you to see your dreams to completion. Success comes from inspiring and motivating people, so that your dream of success becomes their dream as well. Then you all work together, and you all succeed together.

"I get a lot of credit for motivating other people. But when I motivate others, I am actually motivating myself. I gain a lot of enthusiasm from an audience. I inspire them and they inspire me, and together we go forth and have an impact on the world.

"My dad inspired me to believe that there are opportunities all around us, and we can seize them whenever they come our way. So if you fail at one thing, you don't have to despair. There's another opportunity for success just around the corner. That principle has enabled me to maintain an optimistic attitude in the face of trials and disappointments.

"Many successful people today are told that they should feel guilty for their success, as if their wealth came at the expense of the poor. People who create wealth, opportunity and jobs should never have to feel guilty for that. I believe my success has come from helping other people to become successful. So I don't apologize for my success and financial accomplishments. Success is not sinful. The Bible doesn't condemn success.

"Poverty is not a virtue. Being poor is not such a wonderful thing. If you are poor, you should do something about it. And if you have your health and a good dose of common sense, you can."

"I have seen countless people make a choice to be confident," Rich says. "If you don't naturally feel bold and confident, you can choose an attitude of confidence. Again and again, I've seen people who, when they started out in direct selling, were nervous and shaky—but they would take those first small steps toward success. Before long, they discovered abilities they never knew they had. With each small success, they gained new confidence. Eventually these once-timid people were leading hundreds of others, and they were experiencing more success than they had ever dreamed possible. When people aim high, they often surprise themselves by hitting the target!"

In Rich's words, we catch a glimpse of the reason for his phenomenal success and that of Alticor today. Rich DeVos and Jay Van Andel didn't set out to sell products. They sell *confidence*. They fire up people to believe in themselves, and those people sell the product. Bob Vander Weide is married to Rich's daughter, Cheri, and has served as an executive in the Orlando Magic organization. Bob explained to me how Rich has generated success by generating confidence.

"Rich DeVos is a great salesman," he said, "but he's not selling soap and vitamins. He's selling *you* on *you*. He's selling *confidence*. His sales pitch is, 'You can do it! Take a risk! Be the best you can be!' That's how Amway grew. Rich spoke at conventions across America, and when you walked out of one of those meetings, you really believed you could accomplish anything. Rich got millions of people believing in themselves, and a motivated, confident sales force numbering in the millions really can accomplish anything. It was like a runaway forest fire."

Rich's son, Dan, agrees. "Dad is selling more than soap and vitamins (though, of course, no one sells soap and vitamins better than he does). He's selling ideas, truth, faith in God, belief in America, the free enterprise system and compassion for the needy and less fortunate. He's selling the Grand Rapids community, the arts, education and charitable causes. Most of all, he's selling a positive attitude and the fact that we should aim high and believe in ourselves. He's selling optimism and confidence. Dad has always used his talents as a salesman to make the world a better place."

Don't ever let your lack of confidence limit your dreams. Don't let other people tear down your confidence. Don't wait until you have learned more or accomplished more before you start believing in yourself. Begin now. Believe in yourself now. Make a choice to be confident, then hold your head high and go after your dreams.

"God has confidence in you," Rich concludes. "He made you for a purpose, and he designed you with a wonderful mind and a healthy body because he has some important work for you to do. God is in the success business; he has a plan for your life, and he didn't plan for you to fail. Even if you don't have confidence in yourself, have confidence in God, and he will work out his plan for success through you."

Salesmanship ingredient no. 4: courage

All great salespeople are courageous. Why do you need courage in order to sell? Because all salespeople face one great fear: the fear of rejection, a fear that is expressed by such questions as, "What will other people think of me?" or "What if they say no?" Psychological studies show that high-achieving, successful people are not overly concerned about what others think. This suggests that in order to become successful in any endeavor—especially sales—we must overcome our fear of rejection.

> *"Confidence, like every good gift, comes from God. If you didn't receive the gift, you can make the choice. And when you make the choice, you receive the gift."*
>
> Rich DeVos

For most of us, fear of rejection is a pattern of thinking that we learned in childhood. Psychologists call this pattern "excessive self-monitoring," and it is often rooted in destructive messages we send ourselves: "I don't want to be a bother to people," "People won't like me if I'm too assertive and try to sell them something," "I'm afraid to meet new people," or "I don't deserve to succeed."

Fear of rejection often leads to procrastination—the fear of beginning a difficult task. The fear of rejection also makes us feel like quitting after we have started. Many people say, "I will sell when I feel more motivated. Right now, I lack motivation, so what's the use of trying?" To become a fearless seller, you've got to push past your natural human tendency to procrastinate. You have to step out, take action (even if it's only a baby step) and just *do* it! The only way to defeat your fears is to stand up to them, face them squarely and attack them head-on.

> *"Rich DeVos is not just selling a product. He's motivating people to achieve their dreams."*
>
> Josie Luster-McGlamory
> Alticor Employee

The reality of selling is that hardly anybody feels like selling at first. The urge to procrastinate is normal and near-universal. Almost every successful salesperson will tell you that his or her successes have usually come about as a result of disciplining themselves to sell even when they didn't feel like selling.

Successful salespeople have good habits and good discipline. And what is discipline? It is simply doing something you don't want to do in order to achieve something you want to achieve. Once you start to do it, once you will yourself and discipline yourself to do it despite your feelings, you'll usually discover that the feelings will follow. You'll feel motivated to sell once you get into a habit of selling—and that habit only comes about as a result of good self-discipline.

Another solution to the fear of rejection is *good preparation*. One source of fear of rejection is a sense of being inadequate to the task. "What if I bungle my sales talk? What if the customer asks me questions that expose my ignorance? What if I make a fool of myself?" If you are well-prepared, if you know how to answer every question and every objection, then you can lay this fear to rest.

> *"You overcome rejection by doing things that give you positive reinforcement. The first time that you make a sale, you are scared. But when someone buys something, you get confidence. You do that enough and, pretty soon, you gain confidence in yourself and in what you are selling. You begin to not worry about rejection anymore because rejection is just part of the process."*
>
> RICH DEVOS

Another solution to the fear of rejection is to seek the company of other salespeople. Everyone who sells is in the same boat, facing the same issues. Make a point of seeking out people who appear confident and successful. Ask them how they faced the fear of rejection, the fear of cold calling, the fear of the telephone or the fear of meeting new people. In the process, you'll pick up tips from people who have been in your shoes—and you'll gain the encouragement of knowing you're not alone in your fears.

But remember: Even though other people can encourage you and share their insights and ideas, only you can make your success happen. Only you can make your calls and meet your customers. Only you can build good habits and good self-discipline. No one else can do it for you.

One thing is certain: If you sell, you *will* be rejected. It's not a question of *if* you'll be rejected, but *how many times a day* you will be rejected. So get used to rejection—and don't take it personally. Remember that the people you call on deal with a number of salespeople every week—and they reject most of them. It's not personal.

If your sales call is rejected, it's not a rejection of you. When you are rejected, smile, say, "Thank you for your time," and move on.

Don't dwell on rejection. Don't obsess over a customer who said "no." Rejection doesn't mean you're doing it wrong. You are not being singled out for persecution. Rejection is simply part of the territory.

Look at it this way: Suppose you get rejected—what's the worst that could happen? Your customer is not going to physically assault you when you make a sales call. Your customer can't get you fired or take your first-born child from you. In fact, the worst that could happen is that your customer will say "no." And if the customer says no, you won't get the sale. But so what? If you don't make the call, you won't get the sale either—so you might as well summon your courage and make the call!

> *"Rich DeVos isn't selling a product or a specific item. He is selling people on their own potential. He's selling the American Dream."*
>
> STEVE VAN ANDEL, JAY'S OLDEST SON AND CHAIRMAN OF ALTICOR

If you make a lot of sales calls, you'll get a lot of rejections—but you'll also get a lot of sales. With each success, you'll gain confidence and courage, and you'll overcome your fear of rejection. "If people don't buy your product," says Rich, "you may feel rejected. That's not important. Don't worry about rejection. Just get out there and sell. Once you have reached your goals and achieved your dreams, those moments of rejection will fade to nothing. All you'll remember is how good it feels to succeed."

Tom Michmershuizen, a retired longtime employee, told me a story about Rich's salesmanship. "This goes back years ago," Tom said, "when Amway was doing about a hundred million dollars a year. I was a young sales coordinator, and Rich took me with him to a meeting of the Sales and Marketing Club of Detroit.

"Rich sat at the speakers table, next to the president of General Motors. Being a visitor, I sat at a table with a vice president of the Bank of Detroit and a vice president of the Goodyear Tire and Rubber Company. The fellow from the Bank of Detroit asked where I was employed, and I said, 'I'm with Amway.' The man replied, 'Amway? Never heard of it.'

"The man from Goodyear was shocked! He said, 'You're from Michigan and you've never heard of the Amway Corporation? It's one of the fastest-growing companies in America!'

"Hearing this, the banker changed his mind in a hurry, and he asked me to contact him about Amway Corporation's banking needs. That room was so full of industrial heavyweights, he had no idea how little clout I actually had in the company!

"Overcoming fear has been one of the keys to my success. Fear stops us from attempting new things. I've learned to overcome fear because God is the guiding force in my life. Doors have opened for me through the grace of God. So many people fail to take advantage of their opportunities because they fear rejection or failure."

RICH DEVOS

"Well, the meeting progressed, and Rich got up and gave his speech—a great speech, very motivational and inspiring as usual. After the meeting I asked Rich what he and the president of General Motors had been talking about during the meal. Rich told me that he had sold the president of GM a full year's supply of Nutrilite Double X—and the president of GM had sold Rich a new car! He said, 'You know, I thought I was a pretty good salesman—but I think I met my match!'

"Then Rich told me something that has stuck with me ever since: 'A good salesman never stops selling.'"

If you want to be successful like Rich, then get out and sell!

Chapter Ten

Give Till It Feels Good!

TOM MICHMERSHUIZEN BECAME an Amway employee in 1962. An incident from those early Amway days made a big impression on Tom. "In the early 1960s," he told me, "we had a fellow working in the warehouse who got himself in a lot of trouble on a Saturday night. He and his best friend were out with their girlfriends, and they were drinking.

"One fellow and his girl left the tavern a little early and headed home. At a turn in the road, he ran out of gas. He got out of the car and started pushing while his girlfriend steered.

"Just then, his friend—the fellow who worked at the Amway warehouse—approached that very turn, driving his own car while legally drunk. There in the road ahead of him was his pal, pushing the stalled car. Unable to react in time, the Amway employee plowed right into his best friend, killing him.

"The grieving parents of the dead young man forgave the driver, and they interceded on the young man's behalf. They told the judge, 'Sending this young man to prison for manslaughter won't bring our son back, and it won't help this young man, either.'

> *"Many people know that Rich is one of the finest business leaders of his generation. But few people know what a tender spirit and loving heart he has. He is one of history's greatest motivators, precisely because he is motivated by the love of God and a desire to be faithful to his Lord."*
>
> Billy Zeoli, President
> Gospel Communications International

"Rich DeVos, the young man's employer, also wanted to keep him out of prison. Rich could see the grief and guilt the young man felt for having killed his best friend in a senseless accident. He worried that it would do more harm than good to toss the young man into prison with a lot of hardened criminals. So Rich pleaded with the judge to go light on his sentence. 'If the young man has to spend time in prison,' Rich said, 'keep him in solitary with a few good books, away from the other prisoners.' The judge said he had to give the fellow a six-month term, and he fined the boy fifteen hundred dollars—which, for the young man, might as well have been a million. He didn't have it.

"So Rich paid the fine, putting it on the basis of a loan. The young man got to serve his term away from the hardened criminals. As Rich had asked him to, the fellow read good books during those six months and was given favorable evaluations from the prison board. After his release from prison, the young man returned to work at Amway and I believe he stayed there until he retired.

"Understand, in the early 1960s, Rich DeVos was not the billionaire he is today. So when he paid that fellow's fine, it was a costly act of true generosity, motivated by Rich's sincere love and compassion for people. When I saw what Rich did for that young man, I knew that I was part of an organization with a heart. I was proud to work for a man like Richard M. DeVos."

A Good Citizen

"We must not get cynical or pessimistic. We don't have to do everything ourselves, and we don't have to do it all today. All compassion requires from us is that we take that first small step."

RICH DEVOS

What drives Rich DeVos?

He has money, influence, fame, beautiful homes, pleasure boats and the freedom to live his life as he chooses. But I know Rich, and I can tell you that these are not the things that drive him. There is a deeper motivation at work in his heart. All his life, he has been driven to be successful—but not so that he can lavish the rewards of success upon himself. He is motivated by a desire to honor God and improve the lives of people everywhere.

One of Michigan's most distinguished citizens—and a man who knows Rich DeVos well—offers an insight into Rich's generosity. "Rich DeVos has a simple business philosophy," says former President Gerald R. Ford, "and it is this: If you are successful, then you give something back to your community. Rich has given so much back to the Grand Rapids community and to the world community. When he gives, he challenges others to give as well, so that whatever Rich contributes is magnified and multiplied. Rich and his partner, Jay Van Andel, have stimulated the rebirth of downtown Grand Rapids, they have contributed to health care and education, and they have helped to raise the standard of living for people in other parts of the world. Rich DeVos is a classic example of what it means to be a good citizen."

President Ford's appraisal of Rich DeVos is echoed by another distinguished American, Edwin Meese III, who was U.S. Attorney General under President Reagan. He told me, "Rich DeVos is an example to us all—an example of generosity, caring and compassion. He typifies all that is good about America, both in his success and in the way he uses his success to improve the lives of people everywhere. He has made an enormous amount of money through good judgment, hard work and inspiring others to achieve their dreams. Many people in his position would use their wealth in a self-serving way, but Rich uses his money to help others and to make the world a better place."

Former Michigan Governor John Engler adds, "Rich DeVos is a generous man—and not just with his wealth. He gives of himself—he gives generously of his time, his emotional support and his wise counsel. He gives without hesitation because he wants to make a difference in people's lives. Rich has a loving spirit for all people, and that is why he is such a great role model."

> *"Rich and I are loyal to the Grand Rapids community. We made our money here and want to invest it here. For example, the Amway Distribution Center was built here even though it would have been less costly to build it elsewhere. Building it in Grand Rapids was not the best operational or economic decision, but it was the right thing to do."*
>
> JAY VAN ANDEL
> AMWAY COFOUNDER

John H. Logie, former mayor of Grand Rapids, compares Rich DeVos with other wealthy benefactors and explains why Rich stands out as unique. "Throughout our country's history," the mayor says, "wealthy entrepreneurs and industrialists have been content to show their generosity through their last will and testament. Men like Rockefeller, Vanderbilt, Harriman, Ford and others have left endowments and foundations after their deaths. In life, they couldn't part with their wealth—they waited until they died. But how generous is it to bequeath a sum of money when you no longer have any use for money? Rich DeVos is a different kind of business leader. His generosity is authentic. He has been an example of generous giving throughout his life.

Just as important, he has inspired others to give by his example of civic leadership."

Not only does Rich give generously of his own time and treasure, but he is a cheerleader for increased generosity and compassion wherever he goes. "Dad is a terrific fundraiser," says Rich's son, Dick DeVos. "He doesn't hesitate to ask other people to make big donations because he is already giving so generously. His challenge is, 'I'm asking you to join in and become a part of this civic effort or that compassionate cause. I'm offering you the privilege and joy of giving. This is a great cause, and I'm already contributing to it. Don't you want to be involved, too?' People respond by giving money, time and services. So he is not only generous, but he is able to mobilize generosity and involvement throughout the community."

Grand Rapids business and community leader John Canepa agrees: "Rich DeVos's philanthropy is not just about the money he gives, but the leadership role he plays. He gets others involved in improving the community. For example, when we launched the expansion of the Grand Rapids Convention Center, Rich made the major gift. There was another wealthy man whom we had approached, but he refused to give a penny toward the building fund. I called Rich and said, 'I'd appreciate it if you would send this man a letter and request a fifty-thousand-dollar gift. It would mean so much more coming from you.' Rich was glad to do it, and he sent the letter. A few days later, the man called me and asked, 'Can I make this contribution over three years?' Rich has a way of reaching the heart—even the heart of a cheapskate! I call that Rich's 'moral suasion.' It's a key reason for the great things that have been taking place in West Michigan."

> *"The reason Rich likes to make money is that he enjoys giving it away. He takes pleasure in sharing his success with those who are less fortunate."*
>
> Bill Nicholson, Former Amway Chief Operating Officer

Rich DeVos has been widely recognized for his giving. Because of his generosity, Rich's name appears on buildings in Grand Rapids, including the DeVos Children's Hospital, DeVos Performance Hall, the DeVos Center at Grand Valley State University and the DeVos Place Convention Center. I'm sure Rich is grateful that people have chosen to honor him in this way, but I know Rich's heart, and I know that his giving is not motivated by ego or the desire for recognition. He has given literally millions of dollars without any fanfare or recognition, purely because he believed in a cause and wanted to help make a difference.

Grand Rapids attorney Carl Ver Beek recalls, "Jay Van Andel once made a major gift to an Alzheimer's care center at our senior-citizen facility. In gratitude for Jay's enormous gift, we named it the Van Andel Pavilion. What no one knows is that Rich DeVos also contributed to the building. Rich insisted that there be no publicity. 'That's Jay's project,' he said. 'He made it happen, and I just want to help.'" And former Grand Rapids TV broadcaster Jack Hogan recalls, "Sometimes local charities come up short at the end of the year. If they don't meet their budget, they have to cut back services the following year. Rich frequently steps in and makes up any shortfall so these charities can keep serving the needy—but he always does so behind the scenes. He never takes any bows for it."

Max DePree, former CEO of Herman Miller, Inc., and best-selling author of *Leadership Is an Art,* told me, "Rich DeVos is not only generous, he's compassionate. Some wealthy men are generous because they feel it's expected of them, or because an image of generosity is good for business, or because their wealth makes them feel guilty. But Rich's generosity is motivated by his genuine compassion for people. Whether he gives to support improved health care, better education or Christian evangelism, it is Rich's compassion for people that motivates him. Let me tell you a story to show you what I mean:

"My granddaughter, Zoe, was born sixteen weeks early and weighed one pound, seven ounces. She's now fourteen years old and doing beautifully. By the way, *zoe* is a Greek word meaning 'life.' Zoe was cared for at the DeVos Children's Hospital in Grand Rapids. For the first six years of her life, I wrote her a series of letters that were compiled into a book called *Dear Zoe.* I sent Rich a copy of the book, along with a note thanking him for his hospital and the great medical staff that serves there. A few days later, Rich called me from Florida. He was in tears after reading my book. That's a glimpse into the heart of this great man. His compassion always comes out in his generosity."

> *"Rich teaches us to give back to the community. 'Profit is good, not evil,' he says, 'but you must share with your community.'"*
>
> Peter Secchia, Grand Rapids Business and Community Leader

Investing in the Things That Matter

Rich DeVos and his wife Helen have always been a generous couple. They donate time and money to many worthy organizations, including churches, civic and community organizations, charitable organizations and hospitals. "We have the joy of giving away money," Rich says. "From the first days of our marriage, Helen made sure that we tithed our income. 'Tithe' means 'tenth.' So we always gave at least a tenth of everything we earned to the Lord and to people in need. Tithing helps you to see material blessings as coming from the Lord and belonging to the Lord. If you don't possess your money, then your money won't possess you.

"Giving is hard work because there are so many worthy causes. We don't just write a check to every organization that asks us. We spend a lot of time researching each organization or need, and we pray for wisdom. We see tithing and giving as a way of investing in the things that truly matter—investing in human lives, investing in eternity. So we do our homework because we want our giving to be used by God in the most effective way possible, according to his will.

"You should always set the tithe aside first, as soon as the money comes in. And make sure you tithe on the gross, not the after-tax net. Don't think of it as your money. Think of it as the Lord's. If you don't claim it as your own, you won't miss it when you give it to God. But if you put it in your pocket first, it will be hard to give it away. Something inside you will say, *No! That's* my *money!* So tithe off the top—giving is easier when you set your tithe aside the moment you get it.

"'Bring the whole tithe into the storehouse, that there may be food in my house. Test me in this,' says the Lord Almighty, 'and see if I will not throw open the floodgates of heaven and pour out so much blessing that you will not have room enough for it.'"

MALACHI 3:10 (NIV)

"The Lord has enabled me to have financial success, and I don't apologize for the success I've received. But whether you have a little or a lot, something miraculous happens when you tithe. We tithed when we were poor, when I was making a hundred dollars a week, and we tithe today. I encourage everyone to do the same."

Rich and Helen's children have carried on the tithing tradition they learned from their generous parents. Doug DeVos told me, "Dad believes the money you make is not yours, it's God's. He gives us the ability to work and earn money. So we must handle our money wisely, give it away wisely and use it well. Never love money, because money will not make you happy. If God gives money to you, be a good steward of that money so that in the end he will say, 'Well done, good and faithful servant.'" And Dan DeVos adds, "Dad's philosophy on money is that you give first and give freely of everything you have—your time, your talent and your treasure. Dad enjoys giving, and he has always taught us to do the same."

Tom Michmershuizen recalls, "I once heard an Amway distributor ask Rich, 'When did you know that you had arrived financially? I mean, when did you quit worrying about money?' Rich answered, 'How much do you give to your church? When you tithe to the Lord, your money worries will be over!' I heard that, and I gulped hard. I felt convicted that I should start tithing—but it was several years before I got up the nerve to actually try it. But Rich was right. When I started giving 10 percent to the Lord, my money worries went away!"

Rich does not view tithing as a matter of giving your money away. In fact, many people are surprised to discover that Rich views tithing as part of an overall strategy for success. "The tithing principle works," Rich says. "The more generous you are in giving to God and helping those in need, the more you have with which to be generous. You can't out-give God. Try it! Give at least 10 percent of your gross income to the church and charities every month! Find a need and meet it! Then see what God does in your life. There's an old saying: 'Give till it hurts.' I say, 'Give till it feels good!'"

Rich talked with me about some simple components of an overall wealth-producing strategy. "Spend less than you take in," he says. "That's a simple rule of life. We built Amway that way. We never borrowed any significant money. When we made a profit, we left it in the company and let it grow. We built with cash on hand, not bank loans.

"In the early years you work for money. In the later years the money works for you. This is a principle I teach to the Orlando Magic players. These guys make a lot of money, and many of them have never been taught how to manage large sums of money. I tell them, 'You need to set aside 10 million dollars and never touch it. If you earn 10 percent annual interest on that 10 million, you'll have a million dollars a year to live on. That way, you're a millionaire every year. You can live comfortably off the return for the rest of your life.'

> *"Grandpa talks to us about saving money. He says, 'Start with a penny, and it grows.'"*
>
> Hannah Vander Weide, Rich's Granddaughter (Bob and Cheri's Daughter)

"Buying a nice house is a good investment, but most of the other stuff people buy is a poor use of money. Usually, when people suddenly become wealthy, they buy a lot of expensive toys and waste their money. It's not unusual for a newly wealthy person to be right back where he started, as poor as before, within a few years. You see it all the time with highly paid sports figures, entertainers and lottery winners.

"The key to maintaining wealth is to be willing to forego current luxuries in order to invest in the future and live on the interest of that investment. As the saying goes, 'Watch your pennies and the dollars will take care of themselves.'"

Bob Schierbeek, a member of Rich DeVos's business advisory team, recalls, "Once, when I was in a board meeting with Rich, he told me, 'Bob, you have to be careful with an investment or a business. The more dollars you have, the easier it is to let money slip through your fingers.' Rich is always encouraging people to look at the big picture and adopt a simple financial strategy for acquiring and conserving wealth."

Impacting Communities, Impacting Lives

I could fill an entire book with stories of acts of kindness and compassion that Rich has shown to individuals in need. But let me just share a few.

Billy Zeoli, the president of Gospel Communications

International and the man who introduced me to Rich DeVos, has been Rich's friend for many years. Z told me, "My dad, Anthony Zeoli, called him 'Richie.' No one else ever called him that. After Rich's father died, my dad unofficially 'adopted' Rich and made a point of praying daily for him. My dad had a ministry of talking to people, witnessing to them about his faith and leading them to Christ. Rich supported my dad's ministry, and my dad made himself accountable to Rich.

"Every Sunday morning at 8:45 sharp, Rich's phone would ring and it was my dad. He would tell Rich what he had done that week, how many people he had led to Christ, and so forth. This went on for about fifteen years."

Rich picks up the story at this point. "Anthony Zeoli had become a Christian while in prison," Rich told me. "He went on to become a widely respected evangelist. He memorized so much Scripture that he was known as 'The Walking Bible.' I supported Anthony's work, and he reported to me all that he did. Every Sunday morning, my phone would ring and I always knew who it was. I'd say, 'Good morning, Anthony,' and he would proceed to tell me all the things he had done that week. One week I finally said, 'Anthony, you don't have to call me like this.' He said, 'Yes, I do. You pay me, and I'm accountable to you for what I do with the money. All of us are accountable to someone.'"

> *"One time we were on Peter Island with Rich. He said, 'Herb, how much do you give to the church and other charities?' I said, 'Five or ten percent, I guess.' Rich replied, 'Why don't you try twenty percent of the gross? Or even twenty-five? You'll never miss it, and you'll be blessed in the process.' What a challenge! And I've done it ever since."*
>
> Herb VanderMey
> Longtime Friend of Rich DeVos

Anthony Zeoli eventually reached a point in his life where

age and ill health forced him to slow down. But even though he could no longer walk the city sidewalks and share his faith with everyone he met, Anthony still had a job he could do for God: He could *pray.*

"Dad went to Rich," Billy Zeoli recalls, "and he said, 'Richie, have I got a deal for you. I'm getting old and need to leave Philadelphia and move to Florida. I'll send you a budget for my living expenses. I'll move down near you and support you in prayer.' Dad's total budget came to around sixty-two hundred dollars.

"Rich said, 'Anthony, I'll have to turn that down.'

"Dad nodded. 'Well, I understand.'

"Rich said, 'No, you don't understand. I can't do it for sixty-two hundred dollars. I'll do it for twelve thousand dollars.' Rich put up my dad in a condo near his place in Florida, and my dad supported Rich in prayer. In fact, he could see Rich's Florida home from his window, and whenever he saw Rich's boat set out to sea, he'd pray for Rich's safety.

"One of the reasons Rich is like a brother to me is that he was so much like a son to Dad. When Dad was in the hospital, Rich and I went together to see him. Dad called Rich 'my oldest son' because Rich is six years older than I am. Rich and I both knelt at my dad's bedside, and he gave us his blessing, just as Isaac blessed his sons from his deathbed in the Old Testament. While we were kneeling, I whispered to Rich, 'You're stealing my birthright!' It was a solemn moment, but I couldn't resist. Seriously, it was an honor to share my father's blessing with Rich DeVos. He gave so much so that Dad could be used in a big way by God."

That's the way Rich is. His giving always begins with a love for the individual. Rich loves people, and he has a special place in his heart for those who have spent themselves serving God and serving others. He also has a special place in his heart for those who have served their country.

Patrick Cleburne "Clebe" McClary III is a Marine veteran (don't ever say "ex-Marine"—a Marine is a Marine for life). On March 3, 1968, Clebe McClary was a platoon leader with the First Marine Division in Vietnam. Just after midnight, while Clebe and his men were on Hill 146 behind enemy lines, his platoon ran into an ambush. A satchel charge exploded near him, severing his left arm.

Ignoring the unbelievable pain, Clebe McClary continued to fight and lead his men. When he saw a grenade coming toward him, he shielded his face with his right hand. The grenade exploded, destroying his left eye and both eardrums, and mutilating his remaining hand. Another grenade blasted his legs. The platoon beat back the enemy assault, and Clebe and his men were finally choppered to safety.

> *"I learned how to give from Rich DeVos. As our company grew successfully, we had money to give away. In most communities, there are no expectations placed on you to give. However, in Grand Rapids, Rich sets the example for everyone. He has set the bar incredibly high. We have given millions away because of the example of Rich DeVos."*
>
> JOHN KENNEDY
> GRAND RAPIDS BUSINESS LEADER

Clebe spent more than two years in Stateside hospitals, undergoing thirty-four major surgeries and endless rounds of physical therapy. Doctors repeatedly told him he would never walk again—but he was determined to make liars of his doctors! In the years since, he has amazed his doctors by running marathons. Today Clebe McClary *(www.clebemcclary.net)* is in demand as a motivational and inspirational speaker, and Billy Zeoli has made a film of his story entitled *Clebe McClary: Portrait of an American Hero.*

"After I got shot up in Vietnam," Clebe told me, "I came back to the States with nothing. My wife, Deanna, and I lived in government housing, and we had no furniture. Things looked pretty bleak until I met Billy Zeoli."

Billy Zeoli picks up the story. "I met Clebe," Z told me, "while I was doing an evangelistic crusade in Florence, South Carolina. After I preached, I invited people to come forward and give their lives to Jesus Christ. One of those who came forward was Clebe McClary. He was missing an arm and an eye, and he needed help getting down the aisle. I prayed with him, and he received Jesus as his Lord and Savior that night."

"Z and I became good friends after that," Clebe recalls. "He called Rich DeVos and told him about me. Rich asked Z if I needed anything, and Z said, 'Yes. Clebe and his wife need a bed.' Rich said, 'Tell them to order a full bedroom suite and send me the bill.' We had never met the man, but he wanted to help us. We've used that furniture ever since, thirty-five years, and we still have it to this day."

Don Maine, former president and chancellor of Davenport University, has known Rich for a number of years, and he told me, "I used to hear Rich DeVos speak at different events around Grand Rapids, and he was a spellbinding speaker. He talked openly about his faith, and I thought, *Well, that's fine for him, if he wants to be religious—but I'm getting along fine without religion.* I didn't understand that Rich wasn't talking about *religion,* but about a *relationship* with God. But one thing Rich said many times stuck in my mind: 'I'm just a sinner saved by grace.' I thought, *If he's a sinner, what am I?*

"Finally, I reached a point where I knew I had to get serious about my faith. I made a decision to follow Jesus Christ, and I started attending church and studying the Bible. Not long after this, I became sick. I had muscular dystrophy, and then I underwent heart-bypass surgery. Over the next few months, I had thirteen different heart procedures. After every surgery, Rich would call to check on me and encourage me.

"One day, after I got home from the hospital, the phone rang. It was Rich DeVos. He said, 'Don, how you doing? Boy, you scared all of us. I want you to know I'm praying for you. You're a

Christian now, so you know where you're going if you die. You're at peace? Good! Don, that's wonderful!'

"Most people see Rich DeVos as Mr. Amway, as a wealthy businessman, as the owner of the Orlando Magic. I see him as a Christian servant who is genuinely interested in everyone he meets. Rich wants you to find the place God has for you in life. His caring and compassion are genuine."

The compassion and caring of Rich DeVos begins with individuals, and then it extends out into the community. He cares about making the West Michigan and Orlando communities better places in which all can live. Rich's friend and Grand Rapids business leader Chuck Royce told me, "Rich and Jay have done wonders for downtown Grand Rapids. Twenty years ago, they purchased the old Pantlind Hotel, which was one of the ten finest hotels in America when it was built in 1913. By the 1980s, it had become a rundown eyesore. They completely renovated the place and renamed it the Amway Grand Plaza Hotel, and it has become the anchor for the city's renewal and renovation. Today, the area around the Amway Grand Plaza is a popular, desirable place to live. In fact, my wife and I have lived in a condo across the street for seventeen years."

"I have lived in Egypt, Cuba, Israel and Haiti, and I have learned that the thing that destroys most countries is that they neglect people at the bottom of the social chain. Revolutions start at the bottom. In Grand Rapids and other cities, Rich DeVos has set an example by putting dollars back into the inner cities. Grand Rapids is a microcosm of what all countries should be. Share the wealth with the disadvantaged so they feel part of the process."

PAUL COLLINS
AWARD-WINNING ARTIST

The hotel is just one of many downtown buildings Rich has helped to restore, creating a compete turnaround in the heart of Grand Rapids. "Rich DeVos and Jay Van Andel have been restoring old buildings and constructing new ones," says Ralph W. Hauenstein, another Grand Rapids business leader. "The results are remarkable. Grand Rapids has been experiencing a renaissance, thanks to the generosity of Rich and Jay."

Rich and Helen DeVos are well known as leading patrons of the arts in Grand Rapids. "Rich and Helen are responsible for Grand Rapids having a marvelous symphony orchestra," says Chuck Royce. "They also made possible the construction of an acoustically superior hall in which to perform. They started the Artist-in-Residence program and funded the DeVos String Quartet. With their assistance, the then-conductor, Theo Alcantara, was able to transform a community volunteer orchestra into a world-class symphony with thirty-one paid positions."

Rich has a big heart where health care is concerned—especially health care for children. Rich and Helen's generous financial endowment made possible the founding of the DeVos Children's Hospital in Grand Rapids, one of the leading pediatric hospitals in the nation. "Today, West Michigan kids who would have had to go across the state or out of state to be treated for cancer and other life-threatening conditions can be treated right here," says Dr. James Fahner, chief of pediatric hematology and oncology at DeVos Children's Hospital. "When Rich and Helen began working with us to lay the groundwork for this hospital, Rich set only one condition. He said, 'In everything you do, never, ever settle for mediocrity. Always strive for magnificence!' They have given millions to make this hospital a magnificent reality.

> *"Rich is generous because he believes that to whom much is given, much is expected. It's called 'stewardship.'"*
>
> JAY VAN ANDEL
> AMWAY COFOUNDER

"Every Christmastime, Rich and Helen join with us for a luncheon where we present the progress that has been made during the year. The DeVoses are the inspirational and spiritual cornerstone of our hospital, and when we share together about the young lives that have been touched in this place, no one is able to come through it with dry eyes."

Jim Hiaeshutter, former head of security at Amway, recalls an incident that illustrates another facet of Rich's concern for healthcare. "After Rich's first heart attack," Hiaeshutter recalls, "I went with the DeVoses while they vacationed in Fiji. We docked the sailboat at a private island and attended a party. The next morning, Rich wasn't feeling well, so I told the owner of the private island that we needed help. He got a private plane to fly Rich to a hospital on the big island. Rich ended up staying in that hospital for two days.

"When he was feeling better and getting ready to leave, Rich asked the doctor, 'What kind of equipment do you have in this place?' The doctor showed him around, and Rich could see that much of the hospital equipment was old and obsolete. So Rich took me aside and said, 'Find out what the doctor needs to run a modern hospital.' I talked to the doctor and wrote down a few items he needed. Then Rich said, 'You'll be hearing from us.'

"When we got back to Grand Rapids, Rich said to me, 'Go to Butterworth Hospital and tell them to purchase everything on that list and ship it to the hospital in Fiji. Have them send the bill to me.' I don't know what it cost, but Rich paid it all."

Another cause that is dear to Rich DeVos is education. (After all, he married a schoolteacher.) Dr. Gaylen Byker, president of Calvin College, told me, "We needed to build a center for communication arts and sciences on our campus, so I approached Rich for a lead gift. My proposal was laid out on one side of a sheet of paper. I told Rich I could get him a full-blown proposal, but he said, 'I don't need to see any more. I trust you.' The next day, Rich told me, 'We'll do it.'"

> *"Rich DeVos is really just a basic guy who came up with an incredible product and became very wealthy. I believe God wanted him to have all of this money and influence because he knew that Rich would do the right thing with it."*
>
> PATRICK BROSKI, LONGTIME EMPLOYEE OF RICH AND HELEN DEVOS

Arend Lubbers told me, "I was president of Grand Valley State University, and Rich was on our board. We were located twelve miles west of downtown, and we felt we needed a downtown location. Rich is a man of vision, and he saw that this move made sense. He located a piece of property and helped finance it. We dedicated the DeVos Center in 2000."

Rich's sports enterprises in Orlando have also benefited worthy causes and needy people. A study by CSL International (Convention Sports & Leisure) showed that the Orlando Magic has had an economic impact of well over a billion dollars on the Orlando community since it was founded in 1989—an impact that means jobs and economic improvement for the central Florida community. Rich DeVos has personally donated millions to Orlando-area charities and the University of Central Florida. The Magic's parent organization, RDV Sports, has distributed millions more to local charities and central Florida public schools, and was recently named Outstanding Philanthropic Organization of the Year by the National Society of Fundraising Executives.

Through the Rich and Helen DeVos Community Enrichment Award, Rich and Helen encourage Orlando Magic players to use their NBA star status to enrich human lives in the larger community. Every year, this program honors a player who sets a good example, displays a respectable attitude and makes an outstanding contribution to his community. The award includes a fifty-thousand-dollar donation to a charity of the player's choice.

There is no cause closer to the heart of Rich DeVos than the cause of Jesus Christ. That is why Rich and Helen have contributed to ministries that advance the good news of the Christian gospel, such as the DeVos Urban Leadership Initiative, which trains inner-city youth workers to perform evangelism, social action, crisis intervention and other forms of urban Christian ministry.

Billy Zeoli, president of Gospel Communications International, told me, "Rich has paid the production costs for dozens of films which have allowed hundreds of thousands to hear the Gospel of Jesus Christ. One day, Rich and I had lunch with D. James Kennedy, president of Evangelism Explosion International. Jim Kennedy and I had a film we wanted to make, and we were asking Rich to provide the funding. Jim explained the film to Rich, and by the end of lunch Rich said, 'I'll underwrite it.' Just like that.

"Later, Jim said to me, 'How much money is he willing to put up? We never discussed price.' I said, 'If he said he'll underwrite it, he'll take all of it, whatever it comes to.' We made the film. It was called *Like a Mighty Army,* and it was an extraordinarily successful film. Many people made decisions to follow Christ as a result of that film."

> *"Rich DeVos is the epitome of a good corporate citizen. He has done so much for the Orlando community, most of it behind the scenes and without recognition. He doesn't do these things because he wants to puff up his ego or his reputation. He gives to the community because he loves God, he loves people, and he loves the city of Orlando."*
>
> JIMMY HEWITT, ORLANDO CIVIC AND BUSINESS LEADER

Another cause that is near and dear to Rich's heart (literally) is the issue of organ donation. "Every day," says Rich, "sixteen people in America die waiting for an organ donation. And while those people are dying, the organs they need are being buried or cremated with the deceased because we can't get family consent for the donation. I have been on that waiting list. I know what the wait is like. That is why I'm now campaigning to make organ donations more readily available to the people who need them."

The plan Rich supports is called Project Organ Donor, a proposal that would create either an insurance-style policy or an income tax credit of ten thousand dollars for the named beneficiary of any person who agrees to eventually donate organs after his or her death. The organs would be distributed (as they currently are) through UNOS, the United Network for Organ Sharing. The donor would file a signed, witnessed organ donation document that would be activated only after the individual has been declared brain dead, and the family has been notified. This takes the burden of the decision off the shoulders of the family and places it in the hands of the organ donor. (Such decisions can be extremely painful and difficult for family members in a time of grief.)

The ten thousand dollars would be paid by insurance companies or Medicare—and these payments would actually *save money.* For example, kidney patients routinely run up medical bills of between two hundred thousand dollars and four hundred thousand dollars while in dialysis waiting for a transplant. A payment of ten thousand dollars to a beneficiary would save hundreds of thousands of dollars, even after allowing for the cost of the transplant procedure and post-operative care.

"As Rich gets older, he gets more and more generous. He is showering the world with his benevolence."

LARRY ERHARDT SR., GRAND RAPIDS CONSTRUCTION EXECUTIVE

The world is a better place because Rich DeVos has used his success to benefit medicine, education, community development, the arts, the environment, and institutions and outreach efforts of the Christian faith. I am convinced that God entrusted great wealth and great influence to Rich DeVos with the knowledge that Rich would invest it in people.

But in addition to wealth and influence, I believe that God also entrusted some enormous personal challenges to Rich DeVos. God knew that he could entrust life-threatening health problems to Rich DeVos, knowing that Rich would take his own trials and hurts, and use them to bring help and healing to others. Rich's own heart problems and his experience with an organ transplant give him a platform to speak about these issues with credibility and authority.

Rich DeVos doesn't just give his money. He doesn't just donate his time. He literally pours his pain, his suffering and his heart into the cause of helping other people. He impacts his community, he impacts individual lives, and he impacts eternity.

"I was a young CPA just starting out in Grand Rapids. Rich had a lasting influence on my business career. He set a good example in the community of giving his time, energy, ideas and talents—not just money. It would have been easier for Rich to just write a check and be done with it, but he always did more than that."

MIKE JANDERNOA
GRAND RAPIDS BUSINESS LEADER

If we want to be successful and influential like Rich DeVos, then we need to learn what it means to give like Rich.

Biblical Principles of Charitable Giving

Rich DeVos enjoys giving more than he enjoys spending. "Every time Rich buys a big-ticket item, he wrestles with it," says employee Patrick Broski. "He says, 'This money could be put to better use helping others.' His kids have to tell him, 'Dad, you've done so much for others. Do something for yourself without feeling guilty about it.'"

"I was always bashful about my wealth," Rich says, "but one day one of my sons said, 'Dad, stop apologizing for being a billionaire.'

So I've stopped apologizing. Today, I focus on spending it well, investing it well, using it as God would have us use it. My wife and I pray about it, then we decide where it goes."

Rich DeVos bases his giving on biblical principles of Christian charity. His friend, inner-city pastor Orlando Rivera, says, "Rich DeVos's financial giving comes from a true faith commitment. Because God has blessed him, Rich believes that giving is a duty and a joy. His desire to give is inspired by his faith in God." If we want to give like Rich, then we need to understand the principles of biblical giving that underlie every decision Rich makes regarding the wise use of his money:

Giving principle no. 1: biblical giving is systematic

In 1 Corinthians 16:2 (NIV), the apostle Paul writes, "On the first day of every week, each one of you should set aside a sum of money" for charitable giving. Paul sets forth the principle that giving should be regular and habitual. It should be systematic.

Giving principle no. 2: biblical giving is proportionate to our income

Paul continues: ". . . in keeping with his income. . . ." God does not demand more of us than we can afford. Our giving is to be proportionate to the level of our material blessing.

Giving principle no. 3: biblical giving is cheerful

In 2 Corinthians 9:7 (NIV), Paul writes, "Each man should give what he has decided in his heart to give, not reluctantly or under compulsion, for God loves a cheerful giver." When you give to God with the right attitude, giving is a joy, not a burden. A cheerful giver feels a warmth in the heart whenever signing a donation check. That warmth comes from a sense of gratitude over being blessed by God and used by God to bring blessing to others.

Giving principle no. 4: biblical giving is generous

1 Chronicles 29:9 (NIV) tells us, "The people rejoiced at the willing response of their leaders, for they had given freely and wholeheartedly to the Lord. David the king also rejoiced greatly." Our giving should be free, wholehearted and generous. We give not to advance our reputation or to be recognized by other people, but out of a heart full of gratitude to God.

> *"Rich enjoys giving his money away—big-time! And the older he gets, the more he enjoys it."*
>
> John Boerema
> Friend of Rich DeVos

Giving principle no. 5: biblical giving is sacrificial

The apostle Paul praised the hard-pressed churches in first-century Macedonia for their sacrificial giving, saying, "Out of the most severe trial, their overflowing joy and their extreme poverty welled up in rich generosity. For I testify that they gave as much as they were able, and even beyond their ability" (2 Corinthians 8:2–3). God knows our hearts, and he knows our circumstances. When we give, he evaluates our gift not by the cost in dollars, but by the cost in sacrifice. For one giver, a gift of twenty dollars might be an extreme sacrifice; for another, a gift of twenty thousand dollars might be chump change. Whatever we give, we should be sure that the gift is costly and sacrificial. A donation only feels good if it hurts.

Giving principle no. 6: biblical giving is grateful

Everything we have comes from God. You might say, "I worked hard for everything I've earned." That's true—but where did you get the strength and health to work hard? Did you choose to be born in a land of opportunity? Did you teach yourself the value of hard work—or was it by the sheer grace of God that you learned how to succeed by your own labor? Clearly, we owe God a debt of gratitude for everything we are and everything we have. That gratitude should motivate our giving. In 2 Corinthians 9:11 and 15 (NIV), Paul writes, "You will be made rich in every way so that you can be generous on every occasion, and through us your generosity will result in thanksgiving to God. . . . Thanks be to God for His indescribable gift!"

Giving principle no. 7: biblical giving is faithful

God has entrusted his material blessings to us, and we must be faithful stewards of those blessings, using them to benefit the people around us. In 1 Corinthians 4:2 (NIV), Paul writes, "Now it is required that those who have been given a trust must prove faithful." We should make sure that we give to worthy, deserving causes and individuals who will use those gifts wisely and effectively. God is not honored and people are not helped if we simply write a check that ends up being squandered.

> *"Rich's approach to life is, 'Givers get and takers get taken.' He wants us all to become givers. He wants to see a spirit of generosity duplicated in thousands of lives."*
>
> Tony Renard
> Independent Business Owner

These are the biblical principles that Rich DeVos follows in his own giving. If we will practice these same principles in our personal and business lives, they will produce blessings in our own lives and the lives of people around us.

After all the millions of dollars Rich and Helen DeVos have given to hundreds of important causes, he remains modest and unaffected. Rich's friend Paul Conn, president of Lee University, shared a story with me that illustrates Rich's great humility. "On one occasion," he said, "Rich gave a large gift to our school. We held a big ceremony on the campus to publicly thank Rich and recognize him for his generosity. I introduced Rich to the audience, and I gave him a big buildup about his phenomenal business success.

"Then Rich walked up to the microphone. His first words were, 'You know, I used to be a fairly wealthy man until I met Paul Conn.' Then he proceeded to praise me for extracting such a large gift! He didn't want to take credit for his generosity; he preferred to give all the credit to me! It was a nice touch—and so typical of Rich DeVos."

Even after a heart transplant, his heart's desire remains the same: He is a cheerful, generous, grateful and faithful giver. He knows that true success is measured not by how much he gets, but by how much he gives.

Do you want to experience true success? Then be like Rich DeVos. Give until it feels *great!*

Chapter Eleven

Love Your Family!

RICH'S ENTREPRENEURIAL DRIVE and ambition were shaped by his father, Simon DeVos. Rich's father was not an entrepreneur himself; he was an honest, hard-working electrician who regretted never owning his own business. "Whatever you do, Rich," he would say, "get into business for yourself. That's the only way to control your own future and truly succeed."

Those words of advice resonated in Rich's soul, motivating and inspiring him from a very early age to always be his own boss. Rich's father was only fifty-nine when he died in 1962, but he lived long enough to see his advice bear fruit in his son's life. When Simon died, Amway was in its infancy, just three years old, but he had the satisfaction of knowing that his son's fledgling company was rapidly becoming a huge success. In fact, Simon DeVos hoped his son's enterprise would never become so big and impersonal that it would treat its employees as his company had treated him.

Shortly before his death, Simon took Rich aside and told him, "Always do right by your employees. Never forget that your success was built on a foundation of honesty and fairness to others."

Those words have shaped Rich's life; indeed, they have shaped his business values and his businesses.

Rich DeVos is a product of his family, as well as the love and instruction he received from his mother and father. "I have warm memories of my childhood," he recalls. "My grandparents came to America from Holland, and our family was very close-knit. There were tough times, there were financial struggles, but we met those challenges together. We may have lacked for money at times, but we never lacked for love."

> *"Rich came from a family of ordinary means. His dad was optimistic and outgoing, just like Rich is today. Rich's dad worked for a major electrical company for many years, but while he was in his early fifties the company let him go. He received no pension or benefits after all the years he gave to that company. Seeing the way his father was treated had a big effect on Rich DeVos. It affects the way he treats his employees to this day."*
>
> Marvin Van Dellen
> DeVos Family Friend

Rich's sister, Jan Courts, agrees. "Our house was filled with love," she says, "and we had so much fun growing up. Rich was a great fudge maker, and he made lots of different kinds of fudge. He figured out a way to pass the fudge on a string to the babysitter in the next house.

"Rich liked sports and was very creative in finding ways for us to play sports around our house. He built a homemade basketball hoop, and we played a lot of basketball. When we wanted a place to go skating in winter, he flooded a vacant lot. The lot turned to ice, and we had our own skating rink. I've always been proud of my brother and his ingenuity."

With memories like those, no wonder Rich has such a strong belief in family.

The Family: A Foundation of Faith and Values

Rich's faith and values were shaped by his family. Sometimes Rich's mother had a battle on her hands, dragging her son to church by the scruff of his neck. But the lessons he learned at home and in Sunday school lodged in his mind and his heart, and they lasted a lifetime. His parents taught him the Christian gospel and the meaning of love. They instilled in him the values of Christian integrity and compassion that have been the core of his being throughout his life. Every night around the dinner table, his parents prayed and modeled for him a strong sense of gratitude to God for His grace and blessing in their lives.

Rich's family also shaped within him a love of country and a respect for democracy and freedom. "I believe patriotism begins in the home," he reflects. "The home is the incubator of the American dream. I was fortunate to have parents who raised me to seize the limitless opportunities of this country, and to believe in myself and my dreams."

The Rich DeVos Guide to Stronger Family Relationships

"Family," says Rich DeVos, "is the foundation of our country." Rich shared with me a number of principles that have guided him as a husband, father and grandfather, and he asked me to share them with you:

Keys to a Strong Marriage

1. *Have faith in God.* It is important that a husband and wife share one faith. If a husband and wife cannot worship as one, why get married at all? A strong marriage must be based on biblical principles. Couples often think, *Religion isn't important. Our love will keep us together.* But when children

arrive, a religious tug-of-war usually begins, with each side demanding that the children be raised in "my faith." The children, caught in the middle, end up rejecting *both* faiths. All of this pain could be avoided if couples would make shared faith an unconditional requirement of marriage.

2. *Forgive each other.* Marriages crumble when husbands and wives blame each other. We are all sinners. We all marry imperfect human beings—and we are imperfect ourselves. A forgiving attitude will cover a multitude of sins and flaws—and it will keep you together.

3. *Be cheerleaders for each other.* Praise each other in private and in public.

4. *Find agreement on money issues.* Have regular "board meetings" so that the two of you can agree on a budget. Know what you can afford and what you can't, and agree to be responsible and prudent in all money matters. Money is a major issue in every marriage—and a major blame issue in marriages where husband and wife do not agree and do not manage money responsibly.

Keys to Effective Parenting

1. *Pay attention to your children.* Don't just find time for them—make time! "When my children were in school," Rich recalls, "I would put my calendar together and always mark off the kids' birthdays, sporting events and the family vacation. I built the rest of the calendar around those events. My children always knew that they came first in my schedule."

2. *Listen to your children.* They will know you love them by the way you listen to them. Give them your undivided attention when they talk. Look them in the eye, nod and repeat back to them what they tell you so that they know you have heard them.

3. *Discipline your children.* Notice that "discipline" and "disciple" come from the same root word. Make disciples of your children by lovingly setting boundaries for them and imposing fair and reasonable consequences when they overstep those boundaries.

4. *Know your children's friends.* "Our house was always open to our kids' friends," Rich recalls. "It was the local hang-out place. We built a swimming

pool as a magnet for our kids' friends. We wanted to know who else was influencing our children, and in which direction. And we wanted to be an influence on them."

Keys to Effective Grandparenting

1. *Teach your grandchildren the fundamental lessons of life.* Talk to your grandkids about values, character, attitude, the importance of diligence and hard work, earning and investing, and above all, faith.

2. *Make your home a fun place for your grandchildren to visit.* "We bought our boat so that our grandkids would want to come here and spend time with us," Rich says. "On the boat, we have fun times, good food and long talks. Helen and I referee their games and keep score. Grandkids are a delight."

3. *Maintain a good relationship with your children—the parents of your grandchildren.* If you lose the relationship with your kids, you'll lose your grandkids as well. Avoid interfering with your children's parental role, even if you disagree with how your grandchildren are being raised. Avoid judging or criticizing your children.

4. *Love your grandkids intensely, but also demand mannerly behavior.* "For example," Rich says, "teach them the importance of looking people in the eye and calling people by name. I always insist that my grandkids look me in the eye and say, 'Good morning, Grandpa.' These are good habits of relating to other people, and those habits will serve them well in life."

5. *Give your grandchildren your affection and attention.* "Grandkids love hugs and attention," Rich says. "Whenever they are with me, swimming or doing some other activity, they all say the same thing: 'Grandpa! Look at me!' It means so much to them to receive that attention and affection from their grandparents."

Because his family has had such a profound influence in shaping his own life and values, Rich DeVos is convinced that the family is the ultimate shaper of society—for good or ill. After all, a society is the sum of the individuals who compose it. If the family unit is sound and healthy, it will produce sound and healthy people who will build a sound and healthy society.

But if the family unit is unhealthy, it will produce a society rife with neglect, abuse, abandonment, addiction, illiteracy, immorality, crime, disease and violence. These forms of social blight are, in fact, what we are seeing at all levels of our society today. "We have undervalued the importance of the family," Rich says, "and we are reaping the results of that neglect. Our children no longer have a foundation of faith and spiritual values. Families are failing their children because we, as a society, have failed the family."

"I don't know Rich DeVos, but I do know his son Dick. He's the former president of Amway, and he is so proud of the founders, Rich DeVos and Jay Van Andel. In fact, Dick is awed by them—not intimidated, but respectfully awed. The next generation of DeVoses and Van Andels know they have to build their own legacy and make their own mark on the history of the company—and they will. Rich and Helen have passed their life values along to their children. There's a special glow of confidence in Dick's personality. It's something Rich DeVos passed down to his children."

ALAN SPOON
NEWSPAPER EXECUTIVE

All families have struggles and problems. All parents make mistakes. But love covers a multitude of sins and mistakes. If our children know they are truly loved by their parents, they will probably turn out all right. When we, as parents, create an atmosphere of love and acceptance for our kids, then our kids are much more likely to listen to our teaching and to receive the values and beliefs we are trying to hand down to them.

"Helen and I were not perfect parents," Rich recalls. "We made mistakes. But our children always knew they were loved. We told them and showed them, in as many ways as we knew how, that we believed in them and we were proud of them. We taught them our values and brought them up in our faith. We tried to teach by both words and example. Teaching by example alone is not enough. Our children need to hear us talking about our faith and values every day."

Rich is talking about a biblical principle of parenting that goes all the way back to the days of Moses. The book of Deuteronomy tells us, "Love the Lord your God and keep his requirements, his decrees, his laws and his commands always. . . . Teach them to your children, talking about them when you sit at home and when you walk along the road, when you lie down and when you get up" (Deuteronomy 11:1, 19, NIV).

We can't teach our faith and values to our children unless we make it a priority to spend time with them. Rich often quotes the old saying, "If you're too busy to spend time with your family, you're too busy." There is no substitute for time spent with your family, enjoying good times together, having deep talks together, demonstrating love and affection for each other, and building lasting relationships. There is no substitute for giving your children your total attention, listening to them, answering their questions, hugging them and letting them know they are truly loved.

The Bible says, "Train a child in the way he should go, and when he is old he will not turn from it" (Proverbs 22:6, NIV). How successful were Rich and Helen DeVos in transmitting their faith and values to their children? Today, all four of their grown children are Christians,

> *"Rich is very involved in the lives of his children, grandkids, nieces and nephews. He gets down on the kids' level and takes a genuine interest in everything they do. He talks to them and teaches them. They love him, and they are in awe of him."*
>
> Bernice Heys and Jan Courts, Rich's Sisters

and all are involved in the DeVos family businesses in one capacity or another.

One of the reasons Rich and Helen have been able to successfully raise their children to embrace their own faith and values is that they didn't just talk to their kids. They *listened.* And because their parents listened, Dick, Dan, Cheri and Doug knew they were *loved.*

"My dad and I are very much alike," their daughter Cheri told me. "Dad is a good listener, and he's totally fair. I could debate with him better than my brothers could. Dad and I had a good-natured tug-of-war over a number of issues as I was growing up, but our disagreements always took place within a relationship of mutual respect. For example, when I was a teenager, he gave me a 10 P.M. curfew, and I disputed it. I wrote a paper listing all my logical reasons for why my curfew should be extended to 11 P.M. He read my paper, and he agreed. It means a lot to a young person to know that her parents really listen and really try to be fair."

"What was it like to have Rich DeVos as my dad?" says Dan. "He was there for us. He gave us his time and his attention. He helped us with our homework and went to our games and events. That wasn't easy for him, because he was busy building Amway during the years we were growing up. He couldn't come to every event, but I never felt cheated out of my parents' love and attention, because I knew that they had built their entire schedule around us."

"Everything with Dad is about family," says Doug. "We were a normal American family. We had fellowship, we had fun, and yes, we had fights. But we never doubted the love Dad and Mom had for us. I remember one time when I was in high school, and I came in way past my curfew. I went straight to my dad and said, 'I was wrong, and I'm sorry.' I knew I had consequences coming, but I also knew my dad loved me and that whatever he did would be the fair and loving thing.

"My dad showed his love in many ways, including preparing us for life. I remember one time when I was in the third grade, I complained to my dad that I didn't have any friends. So he gave me a pep talk on the way to school. He said, 'You can make friends. Just be happy, and people will want to be your friend. Happy people attract friends.' As I got out of the car and headed to class, I heard him say, 'Go get 'em, Mr. Happy!' That lesson stuck with me throughout my life, and he was absolutely right."

"Dad always made an effort to attend the significant events in my life," recalls Dick. "If I needed him, he'd be there. I don't recall ever feeling neglected or ignored, no matter how busy Dad was in his business. When you consider how much he traveled and the long hours he worked, that's an amazing accomplishment, and it speaks to how committed he is to his family. All four of us DeVos kids grew up knowing that we were important to him. Young people run into problems with drugs, sex and bad company when their emotional buckets aren't full. Dad made sure our emotional buckets were always filled to overflowing. We knew we were loved."

"To Dad, the boat is not a luxury. He uses the boat to build family relationships. The close quarters of a boat force a family to spend time together. On a boat, the teachable moments are more frequent and longer lasting. For relationship-building, there's nothing like a boat."

DICK DEVOS
RICH'S OLDEST SON

As parents, Rich and Helen have impacted not only the lives of their own children, but the lives of their children's friends. "Dan DeVos and I have been friends since kindergarten," Kevin Solon recalls. "Many Fridays, I would sleep over at Dan's house and wake up Saturday morning to the aroma of banana pancakes. Rich himself was out in the kitchen making them. Spending so much time in the DeVos household, I observed firsthand that Rich's priorities have always been faith, family and friends. I admired it then, and I still do. Rich made an impression on my life that continues to this day. Rich and Helen have had as great an impact on my life as my own parents."

> *"Rich has been a consistently encouraging presence in my life. He's an example to everyone in his family because he's genuine, he's always the same person in public and private. He continually encourages me and takes an interest in what I'm doing."*
>
> Betsy DeVos
> Rich's Daughter-in-Law (Dick's Wife)

Another important part of Rich's parental role was teaching his children the importance of hard work and responsibility. Rich's son Dick first began working for the company at age twelve. Dick earned thirty-five cents an hour pulling weeds and performing other grounds-maintenance tasks during his summer vacations. Over the years, the DeVos kids—Dick, Dan, Cheri and Doug—all worked in various departments of the company, learning what the Amway business was all about from the ground up.

"We didn't want our children to think of themselves as heirs to the Alticor fortune," Rich says. "They had to learn the values of the family business, pay their dues, serve their apprenticeship and earn a leadership position. They all worked at entry-level jobs, and they didn't receive any special treatment. As a result, our children learned the value of hard work, and they learned to appreciate the hard-working people who contributed to the success of Alticor."

As Rich's children grew older, he entrusted them with more and more responsibility—and he continued to encourage them to have confidence in themselves. "I was twenty-four and newly married," Doug recalls, "when Dad sent me to Europe. I ran the corporation's division in Brussels for six months, then the division in England for eighteen months. I was nervous about the assignment. It was a big responsibility, and I didn't know if I could handle it. But before

I got on the plane, Dad told me, 'Step up and take charge—you'll be great at it!' Dad's encouragement prepared us to launch out in life and take on big challenges and responsibilities."

Some of the most important lessons that Rich teaches about family are not taught through words, but through the kind of life he leads. "Uncle Rich lives out his convictions every day," says Rich's nephew, Glenn Heys. "His marriage to Aunt Helen is a testimony to what love and faithfulness are all about. The way he has always cared for Grandma DeVos after Grandpa DeVos died so young—that's another example of what love of family means. Uncle Rich has always made family gatherings a priority, and all of us in the family have great memories of Easter egg hunts, boat rides on Memorial Day, Thanksgiving dinners followed by a swim in the pool, Christmas parties where we all take gifts to the children's hospital. Most important of all, he has made sure that we all know what it means to be a Christian and to have a living faith in God. I feel incredibly blessed to be a part of his family."

My friend Ken Hussar, an author and humorist, offered this keen observation about DeVos family values after he read an early draft of this book. "You know," he said, "I don't think Rich's wife, Helen, gets enough credit in the book. I remember what business guru Tom Peters once said: There's always a price to be paid for success, and people who achieve enormous success tend to do so by sacrificing their marriage, family and friendships on the altar of success.

"But look at Rich's family! Even though he was clearly there for his children in a big way, he was very busy and he had to travel a lot on business. You'd think his kids would have suffered and probably rebelled to some degree—yet every one of Rich's children and grandchildren is a follower of Jesus Christ! That tells me that Helen DeVos must have been an amazingly steadfast, Christlike example to her children. When Rich and Helen look back over all the companies and ministries and buildings they have built, they will know that their true legacy, transcending everything else they have accomplished, is this: 'Our children and grandchildren are followers of Jesus Christ.'"

Reflections of "Grandpa Rich"

Bob Vander Weide, Cheri's husband, recalls an incident that illustrates what a tender heart Rich has for his children. "When our daughter Hannah was born in 1991, we invited Rich and Helen to be in the delivery room with us at Spectrum Health. Rich is from the old school—in his day, expectant fathers were shunted into a waiting room. So this was a unique experience for Rich.

> *"Rich was never reluctant to place his sons in responsible positions in Amway, and he expected them to do well. The boys were able to handle any job their dad gave them. They had self-confidence like Rich. That's how they were raised."*
>
> Boyd Hoffman
> Longtime Friend of Rich DeVos

"Rich and Helen came in and waited with Cheri, and it was a long labor because it was her first child. Rich was thrilled to be there—but it was nerve-wracking for him! Every five minutes, he would get up and walk the halls, and he'd tell the nurses what was going on. He wanted to make sure that nothing went wrong. After he'd talk to the nurses, he'd come back and sit down and fidget.

"It was very revealing to watch Rich hovering around Cheri. It was agonizing for him to watch his only daughter go through the pain of childbirth. Though he was excited to see his granddaughter enter the world, you could see concern and compassion oozing out of him as he watched Cheri going through that pain. Seeing a father's love for his only daughter left an indelible memory with me."

Rich has sixteen grandchildren, and he is deeply involved in their lives. Rich and Helen pray for all sixteen of them by name every day. "That's how we remember their names," he jokes.

Rich's grandchildren have given him a whole new generation of young people to love, encourage and teach. He treats them as he treated his own children, giving them his time and attention, and sharing with them the life lessons that will enable them to grow up to become happy, effective, successful adults.

"Rich is a great family man," recalls Thelma Vander Weide, Bob's mother. "I went with Bob and Cheri on one of Rich's business trips to Asia. I helped Cheri with the children, and I got many firsthand glimpses into the way Rich loves and cares for his grandchildren. It was a business trip, and Rich was very busy. But it didn't matter how busy he was, it didn't matter if he had an appointment with the King of Siam, when his grandchildren came around, Rich made time for them. He gave them his full attention."

Elissa DeVos, daughter of Dick and Betsy, recalls, "When we travel on the boat with Grandpa Rich, we get to spend a lot of time together. All of the DeVos grandchildren love sailing, because it means we get to be with our grandparents." Katie Vander Weide, daughter of Bob and Cheri, also loves boating with Rich. "On the boat at dinner," she says, "Grandpa wants to sit with me and make sure I'm having fun."

Dalton DeVos, son of Doug and Maria, remembers the life lessons his grandfather taught him. "Grandpa teaches us to say five things to people: 'I'm wrong.' 'I'm sorry.' 'Thank you.' 'I love you.' 'I'm proud of you.'"

"To me, Rich is just my uncle—not a world-famous business leader. My most vivid memory of him was going to their cottage one Memorial Day weekend and playing in a giant game of Wiffle Ball."

SUE BRANDSEN, RICH'S NIECE

And Cassie DeVos, daughter of Dan and Pam, says, "Grandpa is always teaching us something. Ask him any question, and he'll give you as much time as you need to understand the answer. I love it that he is such a good listener and that he's always willing to talk with me."

Several of Rich's grandchildren made a point of mentioning one of their grandfather's amusing habits. "Grandpa sings a lot," recalls Ryan DeVos, son of Dick and Betsy. "He makes up songs about us and sings to us. He's funny, and he's nice." Rick DeVos, son of Dick and Betsy, also remembers Rich's songs. "When we're out on the boat, he makes up these little songs. He'll see one of us and make up words about us and rhyme it as he goes."

"He'll make a song out of anything—your name, what you're doing, where you're going," agrees Andrea DeVos, daughter of Dick and Betsy. "He has a wonderful sense of humor." And Elissa adds, "Grandpa's always singing to us. He doesn't even know he's doing it. He's cute!"

> *"I saw Rich with some of his grandchildren recently. He kissed his grandsons and granddaughters on the cheek and hugged them. I love to see men like Rich DeVos—men who are unafraid of displaying emotion and affection to their children and grandchildren."*
>
> Charles W. Colson
> Founder, Prison Fellowship

Micaela DeVos, daughter of Doug and Maria, is grateful for Rich's encouragement and cheerleading. "Grandpa came to my soccer game," she recalls. "He was cheering for us and yelling, 'Get that ball!' He had fun cheering for us, but we lost the game. Afterwards, he told me, 'I'm proud of you. If everyone played as hard as you, your team would win every game.'"

Family traditions are important to Rich, and he is passing the family heritage on to his immediate and extended family. "Family has always been very important to Rich," says Craig Courts, Rich's nephew. "Our entire extended family will gather at Christmas, and Rich will talk about his parents and their impact on him. Then he will encourage all of us to pass on our heritage and our family stories to the next generation. We are all inspired to continue doing what Rich has done in keeping those traditions alive."

As a devoted son, husband, father, uncle and grandfather, Rich DeVos is a man who lives, breathes and exemplifies family values. And because his own family is so important to him, Rich is committed to encouraging family values in all of his business endeavors.

Amway Family Values

There are few corporations that can honestly claim to be as family-oriented as Amway. "The great thing about a direct-selling business like Amway," Rich says, "is that it allows families to work together and grow closer. It's the kind of business in which husbands and wives can work as a team, and they can include their children. Amway values are family values. Family values are extremely important to our corporate culture, and we have created traditions and policies that encourage family involvement. When we recruit independent business owners, we recruit entire family units, not individuals. We have learned that the Amway concept works best when the husband and wife work as a team."

> *"I met Rich DeVos over lunch at his plant in 1989. I even became an Amway distributor—we were buying so many cleaning supplies that it became cheaper for me to join. My eight-year-old daughter took the items out of the starter kit and sold them around the neighborhood."*
>
> Tom Monaghan
> Founder, Domino's Pizza

Unlike most corporate conventions, Amway conventions are family-oriented events. Rich recalls the confusion experienced by hotel operators in the early days of Amway conventions. "Normally," he says, "when a convention comes to town, a hotel must add extra bartenders to keep up with the increased liquor sales. The hotel bar is a big profit center during most conventions—but not during an Amway convention. The Amway crowd is made up of families, not a bunch of lonely guys on the road with nothing better to do than to hang out in a bar. So the hotels would have to take the extra bartenders out of the bar and put on more help in the coffee shop, because that's where all the Amway families were.

"We have always placed families over profit," Rich says. "My family shaped the kind of person I am, and families shape our company and our society. I wish every child in the world could have the kind of loving family background that I have had. Jay and I always wanted Amway to encourage the kind of healthy family values that made us who we are."

Rich's friend, John Bertrand, recalls, "Some years back, I was in Michigan to help launch a new boat, the seventy-foot *Windquest* that Rich's three sons had built for their dad. The party for the christening and launch was held on Father's Day and took place behind Rich's summer home in Holland, Michigan. During the preparation for the party, Rich came down to the dock to see how everything was going. I said, 'It's great that your sons can do something like this for you on Father's Day.'

"Rich said, 'Yes, it is—but aren't you a father, John? I feel terrible that you're here when you should be with your own family on Father's Day. You know, if you leave right now, you could be home with your family tonight.'

> *"Rich DeVos is a man with everything, but nothing in his life is more important to him than his family. His home is always open to other people, and what people see when they visit his home is a family filled with love. Rich has been an example to all of us of what family is all about."*
>
> Ken Koldenhoven
> DeVos Family Friend

"I knew Rich was right. I left right then, rushed to the airport, flew to California and made it home by evening. That's what Rich DeVos is all about. He cares about family—not just his own family, but your family, my family, everyone's family."

Rich DeVos has applied those same family values to the Orlando Magic organization. The mission statement of the Orlando Magic reads: "We enhance the quality of life in our communities by pioneering excellence in the management of sports and wellness through a commitment to family values." I can personally testify that this statement is absolutely true—and this commitment to family starts at the top. Whenever Rich comes to my office, the first thing he wants to talk to me about is my family.

Amway family values, Magic family values—where do they come from? They are a direct reflection of the heart of Rich DeVos. And Rich's love for family is intertwined with his heart for God. His family life exemplifies the words of the Psalmist: "Unless the Lord builds the house, its builders labor in vain" (Psalm 127:1, NIV). The house of Rich DeVos was built by the Lord, and that is why Rich is surrounded by a close and loving family to this day.

Rich was recently looking through fifty-year-old wedding photos as he and his wife, Helen, were preparing to celebrate their golden wedding anniversary in February 2003. His assistant, Carol Cunningham, was there. "As he was looking at those photos," she recalls, "his eyes got misty. 'She was so beautiful,' he said, 'and she still is.' After all these years, he is still so in love with Helen."

The Bible tells us, "Husbands, love your wives, just as Christ loved the church and gave himself up for her" (Ephesians 5:25, NIV). That is the kind of love Rich has for his wife. Authentic love places the needs of others above the needs of the self. That is the kind of love that builds stable, nurturing homes where children grow up emotionally healthy and spiritually strong. When you see your wife or husband as a special gift from God, and when you see your children as a special trust from God, then you are able to love your family as God intended.

"There is no better way to love your children," Rich says, "than to love your spouse. If you want to raise children who are secure and confident, then you have to raise them in a secure, intact family. When the children see that Mom and Dad truly love each other, they never even wonder whether they themselves are loved. It is something they know without questioning."

> *"Helen DeVos has not only supported Rich in his business endeavors, but she has helped him keep his life in balance. Rich knows he couldn't have accomplished it all without Helen at his side. Again and again, he says how thankful he is to God for his wonderful wife."*
>
> Marvin Van Dellen
> DeVos Family Friend

By every account, by any criteria you wish to apply to him, Rich DeVos is a successful man. He has built a successful company; he has accumulated wealth and prestige; he exercises influence in society and American politics. But ask him what the word "success" truly means, and he will say, "Success means having a strong marriage and raising children who are confident and strong in the faith. My father was not a wealthy man or a man of influence, but he was a successful man. He built a successful marriage, he created a successful home, and he instilled in me the values and qualities of real success: faith, confidence, hard work and love. I still look up to him as a role model of success. Everything I know and believe about family, I learned from him."

If you want to be like Rich DeVos, if you want to know true success in life, then do as Rich does: Love your spouse, love your children, love your family.

Chapter Twelve

Love Your Country!

I WAS TALKING WITH U.S. Congressman Vern Ehlers about the politics of Rich DeVos. "What kind of president would he have been?" I asked.

"Oh, Rich would have made a great president," the congressman replied. "And he would have had a good chance of getting elected. Remember, he had a built-in organization of a couple million volunteers—and every one of them was highly knowledgeable about person-to-person marketing. And they were motivated."

"Do you think he would have loved the job?" I asked.

Congressman Ehlers considered for a moment, then said, "No. I think he would have been very frustrated. Rich believes in getting things done. He would have been very impatient with the Washington bureaucracy. Still, he would have put up with it to serve his country. There's nobody in America who loves his country more than Rich DeVos."

Richard M. DeVos is an unabashed, flag-waving patriot and a bold, unapologetic capitalist. He loves America and sells his belief in the American Way wherever he goes. His political enemies attack him as a "right-winger," but when I think of my friend,

Rich DeVos, I don't think of political labels. To me, Rich is just a guy who has always done his best, who has always tried to serve God and honor his country, who always respects the people around him and is compassionate toward people in need. I don't see how anyone could find fault with any of those traits.

> *"I am concerned that too many people have lost sight of the fact that America is what it is today because God has blessed this land. They don't even want to mention him anymore. This country was built on a religious heritage, and we'd better get back to it. We had better start telling people that faith in God is the real strength of America!"*
>
> Rich DeVos

What is the one thing above all else that Rich loves about America? "Freedom," he replies. "I'm excited about the revival of patriotism and the love of freedom we're seeing in America today. I love to see people celebrating the blessings of liberty and the sacrifices of those who have purchased our freedom with their lives and their blood. For all too long, Americans have taken their freedom for granted. Many Americans seemed to think that patriotism had gone out of style. They seemed embarrassed to place their hand on their heart and pledge their allegiance to the flag. But patriotism is back—and it's a great thing to see."

The word "Amway" is more than a catchy, clever name for a direct-selling company; it's a declaration of conviction, principle and personal faith. Rich DeVos and Jay Van Andel named their company Amway as a statement of their belief in the American way. That belief has never wavered.

Selling America

In early 1963, Rich was scheduled to address a group of businesswomen on a business-related topic. But when he arrived at the luncheon, he felt compelled to abandon his prepared remarks and speak on a subject he felt strongly about: America. He had recently heard many speakers and commentators say that America was in decline. Some said that the recent Cuban missile crisis foreshadowed bleak and gloomy days ahead. Some said that the Soviet Union's successes in space, from Sputnik to the first man in orbit, showed that communism was the wave of the future.

> *"A wise and frugal government, which shall leave men free to regulate their own pursuits of industry and improvement, and shall not take from the mouth of labor the bread it has earned—this is the sum of good government."*
>
> Thomas Jefferson
> Third President of the United States

Against that backdrop of pessimism and Cold War fears, Rich DeVos stood up and spoke about the virtues of America, freedom, patriotism and the free-market economic system. He spoke without notes. He spoke from his heart. And when he had finished speaking, a roomful of businesswomen jumped to their feet and gave Rich a standing ovation. It had been a long time since anyone had talked about what was right with America—and Rich's audience was overjoyed to hear it.

Within days, Rich was flooded with requests that he deliver that same speech to groups all across America. So he refined the speech and gave it before hundreds of audiences over the next ten years. That speech became known as "Selling America," and it was recorded and distributed around the world as both an audiocassette and an LP record. It received several awards, including the Freedom Foundation's prestigious Alexander Hamilton Award.

History has proven Rich DeVos right. Despite a few early successes, Soviet-style communism was never able to compete with a free society and free-market economy. It couldn't compete technologically, economically, educationally, socially, militarily or in any other way. The Soviet Union has gone the way of the dodo and the dinosaur. The old Eastern bloc nations, such as Poland, Hungary and Romania, are now free-market societies and allies of America. Cuba is on its last legs, and mainland China has had to adopt free-market compromises in order to maintain its survival.

Rich speaks with unabashed pride of the achievements and nobility of the American spirit. More than once, I have sat and listened spellbound as he spoke of immigrants streaming to this land from around the world, seeking freedom, building new lives, forging a bold new legacy. I've heard him retell the story of those ill-equipped, outnumbered American patriots who defended Bunker Hill against Gen. Howe's vastly superior forces—a battle that rallied American resistance against British rule. I've heard him describe how, at the Battle of New Orleans, thirty-five hundred Americans under Andrew Jackson routed sixty-six hundred British troops from a fortress made of cotton bales and sugar barrels.

I've heard Rich speak with passion about the Americans who battled tropical heat and fever to dig a canal across the isthmus of Panama; about the uniquely American daring of Charles Lindbergh, the first man to fly across the Atlantic; about the American genius of Thomas Edison, who rolled back the darkness with a shining filament inside a globe of glass; about Neil Armstrong, an American who went to the moon for all mankind, boldly leaving footprints where no man had gone before.

> *"Rich once told me his political views. He said, 'Those people who write the laws need to come back here to the real world and have to live under them.'"*
>
> Milt Weeks
> Retired Amway Employee

Again and again, shortsighted pessimists have declared that America's best days are past—but Rich DeVos doesn't let those statements of gloom and doom go unchallenged. Yes, our past is full of greatness and heroism—but as long as we are free, as long as we believe in God and believe in ourselves, there is greatness and heroism in our future as well.

The two great sources of America's greatness, Rich tells us, are faith and freedom. America was founded on a belief in God and the belief that we are all created in God's image to dream great dreams. Our founding documents declare both a belief in God the Creator and a belief in the equality of all human beings. "We hold these truths to be self-evident," says the Declaration of Independence, "that all men are created equal, that they are endowed by their Creator with certain unalienable rights, that among these are life, liberty and the pursuit of happiness."

All people are created in God's image, and all should be free to pursue their dreams. "The only answer to the problems that plague our world and our nation," Rich says, "is the answer Jesus gave his disciples just before he was crucified: 'This is my commandment, that you love one another.'" In other words, America can only *be* America if we treat one another as we wish to be treated; if we see every human being as a child of God, made in God's image; if we treat all people everywhere as people of worth, dignity and unique potential.

That is Rich DeVos's deeply held vision of America, and he takes it personally when people sneer at the opportunities this land affords. Retired longtime Amway employee Tom Michmershuizen told me, "For years, Rich got his hair cut in a certain barbershop in Grand Rapids. It's the same barbershop where Jerry Ford got his hair cut when he lived in Grand Rapids. I still get my hair cut in that shop.

> *"Rich DeVos is as patriotic a citizen as I have ever known. He has always believed in doing the right thing for the American people and the nation at large."*
>
> GEN. ALEXANDER M. HAIG JR.
> FORMER U.S. SECRETARY OF STATE

"One time, in the early 1960s, Rich went in and had Fred the barber cut his hair. There was another customer in the place, a railroad worker, and he did nothing but gripe about his job. 'The company doesn't pay me enough! They make me work too much overtime!' He went on and on, gripe after gripe about his job with the railroad.

"While this was going on, Fred could see that Rich was seething. Finally, Rich had heard enough. 'Listen,' he told the railroad worker, 'you're lucky to have a good job, working for a good company, living in the greatest country on Earth. If you hate it so much, why don't you quit the railroad? Why don't you leave this country and go someplace more to your liking? In fact, I've got enough money in my pocket to buy you a one-way ticket to Russia!'

> *"I believe in life with a large YES and a small no. I believe that life is good, that people are good, that God is good. And I believe in affirming every day that I live, proudly and enthusiastically, that life in America under God is a positive experience."*
>
> RICH DEVOS

"After that, Rich added the barbershop story to his 'Selling America' speech, and it became a pretty famous anecdote. A few months after that happened, I was in the shop for a haircut. I sat in the chair and, as Fred was getting ready to give me a trim, he pointed to another fellow in the shop. 'See that guy?' he said. 'He's the one Mr. DeVos talks about—the guy with the railroad job.' Then Fred told the railroad man that I worked at Amway with Rich DeVos.

"The railroad man frowned. 'Oh, yeah?' he said. 'Let me tell you something! The day that guy gave me his speech about how lucky I am to work for the railroad, I went home and found out my wife was using Amway laundry soap! I made her throw it in the trash!'

"The next time I saw Rich, I told him what the railroad man had done. He chuckled and said, 'That's fine—we don't need customers like him anyway!' That's who Rich is. He loves selling Amway products, but if it comes down to a choice between selling Amway or selling America, he'll sell America every time."

The Formula for Success

When Amway Corporation began, the executive office was a kitchen table and the production plant was a basement. Today, parent company Alticor has office buildings, industrial plants and warehouses around the world to facilitate the strength of its business opportunities and distribution of its product lines. This success story is a tribute to one of the most ignored and underestimated blessings in America: *the free enterprise system.*

> *"We were always 'that soap company.' But 'that soap company' gave a lot of people the chance to succeed. Anyone could get a kit and start selling it."*
>
> CHERI VANDER WEIDE
> RICH'S DAUGHTER

What is the free enterprise system? It is an economy that relies on market forces (such as supply and demand) to determine the prices and distribution of goods and services. The free-enterprise system allows private businesses to compete for profits in an open marketplace with the least possible government regulation. The free enterprise system is only possible in an atmosphere of capitalism, an economic system based on the private ownership of capital (wealth).

Rich has been unabashedly preaching about the blessings of America and the free market system since the 1960s—back when capitalism wasn't "cool." In those days, socialism was on the march and free market capitalism was in retreat. To young Americans, "capitalism" was a dirty word, right alongside such phrases as "the

Establishment," "the draft" and "Vietnam War."

Independent business owner Jim Dornan remembers those days. "I was in school during the '60s," he says, "so I grew up with the Vietnam War, the hippies, the whole anti-America mind-set. I bought into the counterculture view. Then, in the early 1970s, I heard Rich speak at a patriotic rally. I was surrounded by people dressed up in red, white and blue, waving American flags. Talk about culture shock! I was a '60s guy—but Rich DeVos turned my head around."

Rich describes the mind-set of those times in his 1975 book, *Believe!* "Unfortunately," he observes, "words like 'free enterprise,' 'profit' and 'capitalism' conjure up visions of money-hungry industrialists greedily stuffing dollars into their pockets while the poor masses become more and more destitute. Free enterprise is fast becoming the all-purpose scapegoat of this half-century. The critics will tell you that all the evils of the 1970s are laid at its door. The air and streams are polluted because of capitalism, people are poor because of capitalism, wars are fought because of capitalism. The free enterprise system is evil, their argument goes, and it poisons the whole society. What ignorance! What foolish, unfortunate ignorance!"

> *"I owe my whole life to Rich and Jay, as do millions of others. This company has given hope to people by making the free enterprise system available to people around the world. Rich DeVos is a hero because he gives people the opportunity to live out their dreams. Rich's own dreams are vast enough to contain the dreams of millions of others."*
>
> Ron Puryear
> Independent Business Owner

What is the opposite of capitalism? Socialism. And history has shown that problems of pollution, poverty, war and unrest are always greater under socialist economies (such as the old Soviet Union and its client states) than under capitalist economies. In free societies, people are free to invent, solve problems, and reap the rewards of their hard work and innovation. That is why free societies are always the cleanest and least polluted, the most economically stable, and the most peaceful and secure.

As Rich DeVos is quick to point out, "The free enterprise system is the greatest single source of our country's economic success." The free enterprise system is also a major reason for our country's great tradition of compassionate charitable giving. One of the striking features of the old failed socialist economies is that they couldn't support charitable organizations. The old Soviet Union never had the equivalent of a United Way or Community Chest because nobody in a socialist economy has any money to donate!

Rich DeVos sees a nation's economic system as intertwined with, and inseparable from, the political life, religious life and cultural values of a nation. Economic freedom is intimately connected with religious freedom, political freedom and free speech. As we have seen in various experiments with socialism over the past century, when a government takes over the economy, it doesn't stop there. All freedom disappears—and so does prosperity. Unfortunately, many Americans enjoy the blessings of the free enterprise system—historically unprecedented choice and quality of food, housing, cars, and other products and services—while at the same time they complain about that system as "evil" and "greedy."

"Private ownership is basic to freedom. Take it away, and the economy is doomed to failure. Deny people the freedom to be what they want and to do what they want, and an economy will collapse. It is useless to talk about economic freedom as separate from political or social freedom. . . . The freedom to work at whatever you want to goes hand in hand with freedom of every kind."

RICH DEVOS

Many people use the word

"greed" without realizing what it really means. Some mistake the profit motive of capitalism for "greed." It is not "greed" to want to make a profit. It is not "greed" to want to accumulate wealth for your family or pass that wealth on to your children after you die. It is not "greed" to want to enjoy the fruit of your labors.

True greed is an excessive desire to acquire wealth that is unearned and undeserved, or to accumulate excessive wealth without a willingness to show generosity to people in need. Obviously, greed does rear its ugly head within the free market system. In 1985, stock speculator Ivan Boesky declared, "Greed is healthy," and the following year he was fined $100 million by the Securities and Exchange Commission for insider trading. Boesky's greedy excesses were caricatured in Oliver Stone's movie *Wall Street* (1987), in which a greedy tycoon played by Michael Douglas uttered the famous line, "Greed is good."

> *"People were down on America in the sixties, but Rich has always been a patriot, a booster for America and American values. Whenever the subject is God and country, Rich speaks passionately and movingly from the heart."*
>
> BETSY DEVOS
> RICH'S DAUGHTER-IN-LAW (DICK'S WIFE)

The recent financial scandals at such companies as Enron, WorldCom and Global Crossing have shown that evil and greed are alive in the free enterprise system—but these excesses do not mean that the free enterprise system itself is at fault. When rich and powerful people break the law and steal from employees and investors, they are behaving as criminals, not capitalists. It is wrong to assume that a wealthy person is automatically a greedy person. True, some rich people are greedy—but there are greedy poor people and there are generous rich people. "Greedy" is a word that describes a person's heart, not his bankbook.

The Bible tells us that God gives us wealth for our benefit and enjoyment. Proverbs 10:22 (NIV) says, "The blessing of the Lord brings wealth, and he adds no trouble to it." And Jeremiah 29:11 (NIV) tells us, "'For I know the plans I have for you,' declares the Lord, 'plans to prosper you and not to harm you, plans to give you hope and a future.'" And Ecclesiastes 5:19 (NIV) says, "Moreover, when God gives any man wealth and possessions, and enables him to enjoy them, to accept his lot and be happy in his work—this is a gift of God."

But wealth becomes a curse instead of a blessing when we become arrogant about the money and property we have acquired, when we lose our compassion for the less fortunate, and when we forget that God is ultimately the source of everything we are and everything we have. As Deuteronomy 8:18 (NIV) warns us, "But remember the Lord your God, for it is he who gives you the ability to produce wealth."

In his book *Compassionate Capitalism,* Rich laments the fact that fully two-thirds of young Americans know so little about capitalism that they cannot even define the word *profit.* If the American people don't even understand what *profit* is (the basic definition: "revenue minus costs"), then how can they ever appreciate the free market system that makes possible the very standard of living they enjoy?

"Rich DeVos is a true American patriot. If he had lived in 1776, he would have signed the Declaration of Independence. He'd have been the first to sign it, and his signature would have dwarfed John Hancock's. The history books would tell about Jefferson, Washington, Franklin and DeVos."

BILL NICHOLSON, FORMER AMWAY CHIEF OPERATING OFFICER

Rich loves to quote a little couplet by Oliver Wendell Holmes to explain what profit is all about:

I only ask that Fortune send
A little more than I shall spend.

Profit—making more money than we spend—is the basis of the free market capitalist system. Profit enables a business to succeed and grow. Profit enables a business to improve the lives of its owners (or shareholders), its employees and its customers. Profit enables a business to practice compassion, generosity and charity, helping to alleviate social problems from pollution to hunger to homelessness; in this way, profits benefit all of society.

In the 1960s, Rich DeVos used a simple formula to explain in clear, straightforward terms how capitalism works:

$$MW = NR + HE \times T$$

What does that formula mean? Rich explains: "Our *material welfare* (MW) comes from *natural resources* (NR) that are transformed by *human energy* (HE) that has been made more effective through the use of *tools* (T)."

Material welfare consists of the wealth, possessions and lifestyle we acquire that make life easier and more enjoyable. *Natural resources* are such things as the cotton that can be transformed into clothing, the iron ore and glass that can transformed into automobiles, the petroleum that can be transformed into plastics and fuel, and the vegetables and livestock that can be transformed into food. *Human energy* is the ingenuity and work that perform those transformations.

> *"The reason I became a Republican was because I thought all Republicans were like Rich DeVos."*
>
> PAUL COLLINS
> AWARD-WINNING ARTIST

Tools are the ideas or machines that magnify human ingenuity and work so that human energy is more effective and efficient. For example, one man with an ox-drawn plow (a primitive tool) can plant a field; but in the same amount of time, one man with a modern tractor can plant a hundred fields because a more advanced tool can multiply the effectiveness of that one man's human energy.

For years, Rich DeVos preached this formula for success. But then he realized that there was an ingredient missing from this formula.

Compassionate Capitalism

In recent years, Rich has added another factor to that equation: *compassion.* "The secret to real, lasting success in business," he says today, "is compassion. Now when I present the formula, I add compassion to every stage of the process." Rich's new, compassionate formula for success looks like this:

$$MW = (NR + HE \times T) \times C$$

The letter C, of course, stands for *compassion.* "There are those who laugh when I say compassion, not profit, is the ultimate goal of capitalism," Rich writes in *Compassionate Capitalism.* "Say it any way you want, but know this: When compassion inspires and informs free enterprise, profits follow, the quality of human life is advanced, and the Earth is restored and renewed." He goes on to say that capitalism without compassion may yield short-term profits, but it inevitably extracts a toll in human suffering and the depletion of the Earth.

The goal of DeVos-style compassionate capitalism is to make the American dream of success and financial security available to the many, not just the few. "Capitalism isn't great because it allows a handful to make millions," Rich concludes. "It is great because it allows millions of people to become what they want to be."

During the turbulent and rebellious 1960s, Rich spoke to a student audience on a college campus. He explained that the American economic system is actually the best way to create an

> *"The level of patriotism in America has risen dramatically since we were attacked on September 11, 2001. This kind of flag-waving, God-bless-America patriotism may be a new experience for a lot of people, but it has been the cornerstone of Rich DeVos's entire life. When America changed after 9–11, it rediscovered the love of country that Rich has had all along."*
>
> Dr. Richard Lapchick
> Director, DeVos Sports Business Management Program,
> University of Central Florida

environment of compassion and generosity toward the poor. As he spoke, Rich mentioned that the car he drove was a Cadillac. This brought one impassioned student to his feet with a question. "Mr. DeVos," the young man said, "if you really have compassion for the poor, why don't you get rid of that Cadillac? Why don't you get a cheap, basic transportation car that will get you where you want to go without the expense and luxury of a Cadillac?"

"Suppose I do as you say and get rid of my Cadillac," Rich replied. "Exactly how will the poor have more if I have less?"

"Isn't it obvious?" the student asked. "You can take the money you save by driving a cheaper car and you can give it to the poor."

"You are mistaken," Rich said, "if you think that the poor will have more if the rich have less. In reality, if the rich have less, then everyone will have less, including the poor."

The student looked skeptical.

"I understand your skepticism," Rich continued, "but I can easily illustrate my point. When I purchased my Cadillac, I paid a certain amount of money for it. Some of that money went to the dealer who sold it to me, some went to General Motors Corporation, and some went into the paychecks of the assembly-line workers who built it. If I had not purchased that Cadillac, those workers would have been poorer. Every product or service I buy puts money into circulation in the free market economy.

The more money circulates in the economy, the more jobs there are, and the more opportunities there are for the poor to get out of poverty."

At that moment, a light of understanding dawned on the student's face.

"Of course," Rich continued, "charitable giving is important. When people are starving or homeless, they need emergency help. But charity is only a short-term solution. The only way to lift the poor out of their poverty and give them a brighter future is to educate them and inspire them to access the opportunities of the free market society."

"Capitalism and communism stand at opposite poles. Their essential difference is this: The communist, seeing the rich man and his fine home, says: 'No man should have so much.' The capitalist, seeing the same thing, says: 'All men should have as much.'"

PHELPS ADAMS
AMERICAN JOURNALIST

The genius of the American free enterprise system is that it works with human nature, not against it, as socialism does. In a free economy, there is a built-in incentive for people to work hard, better themselves and take care of their possessions. A free person in a free economy is allowed to reap the rewards of his or her labor.

In a socialist system, the state owns the possessions and the tools, and the state takes the rewards of labor and redistributes them in a way that destroys incentive. Let's say that you and I work side-by-side in the state-controlled widget factory. You work hard, producing a hundred widgets per day; but I'm lazy and see no reason to knock myself out, so I only produce twenty widgets per day. But because we live in a socialist society, we are each paid the same amount of money. Hard work receives no reward; laziness is never punished. What happens to your incentive to work hard? You realize that hard work doesn't pay—and soon you are producing only twenty widgets a day, the same as me. That is why socialism has failed every time it has been tried.

Rich DeVos quotes psychologist Albert Bandura's analogy to explain why socialism doesn't work: "No single snowflake in an avalanche ever feels responsible." If I make my living from the tools I bought with my own labor, I will take good care of them; but if the tools I use belong to the state, why should I care what happens to them? If I think up an idea for a more efficient tool, and I know that idea can make me rich, I'll patent my idea and put it into production; but if the state takes away all new ideas without paying for them, then why bother dreaming and innovating?

The free enterprise system creates incentives for people to think, innovate, invent, work hard and take good care of their possessions. Socialism kills dreams, stifles creativity, discourages industriousness and destroys pride of ownership. No matter how well-intentioned socialism might be, it always ends up hurting the very people it was intended to help: the poor and disadvantaged.

"Rich DeVos has always been a bold advocate of the free enterprise system. He believes that economic freedom and political freedom are two sides of the same coin."

DAVE VAN ANDEL
JAY'S YOUNGEST SON

In his book *Compassionate Capitalism,* Rich tells of a couple he met when he visited Berlin soon after the collapse of the communist regime in East Germany. Rich had just spoken on the theme of compassionate capitalism before an Amway convention in Berlin. After his talk, he remained in the hotel ballroom for a while, chatting with people, when a couple approached him, holding their twin baby boys.

"Mr. DeVos," the husband said, "I am Andrej Zubail. This is my wife, Maria. When freedom came to East Germany, I didn't know what to do. . . . We wanted to start a business of our own, but how? So I say to Maria, 'What shall we do?' And she answer, 'Now we are free. We can do anything.'"

That is what freedom does. It opens up endless possibilities. It enables people to dream big dreams. When people are free, they can do anything.

Andrej and Maria Zubail started their own Amway distributorship just six months before they met Rich DeVos, and they built it into a successful business. They wanted to tell Rich DeVos what their newfound freedom meant to them: "Now we are free. We can do anything."

> *"Socialism's results have ranged between the merely shabby and the truly catastrophic—poverty, strife, oppression and, on the killing fields of communism, the deaths . . . of perhaps 100 million people. Against that doctrine was set a contrary, conservative belief in a law-governed liberty. It was this view which triumphed with the crumbling of the Berlin Wall."*
>
> MARGARET THATCHER
> FORMER PRIME MINISTER OF ENGLAND

If you want to know why Rich DeVos is an old-fashioned, hand-on-the-heart, flag-waving cheerleader for America, it's because he knows what many Americans have tragically forgotten: This is a land of endless opportunity. Because Americans are free, they can do anything. That is why Americans have built the greatest economy the world has ever seen. That is why there are American footprints on the moon and American-made robot spacecraft touring the outer planets and speeding toward the stars.

We are free. We are Americans. We can do anything we set our minds to.

Rich DeVos believes that the free enterprise system is nothing less than a gift from God to humanity, making possible the unparalleled standard of living we enjoy today. All of the wonders of our modern world, from advances in medical technology to new frontiers in space technology, are a direct result of America's economic freedom.

In America, no one is excluded from the economic system. Your race and skin color don't matter. Your religious beliefs (or lack thereof) do not matter. Your gender doesn't matter, nor does your sexual orientation. Freedom is your right, guaranteed to you by the Constitution. If you can dream it, you can pursue it and achieve it in America.

That's the grand idea that Rich DeVos and Jay Van Andel had in mind when they named their company "Amway." That's the American Way.

Chapter Thirteen

Have Faith!

RICH DEVOS WAS RAISED in the Christian Reformed Church. Sundays were observed as a day of worship and rest, and Rich's parents faithfully took him to church twice every Sunday—morning and evening. "It didn't matter if there was a blizzard or a hailstorm outside," he recalls, "the DeVos family went to church—period, no argument. It was a strict religious upbringing, and I resisted some of the traditions I was raised in. I thought Sunday school was boring, and the sermons and hymns seemed to go on forever.

"Though I didn't appreciate it at the time, I was receiving one of life's greatest gifts. My parents, the pastors and teachers, the deacons and elders and volunteers spent a lot of time in my formative years giving me a road map to God. I'm still following that same road map they laid out for me when I was a boy. It has been a great source of strength and encouragement for some of the trials I've been through. I was also taught the Dutch Calvinist work ethic, which has served me well throughout my life."

Rich is also grateful for the Christian education he received in high school. Grand Rapids Christian High School was not only an academically strong school, but it reinforced the Christian faith that was instilled in him at home and in church. It was also the place where he met his lifelong friend and business partner, Jay Van Andel. Upon his graduation Rich enlisted in the Army Air Corps during World War II.

"Before I went into the service," Rich recalls, "I had never stood up before the church and publicly professed my faith in Jesus Christ. The church leaders had wanted me to do so, but I had argued with them. Having grown up in a Christian home, I assumed I was a Christian. I argued, 'I'm going to heaven, so why do I have to do anything more?'

"After I got back from World War II, my pastor took me aside and told me, 'God calls you, but you have to choose him. You were born with free will, but God knows your answer before you're going to do it.' It's a mystery, and I didn't understand it, but I accepted it. So when I was twenty, I stood up before the church and made a public profession of my faith."

> *"Rich DeVos is one of the most energetic and dedicated Christian laymen I have ever known. I am never in his presence that I don't feel his strength of character and dedication to the things of God."*
>
> Billy Graham
> Evangelist

From the very beginning, Rich made sure that he fully integrated his faith into his business life. His high school classmate, Gale Smith, recalls, "Rich and I worked at the same men's clothing store during our high school years. After World War II, Rich and Jay returned to the States and started their own flying school, Wolverine Air Service. I came out and looked at his operation, and I asked Rich, 'Are you open on Sundays?' He said, 'No, only six days of the week.' I said, 'Well, a lot of your potential customers work during the week, and they'll only be able to take lessons on the weekend. You'll lose a lot of business if you're not open on Sundays.' Rich replied, 'I won't do business on the Lord's Day. If we can't make a profit on a six-day week, then we'll do something else.' Rich was only twenty-two at the time, but his life values were already in place. He has operated by that same set of faith-based values ever since."

A Prodigal's Story

Nicholas De Ruiter, educational director for Global Information Management Systems Corporation, became acquainted with Rich DeVos after the war. "Rich and I attended Calvin Christian Reformed Church in Grand Rapids. After the services, Rich, Jay Van Andel and I sat on the porch of College Hall and discussed the sermon. We each looked at spiritual and theological matters a bit differently from each other, so those discussions were lively and interesting."

Those three young men were profoundly affected by their experiences in the war. "We had seen death and suffering," De Ruiter recalls, "and it had changed us. While serving with the U.S. Navy from 1943 to 1946, I had flown off the carrier USS *Antietam* in the Pacific, and I had seen a lot of terrible things. I was also an observer at Hiroshima, and the horrible annihilation of that city haunted me. It haunts me still. So the three of us war veterans were looking for answers about God, about good and evil, about the meaning of life.

> *"Rich's faith in human potential is rooted in his faith in God. He believes that we are capable of achieving great things—not because we are so great, but because of what a great God can do through us."*
>
> EARL HOLTON
> GRAND RAPIDS BUSINESS LEADER

"Those spiritual discussions with Rich were intense. I remember him being very sincere and passionate about his views, yet he was also humble and a good listener. He always wanted to hear what others had to say. I remember that he had resumed his studies at Calvin College, where his faith was being shaped by some fine theologians and professors. Rich had a few questions and doubts, but overall his faith was rock-solid. He was a man of action who lived his faith, always showing charity and kindness to people in need. He was also very busy in those early postwar years selling Nutrilite products.

"I had a very different focus. I was not a salesman, but a philosopher and a cynic. For me, the Christian faith was not so much a matter of belief, but of investigation and questioning. I had many doubts about God after seeing the destruction caused by the atomic bomb.

"Rich showed a lot of wisdom and patience in our theological discussions. He would listen carefully to my views and questions, and he would respond in a very down-to-earth, humble way."

Nicholas DeRuiter left Grand Rapids in 1960, and he lost touch with Rich and Jay—and he lost touch with God. "I lost my faith in God and the Christian community," he says. "I became very disintegrated in my soul. I served politically with the Democratic Party, then became disillusioned after the assassination of John F. Kennedy. I turned my back on family, church and friends, and plunged into a life of wine, women and jazz."

> *"Rich DeVos taught me how to be who I am by being grounded in Jesus Christ. He never wants you to be anyone but who you are, and he accepts who you are, even with your frailties and faults. In a way, it's ironic that you are calling this book* How to Be Like Rich DeVos. *He would never want anyone to be like him. He just wants you to be like you, and he wants everyone to be more like Jesus."*
>
> Barb Van Andel Gaby
> Jay's daughter

DeRuiter's next encounter with Rich DeVos came more than twenty years later, in the mid-1980s. "I was watching a religious program on television one morning," DeRuiter remembers, "when, much to my surprise, the pastor introduced Rich DeVos. Though I was a prodigal and a cynic, I was intrigued to hear what Rich had to say. His humility and sincerity took me back to our discussions on the porch of College Hall. Here was a man who had reached the top of the business world, yet he expressed his faith in Jesus Christ in simple, honest terms.

"As I listened to Rich speak, I prayed for the first time in years, 'God, what have I done with my life?' Tears rolled down my cheeks. I couldn't help thinking of all I had lost during my prodigal years—but I was also grateful to my old friend, Rich DeVos. He didn't know it yet, but God used Rich to bring a spiritually dead man back to life. I didn't meet Rich in person again until 1998 when we became reacquainted at a Gospel Communications conference in Grand Rapids. I was glad that I had the chance to thank him in person and tell Rich how he had been used by God to bring me back to faith in Christ."

A Sinner Saved by Grace

There is nothing more important to Rich DeVos than living out his faith in Jesus Christ. God has first place in his life, and everything else is, at best, a distant second. I spoke with two of Rich's pastors at La Grave Avenue Christian Reformed Church in Grand Rapids. His current pastor, Dr. Stan Mast, told me, "Rich has a deep personal relationship with Jesus Christ. He believes in Jesus with all his heart, and he thinks you and everyone else should believe in him, too. You might think this would make Rich intolerant of people with different beliefs, but his great humility and love for people enable him to be perfectly accepting of people from other faiths. Although he never hesitates to share his faith, he is eager to hear what others have to say. His boldness for Christ has increased since his heart-transplant operation. Something about that experience deepened his conviction that the Christian faith is the truth, and that every person on Earth needs to hear about Jesus."

> *"Rich DeVos sincerely believes in the Bible and his Christian faith. He's one of the few truly wealthy men I know who treats all people as equals, as human beings made in the image of God. Rich relies on his faith to overcome obstacles, such as the criticism he has taken over the years as a cofounder of Amway and as a leading conservative thinker. His faith and courage set an example for me that I try to emulate."*
>
> Glenn Steil, Former Michigan State Senator and Grand Rapids Business Leader

Rich's former pastor, Rev. Jacob Eppinga, told me a story that illustrates so many facets of Rich's character, including his commitment to Jesus Christ. "Rich served as an elder on our church council," Rev. Eppinga recalls, "even though he was one of the busiest men in the world. He was so committed to serving in the church that he would fly in from Florida just to attend a Monday night council meeting.

"On one occasion, Rich told me he would be at a council meeting. But when it was time for the meeting to begin, Rich wasn't there. One of the elders opened the meeting with prayer—a long, drawn-out prayer. As the elder was praying, the phone in the next room began ringing. It rang and rang as the prayer went on and on. The ringing phone was becoming a distraction, so I got up and went to answer it. I picked up the phone and it was Rich. I said, 'The meeting just started. Where are you?'

"He said, 'I'm two blocks away, at the hospital.'

"I said, 'At the hospital! Rich, are you okay?'

"He said, 'I'm fine. I just walked over here to use the phone.'

(This was in the days before cellular phones, of course.) 'I took a cab from the airport, but when I got to the church, all the doors were locked, and I couldn't get in. So I pounded on the door, but I guess you couldn't hear me. I was beginning to think I had come on the wrong night. Could one of you fellows come out here and pick me up?' So we brought Rich back, and the meeting continued.

"That little incident illustrates exactly the kind of person Rich is. He's committed to his faith and to his church—he'll fly a thousand miles to attend a church board meeting. And he's persistent—he'll pound and pound on the door, and if that doesn't work, he'll find a phone. He'll keep ringing that phone until somebody answers. Those qualities—faith, commitment and persistence—have made Rich the person he is today."

Whenever Rich gets up to speak, he introduces himself in the simplest of terms. He says, "I'm just a sinner, saved by grace." Even in secular settings, before secular audiences, Rich boldly bases his identity on his faith.

Rich explained to me why he introduces himself that way: "Years ago, I was invited to speak at a bankers conference on Mackinac Island. The emcee gave me this huge, flowery introduction. It went on and on. When I finally got up to speak, I said, 'Come on. I know who I really am. I'm just a sinner saved by grace.' The line just came out.

"A few days later, I received a note from a man who was in the audience. He wrote, 'When you said that, something hit me like a lightning bolt. I knew I was a sinner, too, and that I had to change my life.' God had used that line to bring conviction to this man's

"Rich DeVos has made a total commitment to the values he holds deeply—God, free enterprise, family and friends. Inspiration radiates from him, so that everyone around him is inspired as well."

GUY VANDER JAGT
FORMER U.S. CONGRESSMAN

soul. So today, whenever I'm asked to speak, I tell the crowd, 'I'm just a sinner saved by grace.' Regardless of any flowery introductions, that's who I truly am. I say that at almost every session."

For many years, Rich carried cards with him that he would hand out to people he met. The cards were printed with these words:

Excuse me, but could I ask you a question?
I hope it won't offend you, but if you were to die today,
do you know where you would spend eternity? The Bible says it
will either be in Heaven or it will be in Hell. Would you think
about that, please? Thank you and God bless you.

Rich DeVos

That card is a fitting description of the heart and soul of Rich. He is completely devoted to his Lord, Friend and Savior, Jesus Christ—and he wants everyone to know it. Some people believe that faith is a private matter, best kept to oneself. Not Rich. "Faith is not passive and private," he says. "Faith is active. It is something you live and declare."

"Faith is the centerpiece of Rich's life. He has Reagan-like optimism. It's not pollyannaism but a realistic optimism, rooted in Rich's belief that God is in control. Faith in God drives his life."

Jack Kemp, Former U.S. Congressman

Those who have known Rich the longest say that he has always been very open and bold about declaring his faith in God. Former Amway employee Jim DeVoss told me this story: "An employee attended a seminar on the east coast. At the seminar, he became acquainted with a man who served as a sheriff in a town in the Southeast.

"'What company are you with?' the sheriff asked. 'Alticor,' said the employee. 'It's an international direct-sales company with headquarters in Ada, Michigan.' The sheriff said, 'Really? I used to know a fellow from Ada, Michigan. I wonder whatever happened to him.'

"The sheriff went on to explain that, when he was in the military, he had been in the same Air Corps unit with a young man from Ada. This fellow had made such an impression because he was the only man in the barracks who unfailingly knelt by his bunk every evening and said his prayers. Only someone who was totally sure of his faith in God would be that bold.

"The Amway employee asked the sheriff if he recalled the name of the young man who prayed in the barracks. 'Yes, I do,' the sheriff replied. 'His name was DeVos—Rich DeVos. Why, do you know him?' The employee was happy to let this sheriff know what Rich DeVos had done with his life in the years since the war."

> *"Rich believes in absolutes, and his faith is the foundation of his life."*
>
> Helen DeVos
> Rich's Wife

Rich's faith pervades every aspect of his life, including his decision to become involved in the world of professional sports. "When the opportunity to buy the Orlando Magic came up in 1991," Rich recalls, "our family got together and prayed about it. We had earlier discussed buying the Dallas Cowboys, but there was one major problem: Pro football is played on Sundays. The NFL would have completely overwhelmed our lives every Sunday during football season. We felt our church life would have been compromised."

Rich and his family decided they wanted to become involved in pro sports as a way to expand their influence for Jesus Christ. The Orlando Magic gave them the perfect vehicle. Not only does NBA team ownership give Rich access to the national sports pages and ESPN microphones, but it also gives him a whole group of influential celebrities to talk to about his faith. "I pray with the team at the start of every season," Rich says, "and the players respond to that. I let them know that I'm available to them all year 'round. I enjoy talking to the players about faith and life values."

In his book *Hope From My Heart,* Rich writes, "I put my trust in God and in his Son, Jesus Christ. My Christian faith is the foundation on which all else in my life rests; it is my life's most important asset. I believe that genuine success—in every aspect of our lives—depends on an unshakable foundation of Christian faith. Without faith in a personal, creator God, the universe is a meaningless place, nothing in life has direction, and moral principles are impossible. Without faith in the personal God of the Bible, and knowledge of his Word, no one has an accurate road map for life."

What does Rich's faith consist of? How can we know Jesus Christ in a personal way, as Rich knows him? Rich explains the gospel with characteristic simplicity:

> *"Rich DeVos has an uncommon commitment to his faith. Many business leaders are committed to their business. Rich has kept his business subordinate to his faith. Many who claim to be Christians act as if their God is no longer living. You can see that God is alive and well in the life of Rich DeVos."*
>
> MAX DEPREE, BESTSELLING AUTHOR AND FORMER CEO OF HERMAN MILLER, INC.

"Man is separated from God by sin," he says. "But God sent his Son, Jesus Christ, to be born as a child so he could bridge that gap between God and humanity. As a man, Christ died on the cross to pay for our sins. We cannot buy or earn our way to salvation. The good news is that salvation is a free gift from God to all who accept Jesus Christ as their Savior. You can come to know God by admitting that you are a sinner and asking Christ to accept you. All it requires is true faith and a simple prayer. Jesus himself explained it this way: 'For God so loved the world that he gave his one and only Son, that whoever believes in him shall not perish but have eternal life' (John 3:16, NIV).

"Sharing my faith is the simplest thing in the world. All I do is show people I'm interested in them. I enjoy asking people questions and finding out what they believe. I ask, 'What church do you go to? What do you believe in?' We talk about what they believe; and then they ask me what I believe. I never push my faith on other people. I don't have to. They usually ask me, and then I tell them about my Friend, Jesus."

A Foundation of Faith

Only God knows how many people have found faith in Jesus Christ through the simple Christian message of Rich DeVos. One couple who found Christ through Rich's life and words are independent business owners Dan and Bunny Williams. "Rich introduced us to his friend Billy Zeoli," Dan told me. "Billy is Rich's close friend and advisor. Bunny and I could tell that Rich and Billy both had something very special, something we didn't have. We didn't know what it was, but we both wanted it."

> *"Faith is woven into the fabric of Rich's life. His optimism springs from his strong faith in God. Sure, Rich knows there is evil in the world, but he is confident that God is ultimately in control. If things go well for Rich, he gives God the credit. If things go against him, he doesn't blame God. He accepts the defeats along with the successes, and he keeps trusting in God, no matter what comes his way."*
>
> BILL NICHOLSON, FORMER AMWAY CHIEF OPERATING OFFICER

"As we talked to them and got to know them," Bunny said, "it dawned on us that what Rich DeVos and Billy Zeoli had was a deep relationship with the Lord Jesus Christ. Because of those two Christian men and the way they are so open about their faith, Dan and I prayed and asked Jesus to be our Lord and Savior. Our lives have been blessed in so many ways because of our friendship with Rich DeVos, but the greatest blessing of all was when Rich and Billy introduced us to Jesus Christ."

Dennis Delisle is past president of the board of the Independent Business Owners Association International. "The first time Rich DeVos came into my life," he recalls, "I was a junior at San Jose State University. At the time, my mind was captured by the situational ethics and moral relativism that was being taught in my college courses. I tried to explain to Rich why moral relativism was more valid than the faith-based absolutes he believed in. Rich responded, 'Dennis, if it's against the Bible, it's wrong.' I thought about it, and I woke up to the realization that Rich was right and my college professor was wrong.

> *"The riches of life, the love and joy and exhilaration of life, can be found only with an upward look. This is an exciting world. It's cram-packed with opportunity. Great moments wait around every corner."*
>
> RICH DEVOS

"Not long after that, I made a trip with Rich to Rio de Janeiro, and I had a lot of time to sit and talk with Rich and soak up his wisdom. I was a hard-charging, ambitious young man in my twenties, and I thought I was conquering the world. By watching Rich's life, I saw that a person could be successful and influential while maintaining a strong Christian faith. Rich's life made a powerful impact on me. It was at that time that I prayed to receive Jesus Christ as my Lord and Savior.

"Rich wasn't just interested in seeing me become a Christian. He wanted me to grow as a Christian. He once asked me, 'Now that you are a believer, what are you learning? How are you growing?' He encouraged me to study the Bible and pray. He said, 'Ask the Holy Spirit for wisdom. He will guide your life and show you what to believe.'"

Billy Zeoli recalls, "One Sunday, Rich and I spoke at a New York Yankees chapel together. Afterwards, pitcher Ron Guidry came up to us and it was obvious that he was searching. I turned him over to Rich, and he told Ron, 'There are three types of sinners here. There's a business sinner, a preacher sinner and a ballplayer sinner.' Ron was absolutely ready to commit himself to Christ, and Rich had the privilege of praying with Ron to take that step."

> *"Every time I see Rich, he tells me how thrilled he was to see me preach at Mickey Mantle's funeral. Rich loves the Lord, and his greatest joy is to see people hearing and receiving the gospel."*
>
> BOBBY RICHARDSON
> FORMER SECOND BASEMAN,
> NEW YORK YANKEES

Rich is just as eager to share his faith before groups as he is in one-to-one situations. Elsa Prince-Broekhuizen is the mother of Betsy DeVos, the wife of Rich's son, Dick. "Rich's faith is just part of his life," Elsa told me, "and he is completely open about it. He'll be at a banquet or a meeting, and he'll say, 'It's our custom to pray to the Lord at an event like this,' and he will lead in prayer. Since his heart surgery, he is even more bold about his faith because he believes this is why God spared him."

Howard Edington, former senior pastor of the First Presbyterian Church in Orlando, agrees: "Rich DeVos does not divide his life into sacred and secular. In his life, *everything* is sacred. Scratch the surface of his life and you discover that the faith foundation of the man is unmistakable."

Rich's oldest son, Dick, observes, "Dad's faith is woven through his worldview and all that he does. His faith is not a deep, intellectual theology, but a simple, trusting relationship with God. It is absolute in every area of his life. It's the compass he steers by."

Rich's youngest son, Doug, adds, "Dad practices his faith by loving God and loving his neighbor, and he doesn't get all hung up on theological debates. When deep questions come up about the virgin birth or some other theological issue, Dad will say, 'I don't know. It's a mystery. I just accept it by faith. Why get hung up on doctrinal discussions? All I know is that God loves me, and Jesus Christ died for me.'"

Those who know Rich best say that it is the shared Christian faith and values of Rich DeVos and Jay Van Andel that have enabled the two men to maintain such a close and successful business partnership over the years. Jay's son Steve, now chairman of Alticor, says, "Dad and Rich have a common set of beliefs that surround their lives and their business. Faith in Jesus Christ kept dad and Rich together. It smoothed out every rough spot in their business relationship.

"In most family businesses, things can collapse when the second generation takes over. But the DeVos and Van Andel families have based their lives on the same faith and values that the founders have. We are building that same foundation into the lives of our own children."

Rich's son Doug agrees. "The reason Dad and Jay worked so well together," he says, "is that they have always been men of integrity and strong Christian faith. They believed they were part of something bigger than themselves. They wanted to use their business to serve God and impact human lives. They felt that Amway was a special business because it was God's business. If

> *"I admire, respect and love Rich DeVos, and I give thanks to the Lord for him. Over the years, I have known a number of business giants who served the Lord—J. C. Penney, Mr. Kraft of Kraft Foods and Art DeMoss, to name a few. Rich DeVos certainly belongs on that list. Few have accomplished more than Rich, and amid all of his achievements, he has brought thousands into the Kingdom of God."*
>
> Dr. Bill Bright, Founder, Campus Crusade for Christ

something went wrong, they never said, 'It's your fault,' or, 'I told you so.' They never placed blame; they just solved problems. The next generation of DeVoses and Van Andels sees life the same way. We all feel responsible to be good stewards of God's blessings."

Many people think that Rich's brand of unabashed Christianity has gone out of style. You will often hear people say, "Oh, I'm very spiritual—but I'm not religious. I can go out to the forest or the seashore and worship God. I don't need to find God in some building with organ music and stained glass."

To these objections, Rich replies, "We need God, and we need to be part of a worshiping community. I don't think of church as a place I have to go. It's a place I love to go because I get to share my faith with a community of believers and join with them in worshiping God. Church, to me, is not a building. It's people, and I love to be with people. In my worshiping community, we have fellowship together, we build each other up, and we encourage each other so that we can go back out into the world and live out our faith in the trenches of the real world."

Even though Rich DeVos has a firm faith in Jesus Christ, he is fascinated by the religious beliefs of other people. "Rich comes from a Dutch Reformed background," says his friend Paul Conn, "which is not exactly noted for its inclusiveness. Yet Rich practices his faith in a remarkably inclusive way. He is not rigid or judgmental toward other faiths. He's amazingly broad-minded and curious about the beliefs of other people. I have sat in on discussions he's had with people of other religions, and he is always interested to hear other people express their views. He's inquisitive and eager to know where people are coming from."

Arend Lubbers, former president of Grand Valley State University, agrees. "Although Rich is strong in his conservative evangelical beliefs, he always accommodates people who don't believe as he does. He welcomes people as friends, even when their beliefs are very different from his. He finds a comfort zone with people."

Rich's son Doug offers an example of the way Rich boldly and publicly practices his own faith while reaching out to people of other faiths. "Prayer is a natural part of Dad's life," Doug told me. "He'll be speaking at a public event or a meeting, and he'll say, 'Okay, it's time to pray.' On one occasion, Dad prayed at a public gathering, and as he always does, he closed his prayer in the name of Jesus. Afterwards, a Jewish man took Dad aside and said he was offended by the use of Jesus' name. Now, Dad is not going to stop praying in the name of his Lord, but he fully understood the man's problem. So Dad said, 'Okay, next time you pray.' And the Jewish man was fine with that."

> *"I had never spoken publicly about my Christian faith until I met Rich DeVos. He taught me to be confident and bold about my beliefs."*
>
> Dexter Yager
> Independent Business Owner

People have asked Rich if Amway was a Christian organization. "Absolutely not," he replied. "There are many wonderful Christian people in Amway, but there are also many fine people from other faiths involved in Amway. The fact is, an organization can't be Christian. Only people can be Christian, because Christianity is a personal relationship between Jesus Christ and an individual human being. I would never use the Christian gospel to promote Amway, nor do I use Amway as a means of imposing my religious beliefs on other people.

"Now, it's true that I'm not shy about discussing my relationship with Jesus wherever I go, including Amway meetings. I always introduce myself as a sinner saved by grace, because that's what I am. I can't compartmentalize myself and say, 'This is who I am on Sundays, and that is who I am the rest of the week.' I am a Christian twenty-four hours a day, seven days a week. There is no part of my life that I do not place under the Lordship of Jesus Christ.

"Someone once asked Jesus, 'What is the great commandment?' Jesus gave a very simple reply: 'Love God," he said, 'and love your neighbor as you love yourself.' That commandment is the source of all my values. I know that God has put me on this Earth to love him and to love other people as I love myself. That may sound like an oversimplification, but that's what Jesus said, and that's what I base my life on. Sometimes I fail to meet that standard, but it is always my goal."

> *"As the years go on, Rich gets bolder in publicly expressing his faith in Christ. I have seen him do it even in situations where it's not politically correct. He gets away with it because of his obvious sincerity and personal charm."*
>
> VERN EHLERS
> U.S. CONGRESSMAN

Why does Rich DeVos depend so strongly on his faith? He has success. He has wealth. He has fame and influence. Isn't all of that enough to satisfy any human being? "Without faith," Rich says, "no amount of success will satisfy you. Life is empty without God. There is no meaning, no purpose in life, if you don't know Jesus as your Lord and Savior. Jesus himself stated it perfectly when he said, 'What good is it for a man to gain the whole world, yet forfeit his soul?' When you reach the end of your earthly life, what good will money and fame do you? In this life, there is only one thing we can ultimately depend on, and that is God himself."

The Valley of the Shadow of Death

When Rich DeVos talks about human mortality, he speaks from years of experience, having survived strokes, heart failure, one heart bypass surgery in 1983, a stroke, heart attack and a second bypass in 1992, staph infection and diabetes. In 1997, he faced the toughest challenge of his life. His seventy-one-year-old heart was failing,

> *"A poor man might live a lifetime with the delusion that if he only had enough money all his problems would disappear. When he acquires a fortune, he discovers just how limited money can be. Money cannot buy peace of mind. It cannot heal ruptured relationships or build meaning into a life that has none. It cannot relieve guilt or speak to the great agonies of the broken heart."*
>
> RICH DEVOS

and doctors told him he had only one chance for survival: a heart transplant. That one chance was made slimmer because of Rich's age, history of poor health and rare AB-positive blood type. Donor organs for transplants are in short supply to begin with, but the special factors in Rich's case reduced his odds to something like one in a million.

The doctors spent months searching for a surgeon to take Rich's case, but every surgeon they contacted refused. Finally, one doctor agreed to consider Rich as a candidate—Professor Sir Magdi Yacoub, an Egyptian-born thoracic and cardiovascular surgeon at London's Harefield Hospital. Professor Yacoub was a transplant researcher who specialized in unusual and challenging cases that extended the boundaries of medical knowledge. The rare combination of problems in Rich's case presented exactly the kind of challenge that Professor Yacoub was looking for.

In addition to Rich's medical problems, legal obstacles had to be overcome in order for him to receive a new heart. By British law, Rich couldn't receive a new heart if a British subject was also a match for an available organ. "I was literally the last guy on the list to receive a new heart," Rich recalls. "If I was going to get one, it would have to be a genuine miracle. All the odds were against me."

In January 1997, Rich flew to London, accompanied by Helen and two of their sons, to undergo four days of testing and evaluation. There Rich found out that what had originally appeared to be a strike against him—his rare blood type—just might turn out to be a blessing in disguise. Because AB-positive donors are so rare, AB-positive hearts are not easy to come by—but the rarity of that blood type also means that there are few AB-positive patients on the waiting list at any given time. So if there were no British subjects waiting when a heart became available, a non-Briton like Rich could receive a heart that would otherwise be wasted. Rich's rare blood type—a strike against him in the United States—became a factor in his favor in England.

> *"People miss golden opportunities every day because they are afraid of rejection, afraid of what other people might say. You can't let fear of rejection stop you. When I needed a new heart, I battled rejection daily: I was rejected by every heart-transplant surgeon in America. But I didn't let that stop me. Even after successful transplant surgery, I had to deal with the fear of rejection—the possibility that my body might reject my new heart. Throughout my life, I have faced rejection, and I have won. That is why I am alive today."*
>
> RICH DEVOS

Even so, finding a new heart for Rich DeVos wasn't easy. Rich had to remain in a London hotel room, close to a pager at all times. If a donor heart became available, Rich would have to be rushed to the hospital on a moment's notice. A donor heart can remain viable outside the body for no more than four hours. Every second counts. As it turned out, Rich waited in that London hotel room for five months until a heart became available. As the wait dragged on, Rich's own heart continued to deteriorate. He grew weaker with each passing day.

As Rich waited, his wife Helen was constantly with him. His four children (Dick, who was forty-one at the time; Dan, thirty-nine; Cheri, thirty-six; and Doug, thirty-three) took turns visiting him, along with the grandchildren. Every day, Rich and Helen read the Bible together, focusing especially on such beloved passages as Philippians 4:4–7. Verse 4 (NLT) says: "Always be full of joy in the Lord. I say it again—rejoice!"

Finally, in early June 1997, the pager beeped. A heart was available. Rich was whisked away to Harefield Hospital and prepared for surgery.

> *"I know the Lord is in charge of my life. And if he wants me to live longer, then this is going to work well. And if he says, 'That's it,' then that's okay. I know where I'm going, and I am at peace. I have no fear of dying."*
>
> RICH DEVOS, JUST BEFORE HEART-TRANSPLANT SURGERY

A Living Heart Donor

Rich's new heart had become available because of a highly unlikely—even *miraculous*—chain of circumstances. At the same time Rich was waiting for his new heart, a woman was waiting for new lungs—and she had the same rare AB-positive blood type as Rich.

The woman's heart was healthy and strong, because it had been working harder to make up for her weakened lungs. But her heart had an enlarged right ventricle, which made it unsuitable for almost any heart recipients. Miraculously, it was just right for Rich DeVos. His heart was also enlarged on the right side due to the strain caused by pulmonary edema (an accumulation of fluid in the lungs). To those who believe in God, it is more than a mere coincidence that the woman's heart was just the right size, shape and type for Rich's body.

Only one thing prevented Rich from receiving this woman's heart: She was still using it. But one day, after Rich had been waiting five months in a London hotel, everything changed. A victim of a fatal car crash in the Czech Republic was found to have a set of undamaged heart and lungs—and the rare AB-positive blood type. In lung-transplant cases, surgeons prefer to replace the heart and lungs together because this increases survival rates. So the woman would get a new heart and lungs from the Czech crash victim—and Rich DeVos would get the woman's healthy heart. Out of the tragedy of one person's accidental death, two people would receive the gift of life.

Rich was wheeled into the operating room, knowing that his own heart was about to be removed from his body and discarded. If all went well, he would receive a new heart—and a new lease on life. If the operation failed—he knew that the question of his eternal destiny was settled. He would go to sleep on Earth, and he would awaken in God's presence.

The operation lasted five hours and was completed without a hitch. Then came Rich's *real* ordeal—a long postoperative trial of pain, weakness, drug-induced nightmares, waking hallucinations, and fears of rejection and infection. For days afterward, Rich felt disoriented and struggled with depression—a strange experience for the always hard-charging, optimistic Rich DeVos.

I spoke with Professor Yacoub, Rich's London surgeon, and he told me, "Rich is very determined, optimistic and disciplined. All of these traits were on display as he went through the most difficult experience of his life. I'm convinced that those traits enabled him to come through the surgery and the difficult postoperative recovery."

> *"Shortly after Rich's transplant operation, I was talking with him by phone, and I used an expression I often use: 'Bless your heart.' Immediately, Rich said, 'Which one?'"*
>
> John Haggai
> Founder and Chairman, Haggai Institute

The doctors ordered him back on his feet as soon as possible. He needed exercise—and he needed the sensation of living, of getting back into the game of life. One day, as he was walking down a hospital corridor to work his muscles, he met a woman patient who was also walking in the corridor. They were in a transplant ward, so it was obvious that they had something in common. The woman smiled at Rich and said, "So you have a new heart, do you? When did you receive it? What day? What time?"

Rich told her.

The woman's face lit up. "You have my heart!"

It was one of the rarest of all miracles. Rich had just met the woman whose heart was beating in his own chest! Who would have guessed that he would have had the privilege of meeting and thanking the *living donor* of his new heart? "She was alive and well and recovering from her own miracle," Rich later recalled. "We were *both* alive!"

Three weeks after his surgery, Rich was released from the hospital. He spent a month recuperating in the village of Viareggio on the west coast of Italy, then he returned to the United States. He was met at the Gerald R. Ford International Airport in Grand Rapids by a crowd of relatives, friends and supporters that included his ninety-two-year-old mother, Ethel, and Michigan Governor John Engler.

How to Face Death Like Rich

Rich DeVos has been living in the shadow of death for a number of years, and the way he has faced his own mortality is an inspiration to everyone who knows him. Here are some firsthand observations of people who have watched Rich face the greatest crisis of his life with courage, serenity and faith.

Dr. Rick McNamara, One of Rich's Physicians:

"I met Rich in 1992 at the time of his major heart attack. He arrived by ambulance suffering from major chest pains. When he arrived I saw him at his weakest point. A very intense week followed as we fought for his life. I was amazed at how trusting he was.

"Finally, he had bypass surgery and came through the operation just fine. But then a serious monster infection set in. At that point, I saw Rich's true strength. It took three surgeries to get the infection cleaned out.

"Rich's heart attack had left him with a very bad heart muscle, and the infection had left him very weak. His chances weren't great. I talked with Rich, and he told me he was ready to die. He didn't want to die, of course, but his faith was strong and he was prepared to go.

"When the possibility of a heart transplant came up, we suggested it to Rich, and he said he'd consider it. 'I was wondering if you were going to bring that up,' he said. He trusted us to make all the decisions. And he trusted God to take care of the results."

Dick DeVos, Rich's Oldest Son:

"Dad was in a London hotel waiting for a heart transplant to save his life. At the same time, he was very excited about a boat he had designed, the *Independence*. It was being built in Italy. Even though Dad was so weak he could hardly walk, he would sit in that chair, surrounded by boat plans, weather charts and cruising guides.

"I said, 'Dad, how can you do all this? You may never see this boat.'

"'Maybe I'll live to see it, maybe I won't,' he replied. 'It's only a boat. If I die, the boat can be sold. I have faith in God, so I'm not worried about dying. If God grants me more years to live, then the issue is, What is my role? What does he want me to do next?'

"That kind of positive attitude is only possible when you have faith in God. Because Dad believes that God is in control and there is order to the universe, he can live with courage and optimism even when the medical experts were telling him, 'You're too old; there's no hope; this is the end of the line.'"

Fred Meijer, Grand Rapids Business and Community Leader:

"We visited Rich in London eight days before his heart surgery. He was very ill and extremely weak, but he was upbeat and confident that the surgery would be successful. I can't imagine going through something like that, but Rich's optimism and faith carried him through."

Lynne Courts, Rich's Niece:

"When Rich was waiting for his heart transplant in London, I went to see him. He was desperately ill, but he wasn't depressed. In fact, he was sitting in his room making plans for his latest boat! But that's Rich—always looking forward to the next challenge, always planning for the future and working on his next project. Rich won't ever give up because he is so full of life. That is what he's all about."

Joe Tomaselli, Vice President and General Manager, Amway Grand Plaza Hotel:

"When it was time for Rich to get a new heart, I asked him if he was afraid. He said, 'No. I'm at peace with the Lord, and I'm prepared for the outcome. If I die, I know I'm going to a better place.' He was very calm and at peace. It was actually a joyful time for him."

Dr. Oliver Grin, Grand Rapids Physician:

"Rich DeVos has an amazing attitude of optimism and enthusiasm, even when facing a life-threatening illness. I'm sure it's that attitude that has enabled him to survive surgery after surgery. I spoke with his wife Helen about his attitude, and I asked if he was able to remain positive even when death was approaching prior to his heart transplant. She said that even when he became weak to the point of being barely able to talk in the last few weeks before the transplant procedure, his positive attitude never wavered. Even undergoing such an incredible ordeal, he remains optimistic; he always gives two thumbs up."

Gen. Alexander M. Haig Jr., Former U.S. Secretary of State:

"Rich showed remarkable courage during the time he was waiting for a new heart. His old heart was failing, and the odds of a new heart becoming available were very slim. Most people would have given up, but Rich waited patiently in London, leaning on his faith in God."

Bob Vander Weide, Rich's Son-in-Law and Orlando Magic CEO:

"I watched Rich go through his health crisis a few years ago. I observed his peace of mind. There was no panic, no fear. He was completely at ease during that incredibly difficult time because his entire life had been focused on the right things."

Jay Van Andel, Amway Cofounder:

"Since Rich's heart transplant, his faith seems even deeper. He talks more freely about his faith and is more expressive about it. Rich sees what God has given to him and what God expects from him as a result."

Bud Berends, Rich's Longtime Friend:

"Every year, Rich and Jay put on a big Christmas party at Alticor headquarters. The food is tremendous, and there's always outstanding live music. After his heart transplant, Rich started doing something new at the Christmas party. He stops the music and gets up before the crowd and says, 'I've got a new heart. You can have a new heart, too. All you have to do is put your trust in Jesus Christ.' He has never been bashful about his faith, but since his brush with death, he has been even more bold in speaking out about the most important thing in his life, his faith in Jesus Christ."

Looking back, Rich views his close encounter with his mortality as a miracle of God's amazing grace. "Only the spiritually blind could fail to see the hand of God in my circumstances," he reflects in *Hope From My Heart*. "But one question remained: Why me? People die every day waiting for a donor organ. . . . Ultimately, there was only one explanation for a miracle like that: the grace of God and nothing else. God's grace gives hope in the most hopeless situations."

Rich and Helen DeVos look at this new chapter in his life as an exciting adventure—the adventure of faith in Jesus Christ. Rich's experience is a lot like an exciting NBA game. The Orlando Magic is down by three as the clock ticks down to zero. Suddenly, an unbelievable three-point shot falls through the net as the buzzer sounds—and the game goes into overtime.

> *"Grandpa believes in Jesus. He says we should always trust him and believe in him."*
>
> MICAELA DEVOS, RICH'S GRANDDAUGHTER (DOUG AND MARIA'S DAUGHTER)

Rich is playing his game in overtime right now. He's still competing, still battling it out, still having fun, still living his dream of success and influence for God. "God still has something important for Rich to do in this life," his wife Helen says. "I believe that's why he's still alive."

Rich's faith has conquered his fears, freeing him to live the adventure of life. Nothing holds him back, not even his own mortality. "I'm not afraid of dying," he says. "As I went through my heart transplant, I discovered that God's peace is amazing. I know Jesus and his love, and I want to share that love with the entire world."

The new life Rich received through his heart transplant in 1997 is symbolic of the new life God offers to all who place their trust in him through faith in Jesus Christ. Here is what God says in his world about the new heart and the new life that he wants to transplant into each of us:

"I will sprinkle clean water on you, and you will be clean. . . . I will give you a new heart and put a new spirit in you; I will remove from you your heart of stone and give you a heart of flesh. And I will put my Spirit in you" (Ezekiel 36:25–27, NIV). That is the message and the meaning of Rich DeVos's life: *Have faith*—and God will give you a new heart!

Chapter Fourteen

Keep an Upward Look!

YOU HAVE ALREADY READ how, in 1949, Rich DeVos and Jay Van Andel set off on a sailing adventure down the east coast of the United States to the Caribbean. They had planned to sail all the way to South America—but their boat sank in the Bahama Channel. Though they had lost their boat (and with it, a large chunk of their net worth), those two young men in their twenties kept going. They bummed a ride to South America aboard a tramp tanker, then proceeded on their adventure aboard a puddle-jumping airplane, a paddle-wheeled steamboat and a steam-powered railroad. Their journey together was more than just a tropical vacation; it was jam-packed with life lessons about attitude, character and what it takes to succeed in life.

Twenty years later, in 1969, Rich DeVos and Jay Van Andel were business partners in a fast-growing company called Amway—then disaster struck. A fire burned their aerosol manufacturing plant to the ground. The night of the fire, Rich and Jay vowed to rebuild the facility and move on—and they did.

"Rich is positive about everything," Rich's nephew, Randy Heys, told me. "He can even be positive when people unfairly criticize him. One time there was a negative article in the newspaper about some issue he was involved with. I asked him, 'Don't you ever get sick of people attacking you and telling you that you're wrong?' He said, 'No, that never bothers me.' Rich never lets other people's opinions get him down. He's a public personality, and people in the public eye have to put up with a lot of unfair attacks. Some people lash back at their critics. Others say, 'I don't need to put up with this,' and they walk away in disgust. But Rich just puts it behind him and keeps moving forward."

> *"Rich DeVos has taught me about persevering through tough times. Amway has always been attacked and ridiculed as 'that multilevel marketing thing.' Rich kept his head up and moved forward. He's successful because he didn't listen to his critics. He persevered."*
>
> Dr. Robert A. Schuller, Vice President, Crystal Cathedral Ministries

How to Develop Character

Anyone who wishes to be successful and influential like Rich DeVos should recognize one crucial truth: Life is full of hard knocks—and the more successful and influential you become, the harder the knocks. If you want to be like Rich, then you need to develop an attitude like his. You need to develop character like his. There are many attitude and character qualities that define Rich DeVos. As we approach the end of this book, let's focus on just six: persistence, humility, kindness, honesty, hard work and optimism.

Crucial character trait no. 1: persistence

The very existence of Amway is an object lesson in persistence. Back in the early 1960s, during the company's precarious infancy, Rich and Jay planned a huge event in Lansing, Michigan. Their goal: to sign up two hundred new distributors in the Lansing area.

They took out radio ads on several stations and bought expensive display ads in the Lansing newspapers. They rented a two-hundred-seat auditorium. On the day of the event, they walked the streets of Lansing, handing out fliers and personally inviting hundreds of people to come.

That night, they walked out onto the stage of the auditorium and faced an audience of—are you ready for this?—*two people.* They had spent several thousand dollars and uncounted hours to attract a crowd, and the audience that turned out wouldn't have filled a phone booth. Having spent everything they had on promotion, Rich and Jay couldn't afford a hotel room. So they drove home that night, arriving at 2 A.M.

Many people would have called it quits then and there. Rich and Jay persevered. After such a shaky start, how did Amway ultimately succeed? In *Believe!* Rich says there is only one answer: "Persistence—not brilliant planning or blind luck or clever planning—has been the key."

Perseverance has literally been a matter of life and death for Rich DeVos. He has come face-to-face with his own mortality several times since his first heart bypass in 1983. In 1997, when his heart was failing and his only hope was transplant surgery, his London surgeon interviewed Rich, asking him a series of tough, probing questions: How strong is your will to live? Are you a fighter? Are you ready to go through an ordeal of pain and mental suffering in order to stay alive? The doctor wanted to know: Would Rich give up on life when the pain grew too intense—or would he push through the pain and keep fighting to live? Transplant surgery is difficult and expensive, and it would only be worth doing if Rich was willing to persevere. Rich

> *"Persistence is stubbornness with a purpose. It is determination with a goal in mind."*
>
> RICH DEVOS

and the doctor had a good talk—and when it was over, the doctor knew that his patient was a fighter. If anyone had the will to live, Rich did.

Rich has met every challenge of his life with unyielding determination and perseverance. Looking back on a lifetime of challenges and hard-won victories, he reflects, "If I had to select one quality, one personal characteristic that I regard as being the most highly correlated with success in any field, I would choose the trait of persistence. It is the will to endure to the end—to get knocked down seventy times and get up off the floor saying, 'Here comes number seventy-one!'"

His friend Michael Novak, an author and scholar with the American Enterprise Institute, described to me the perseverance of Rich DeVos. "Rich has the capacity to get his teeth into something and then hold on like a bulldog. Once he gets involved, he will stick with it through thick and thin. Many people quit when they see quitting as the reasonable option. But a hard-headed Dutchman like Rich DeVos will never consider quitting a reasonable option. He will just keep going until he wins. That's his genius. That's the secret of his success."

> *"I was at the bottom of the barrel when I started with Amway. Rich knew I was struggling, so he told me, 'Tony, don't you dare give up!' And I never have."*
>
> Tony Renard
> Independent Business Owner

Perseverance is more important in determining a person's success or failure than any other factor. It is more important than intellect, talent, health, speaking ability, personal charisma, physical attractiveness or any other advantages. You can lack most or even all of these advantages—yet you can still win and succeed if you have the dogged determination to never give up. "Persistence comes from a deep place in the soul," Rich says. "It is a God-given compensation for what we lack in other areas of our life. Never underestimate its power."

This message of success-through-persistence has been communicated throughout Rich's extended family. Rich's nephew, Todd Courts, says, "Rich and his two sisters grew up on Baldwin Street and came from an ordinary family. His baby crib was a drawer in the bedroom dresser. From those humble beginnings, Rich achieved incredible wealth by hard work and perseverance. He knows how hard it is to make a dollar, and he shows people what persistence can accomplish. I have a poster on my office wall with a big headline: 'Believe and Succeed!' Underneath that headline is a quote from Rich: 'The only thing that stands between a man and what he wants from life is often merely the will to try it and the faith to believe that it is possible.' That's the lesson of Rich's life: Dream big dreams, believe in your dreams and stick to them no matter what—and you will succeed."

Crucial character trait no. 2: humility

John E. Avellan was an airport manager with Avis Rent A Car when he first met Rich DeVos at the Avis counter at the Orlando airport, just a few months before Rich purchased the Orlando Magic franchise.

"I had never heard of Mr. DeVos before that day," John recalls. "He was returning his rental car, and he mentioned that it was a corporate account, and there should not be any insurance charged. I looked the contract over and said, 'I need to talk to my superior about this.' Unfortunately, it was after hours, and our corporate accounts office was closed, so I had to return to Mr. DeVos and tell him I was unable to get authorization to remove the insurance charges.

"He said, 'Do you know who I am?' Now, I have heard that

question many times before. I have heard it asked by rock stars, CEOs, politicians and sports figures. Whenever someone asks that question, it is usually followed by an angry tirade. I always brace for the worst. But there was something about the way Mr. DeVos asked that question—something about his demeanor—that was very different.

"I said, 'No, I'm sorry. I don't know who you are.'

"He smiled and even chuckled a little. 'Don't worry,' he said. 'I'll have my office take care of the insurance matter. Thank you for looking into it.' And he went to board his plane.

> *"Mr. DeVos is so down-to-earth and humble. He's warm and friendly to everybody."*
>
> FLUTIE TOLONEN
> AMWAY
> GRAND PLAZA HOTEL EMPLOYEE

"Well, I figured he must have been someone very important, but he was also extremely friendly and kind. That made an impression on me. To this day, I remember the details of that encounter—the fact that Mr. DeVos had returned a gray Chevy Corsica with about seven thousand miles on it, the fact that he was wearing a brown tweed jacket and a cream-colored shirt. I remember those details ten years later because that's the kind of impact Mr. DeVos made on me.

"A few days later, I was reading the sports section of the Orlando *Sentinel*—and there was a picture of Mr. DeVos, the very man I had met. I read the article and found out that he was a billionaire, and he was about to become the new owner of the Orlando Magic. And I knew something about him that the newspaper didn't report: Mr. DeVos is a humble, gracious man. Despite all of his wealth and influence, he doesn't feel the need to throw his weight around or intimidate people to get what he wants. He's a true gentleman, which is why he has built an organization of gentlemen such as John Gabriel, Doc Rivers, Pat Williams and many others. His attitude of gentleness and humility must be contagious."

Rich's longtime friend, John Bissell, chairman of Bissell, Inc., affirms John Avellan's impression. "Even with all of Rich's success, wealth and notoriety, he has never become arrogant. Just the opposite. Power usually corrupts people and inflates egos to the bursting point, but Rich has never been captured by his own wealth and power."

Former Amway chief operating officer Bill Nicholson agrees. "Rich's humility remains," he says. "Rich was born poor and raised in an atmosphere of simple homespun values, so Rich knows who he is, and he refuses to let money change him. Deep down, I think he gets up every morning and says, 'Wow! I never dreamed all of this could happen to me! I am so blessed and so undeserving!' I think that is the key to his humility."

> *"Rich DeVos has a humble heart and a proper sense of himself. When he says, 'I'm a sinner saved by grace,' he often adds, 'I hope to do some good in my life.'"*
>
> Edwin Meese III
> Former U.S. Attorney General

Sailing friend John Bertrand agrees. "Rich has a childlike awe of his own success," he says. "He continually expresses amazement over his material blessings, but he doesn't dwell on them. He simply sees his wealth as a means to helping others succeed. Deep down, Rich would be the same optimistic, humble, caring person whether he was wealthy or whether he only had two nickels to rub together."

Rich's daughter, Cheri, offers a similar perspective. "Dad is awed by his success," she says. "He looks at all that has happened in his life, and he kind of chuckles, 'Who would have thought that this would happen to me?' Instead of becoming arrogant about it, he is humbled by it. And he is gratified that God has used him to help other people. Ten thousand people have jobs as a result of Dad's success, and three million people are independent business owners.

Dad never gets over that sense of awe that God has used him to improve the lives of so many people and their families."

Rich's son, Doug, adds that Rich's deep faith in God has also kept him humble. "Dad believes that none of us has any reason to become puffed up with pride and conceit. Rich or poor, we are all the same. That's why Dad says, 'I'm just a sinner saved by grace.' If everyone on the planet had his perspective, there would be a lot more humility in the world and a lot fewer problems. A humble heart is just a part of who Dad is as a Christian. He believes it is important to walk humbly with God because the way we live today is the way we prepare ourselves for eternity."

True humility begins with the biblical truth that "all have sinned and fall short of the glory of God" (Romans 3:23, NIV). When Rich introduces himself as "a sinner saved by grace," he is humbly acknowledging that all success, riches, fame and wisdom come from the hand of God. It is God who deserves the credit, not ourselves. Rich genuinely sees himself as a sinner who has been blessed by God far beyond his own deserving. That recognition is the beginning of true humility.

> *"And what does the Lord require of you? To act justly and to love mercy and to walk humbly with your God."*
>
> Micah 6:8 (NIV)

A humble person is a servant; he doesn't consider any job or task as being beneath his dignity. Billy Zeoli told me, "Some years ago, I went to Dallas to speak at a meeting of the Dallas Cowboys, and Rich went with me. This was back in the Tom Landry days. Before the meeting, quarterback Roger Staubach came up to me and said, 'I thought Rich DeVos was coming with you. I was looking forward to meeting that guy.' I said, 'Oh, he's here. He's in the other room, arranging the chairs for the meeting.' That's the kind of guy he is. Any little job that needs doing, he'll pitch in and do. He's a humble servant, and there are too few of his kind in the world."

A humble person does not abuse wealth, power and position to intimidate others and get what he wants. Debbie Blozinski of Grand Rapids told me a story that speaks volumes about the humility of Rich DeVos. "I was working as a waitress at Charley's Crab in Grand Rapids," she said. "One night, I looked up and saw Rich DeVos come in alone. The restaurant was busy, there were people waiting, and the receptionist told him there would be a twenty-minute wait. So Rich sat down and read the newspaper while he waited. I thought, *Oh, no! We can't tell a billionaire like Mr. DeVos that he has to wait twenty minutes!*

"I quickly set up a table, then I came out and told Rich that his table was ready. He looked around at the others who were still waiting. Then he smiled and said, 'No, thank you, Debbie. Let these people have the table. I'll wait my turn.' I've never met a nicer, more humble man than Rich DeVos."

> *"People with humility don't think less of themselves. They just think about themselves less."*
>
> NORMAN VINCENT PEALE
> AUTHOR AND INSPIRATIONAL SPEAKER

When Grand Valley State University in Grand Rapids began construction of the Richard M. DeVos Center (a 256,000-square-foot building to house a school of business, a library and other facilities), Rich told an interviewer for *The Saturday Evening Post,* "They stuck my name on it. That is nice. But I was thinking that they should have put God's name on it. The money that I gave them wasn't my money. It was money that God entrusted me to take care of and to dispense, so we gave some to the college and they say, 'Good for you, DeVos.' But God gave me the talent to make money, so his name should be on it." That is not a "humble act" on Rich's part. I know that man, and that statement comes from the authentically humble depths of his heart.

How is humility displayed in a person's life? I have seen Rich's humility take many forms. For one thing, Rich listens more than he talks. He is genuinely interested in the opinions of others, and he always takes a variety of viewpoints into consideration before making a decision. His humility makes him a good listener.

Orlando sportswriter Bill Fay recalls, "The day the Magic signed Penny Hardaway to a long-term contract, I saw Rich in the hallway at the Magic arena. He said, 'Well, what do you think of our new guard?' I said, 'He's going to be a star player, but as a season ticket holder I'm not too happy. The money you're paying him will force ticket prices to go up. Eventually, that's going to ruin the game.' He listened to everything I had to say. He wanted to know what the fans really think. That's the thing I admire about Rich—you can talk to him, be totally straight with him, and he never takes offense at your opinion. He never makes you feel like he's the rich tycoon and you're the idiot. He's a good listener."

Doc Rivers, former head coach of the Orlando Magic, agrees. "I'm continually impressed with Rich's humility. He cares about people and about the spirit of life. He is all about helping people and teaching people to help themselves. With Rich, it's never about himself; it's always about others."

> *"Rich has maintained a common touch. People often assume that he's way up there and unapproachable because he has wealth. They are always pleasantly surprised when they talk to him and discover how friendly and humble he is. His attitude is, 'I'm just like you. I've been where you are. I've delivered papers. I've pumped gas.'"*
>
> Helen DeVos
> Rich's Wife

Rich's humility is expressed in his equal treatment of others. He treats all people—from the gardener who pulls his weeds to the several U.S. presidents who he personally knows—as complete equals. In Rich's world, there are no inferior people, no superior people.

Everyone is a child of God, made in his image, worthy of fair treatment and respect.

Writer Brian Schmitz of the Orlando *Sentinel* says, "Rich DeVos is the most approachable guy around. Of all the owners in pro sports, he seems the most human and easy to talk to. To Rich, the Magic is a family business and he's the daddy—anyone can come and talk to him anytime. That is rare in professional sports."

You see Rich's humility in the way he defers to others and steps out of the limelight. Former Amway executive John Gartland recalls, "One time in the late 1980s, Jay Van Andel was invited to a White House state dinner for Queen Beatrix of Holland. I told Rich I could arrange an invitation for him if he wanted to go, but he declined. 'I'll go another time,' Rich said. 'This is Jay's night, and I don't want to interfere.' Rich and Jay are two humble men who often deferred to each other that way. They both have the humility to step back and let the other have the limelight. I'm sure that's one of the reasons they have lasted so long as partners and friends."

Rich's humility is also evident in his sense of humor. He loves to laugh, and his jokes are always at his own expense, never at the expense of others. "Rich can laugh at himself," says Brian Schmitz. "After he received a woman's heart in a transplant operation, he kidded that he would now have a higher voice and could change his mind whenever he wanted to."

> *"Rich has a great sense of humor. One time we did a book signing together, and we spent most of the time laughing."*
>
> Max DePree, Bestselling Author and Former CEO of Herman Miller, Inc.

Retired Michigan bank executive Charles Stoddard told me, "The poet Edgar Guest once said, 'I would rather see a sermon than hear one.' Rich DeVos is a walking sermon on humility. Some years ago, my brother-in-law, Phil Ordway, attended a gala black-tie event in Phoenix. The scheduled speaker for the event was Dr. Henry Kissinger. As Phil was walking into the banquet hall, he accidentally bumped into a man, and this man introduced himself.

"'Hello,' he said, 'my name is Rich DeVos. I'm here from Ada, Michigan.'

"'Really!' Phil said. 'My brother-in-law, Chuck Stoddard, lives in Ada. Do you know him?'

"'Oh, of course!' Rich said. And they chatted for a few minutes, then went their separate ways. Sometime later, it was announced that Dr. Kissinger had to cancel his appearance, and that a substitute speaker had graciously agreed to come at the last minute. Phil was shocked to see that the speaker was Rich DeVos, the very man he had been chatting with. Phil had not had a clue that he was speaking with the billionaire founder of Amway and the evening's keynote speaker. What a great example of humility!"

Some people say that a humble person can't be ambitious and successful—but Rich DeVos proves that humility and the drive to succeed are *not* mutually exclusive. *Newsweek* executive Bill Youngberg has known Rich for years, and he says, "Rich DeVos is a man with drive and ambition, yet he lives his life and wields his influence in a humble, low-key manner. He didn't get where he is by climbing over other people, but by building other people up. He is not only out for himself; he wants to see everybody succeed."

There is a story told of a man who became well-known for his humility. His humble spirit so impressed his fellow citizens that they awarded him a pin that read, "Most Humble Man in Town." The next day, they took the pin away from him when they caught him wearing it!

"Rich and Helen are just regular people—simple people who remember their roots."

PAM DEVOS
RICH'S DAUGHTER-IN-LAW
(DAN'S WIFE)

Rich DeVos is the kind of guy

who, if you gave him a "Most Humble Man" pin, would never wear it. The only pin you would catch him wearing is one that reads "I'm a Sinner Saved by Grace."

Crucial character trait no. 3: kindness

Rich's longtime physician and surgeon, Dr. Luis Tomatis, told me a story about Rich that illustrates one of his most endearing traits: his kindness and compassion. "Rich and I were in Washington, D.C., to call on some senators. It was a cold, raw, rainy day outside. We entered the elevator in the Senate building, and as the elevator doors were closing, a man in a motorized wheelchair arrived. Someone held the doors open, and the man in the wheelchair rolled in. His hair and clothing were wet from the rain. As the elevator started moving up, the man said, 'I need a windshield wiper for my glasses.' The other people in the elevator chuckled.

"The elevator stopped at the fourth floor, and Rich and I got out. So did the man in the wheelchair. I started walking down the hall—then I realized that Rich wasn't with me. I turned and saw that Rich had gone back to the man in the wheelchair. 'Would you like me to wipe your glasses?' Rich asked, and the man said, 'Yes, please.'

"Rich had noticed something that I, a doctor, had missed: The man was unable to use both of his hands, so he was unable to wipe his own glasses! Rich took out his handkerchief, cleaned the man's glasses, then placed them back on the bridge of the man's nose. 'Is that okay?' Rich asked. 'Yes, thank you,' the man said. That's the kind of person Rich DeVos is. He notices when people need help."

Joe Torsella, president of the National Constitution Center in Philadelphia, told me, "I am continually struck by his generosity of spirit. Rich is a classic American story, coming from humble beginnings and achieving great success by accessing America's great freedoms and opportunities. For a lot of successful people, that's where the story ends, but for Rich, success is just the beginning. The larger part of his story is the way he gives back and keeps giving and giving—through his philanthropy, through his speaking, through his involvement with special causes, through the kindness he shows to people on an everyday basis. That's unusual for a man of Rich DeVos's stature, but that's just the kind of man he is."

> *"Rich is so loving to the grandchildren, and he teaches them to be kind to others. He says, 'You are Christians, so be humble and kind like Jesus.'"*
>
> Maria DeVos
> Rich's Daughter-in-Law (Doug's Wife)

Orlando Magic forward Tracy McGrady (a.k.a. "T-Mac") is one of the hottest stars of the NBA. When I asked him his impression of the owner of our team, T-Mac said, "When I think of Rich DeVos, I think of one word: *kindness*. Rich is interested in me as a person, not just as a player. To him, this image they call 'T-Mac' doesn't matter. He wants to know, 'Who is Tracy? What does Tracy need?' And Rich cares about all of his players the same way. I know a lot of guys in this league who have never met the owner of their team. Rich is right there alongside us, in the locker room, behind the bench. He's there for us. He is kindness personified."

Tom Michmershuizen recalls an incident from the early days of Amway that illustrates the kindness of Rich DeVos—and the fact that kindness pays off. "We had an independent distributor named Ruby Bowles who lived in Missoula, on the western edge of Montana. To put it mildly, Missoula is off the beaten path. It's not on the way to anyplace. Because Ruby lived so far off the main delivery routes, she had to buy her Amway products by the truckload—yet she was such a dedicated salesperson that she managed to sell in full-truckload volume!

"Ruby kept asking me to bring Rich out to Missoula to speak at a sales meeting. Rich knew how hard Ruby was working, and he wanted to help her out. But because of the remoteness of her location, we just couldn't fit a trip to Missoula into Rich's travel schedule. One day, Rich was going over his travel itinerary, and he saw that he had a two-day session in Seattle, a two-day sales meeting in Denver, and a travel day in-between.

"Rich said, 'Tom, I could go to Missoula during our travel day from Seattle to Denver.' He explained how we could do it, and it made sense. So I called Ruby, gave her the date and asked her if she could set up the meeting. Ruby was overjoyed! So we went to Seattle, did the two-day event, closing with a rally that kept us up late. The next morning, we got up at five and caught a milk flight that stopped at every little town from Seattle to Missoula. We arrived at noon and had lunch with Ruby.

"Now, Rich was supposedly there to get Ruby and the other distributors in the area fired up to sell Amway. As it turned out, Ruby was so enthused and fired up that Rich and I came away feeling inspired by her! She was a bundle of positive energy! In fact, that meeting in Missoula turned out to be more exciting and worthwhile than either of the two-day events in Seattle and Denver!

"I have always been impressed by the fact that Rich cared about every independent distributor in the Amway family. He had been a distributor himself, and he knew how much it meant to them when he made a personal appearance. No place was too distant or out-of-the-way for Rich. He knew that people like Ruby Bowles were the backbone of Amway, and he would do anything to help them."

Rich DeVos's kindness and

"Be patient and loving with people. You learn to treat people with patience. As you get older you understand that most people are trying to do things right, and the few who aren't just never got their act together. The only problem with being at the top is isolation."

Rich DeVos

caring for his distributors was always repaid in increased sales and recruitment for Amway. That wasn't his motivation for being kind, of course. Serving people and helping people is just a part of what Rich does. It's the kind of person he is. But it's also true that Rich's sincere heart for people is one of the keys to his success.

Crucial character trait no. 4: honesty

Tim Foley played cornerback for the legendary 1972 Miami Dolphins—the only NFL team in history to play an entire season undefeated. As part of the celebrated "No Name Defense," he carved a place for himself in sports history. Though Tim Foley was well-paid as a pro football player, Tim has made a vastly greater fortune as an IBO than he ever made in the NFL. Today he lives in Central Florida and is among the top IBOs in the world.

> *"Rich has always taught that if you sow love and respect, you will reap the same tenfold. Rich has sown love and respect throughout his life, and now he is harvesting in abundance."*
>
> Rev. Neal Plantinga
> President, Calvin Theological Seminary

"The two great encouragers in my life," Tim told me, "have been Dolphins coach Don Shula, the winningest coach in NFL history, and Rich DeVos, one of the most successful men in the history of American business. Don and Rich are amazingly similar men. Both assembled gifted coaching staffs and talented teams. Both are great communicators and motivators. Don Shula patrolled the sideline at every game; Rich patrolled the stage at every rally. Both filled your spirit with hope for a better future. Both are generous men who are admired and loved by their teams. Both men love the heat of battle. They get fired up by a great challenge.

"One of the things that has impressed me the most about Rich

DeVos is his absolute honesty and integrity. If you do business with Rich, you know it will be done correctly, fairly and equitably. If there is a question of right or wrong, Rich will do what is right, even if it costs him in time, money or convenience. That's the kind of person you want to be in business with—and the kind of person you want to emulate.

"Rich DeVos is beyond rare. He's totally unique. His life is built upon principles that never waver. He and Jay Van Andel started a business in their basements and grew it into a worldwide, multibillion-dollar enterprise. While some people in this world get rich by stepping on other people, Rich and Jay have made a fortune by lifting people up and helping others become successful. I have been blessed to learn from the example of Rich DeVos and Jay Van Andel."

> *"Rich is a man of great integrity. If he says it, you can depend on it. That's why people around the world know they can trust him."*
>
> Bill Britt
> Independent Business Owner

Jody Victor, a second-generation independent business owner, says, "One word describes Rich DeVos, and that word is *integrity.* He believes your word is your worth, and your worth is your word. I have watched Rich go from the early days of Amway to the high level of success he has achieved today, and he has never changed. He believes in absolutes like honesty and truth. Those principles are not open to debate. 'Once you lose your good name,' he says, 'you can never get it back.' Rich has kept his good name."

To be an honest person means to be totally, uncompromisingly committed to the truth. It means that your walk matches your talk. The public you and the private you are one and the same. You don't project an image to the world; you show the world who you really are.

Honesty is not a matter of degree. There's no such thing as being "a little bit dishonest." You are either committed to being truthful and real, or you're not. As Tom Peters said, "There is no such thing as a 'minor lapse' of integrity."

Clearly, no one is perfect. But an honest person sets a conscious goal of perfect truthfulness. And when you fail to keep that goal? Just be honest about it! People respect you when you honestly admit your flaws and failings.

Rich DeVos has earned the respect of the people around him, the people who work for him. "Rich DeVos is a stand-up guy," says Horace Grant, a former player for the Orlando Magic. "He's the real deal. Genuine. Honest. As far as NBA owners go, put Rich over on one side, and all the rest over on the other side. Rich is more than just an employer. He's a friend for life. You can trust him."

> *"I've sat on many boards with Rich. He is a man of commitment and integrity. He says, 'Never do what is best for the moment. Just do what is right.'"*
>
> Robert Hooker
> Grand Rapids Business and Community Leader

Crucial character trait no. 5: hard work

"It takes a lot of courage and hard work to start a business," Rich's son Doug told me, "but Dad and Jay were dedicated to doing whatever it took to make it happen. Dad often said, 'You have to work at least eighty hours a week to succeed. You work the first forty hours to survive and the next forty hours to get you somewhere.' And that's what Dad and Jay did when they started out. They operated two full-time businesses every day. They ran a flying school by day and a restaurant at night. Dad says, 'Everyone should be in the restaurant business—once. Just to say you've done it.'"

Rich DeVos works hard, and he expects the people in his employ to put forth their best effort. Recalling some of the pep talks he's given his players before a Magic game, Rich said, "I'll tell the players, 'Some father has saved up his money for tickets so he can bring his family to the game. Don't tell me you're tired. Don't make excuses for a half-hearted effort. Go out and play to your full potential. You owe the fans your best effort.'"

A relentless work ethic is central to Rich's personality, essential to his being. He believes that work is honorable, and gives meaning and dignity to living. He considers a person's work to be a "calling"—a noble position in life given by God. Viewed in this way, work becomes a holy pursuit, almost a sacrament.

> *"You have to have something within you that drives you, that possesses you, that says, 'I have a reason to live and work to do.' I don't care what work that is. Work is worthy at all levels, whether it is running a camera, driving a truck or laying bricks."*
>
> Rich DeVos

In his book *Compassionate Capitalism,* Rich reflects on the fact that work has been viewed differently by different cultures through the ages. The ancient Greeks and Romans, for example, thought that because they had to work hard to earn a living, this was evidence that their gods hated them and wanted to make their lives miserable. In both Greek and Latin, the word for *work* came from a root word meaning *sorrow.*

During the Renaissance and the Reformation, attitudes toward work began to change. Reformers, such as Martin Luther and John Calvin, taught that work was not a curse imposed on humanity by God as a punishment; rather, work was actually a channel for service to God and a source of human dignity. This was the beginning of the "Protestant work ethic" that became the foundation of modern capitalism. "Meaningful work," Rich concludes, "always pays dividends beyond the paycheck when we embrace it with energy and commitment. . . . Work is a powerful force in shaping a person's sense of identity."

Of course, there have been many times and places where work has not been meaningful or ennobling—times when people have been enslaved. Under slavery, people are forced to work under miserable and demeaning conditions, and are not even allowed to enjoy the fruits of their labor. But meaningful work—the act of performing useful labor to support oneself and one's family, and to contribute value to society—is honorable and noble. Those who are privileged to do meaningful labor should be grateful for the opportunity God has given them.

Rich has a deep and abiding respect for people who view their work as a calling from God, and who approach their jobs with diligence and a conscientious attitude. He often tells the old story of an Amway employee named Harry. It was Harry's job to take care of the lawns and gardens around the Amway offices and facilities. One day, Rich approached Harry as the man was on his knees, pulling weeds.

"Harry," Rich said, "why don't you let me get you a better-paying job inside the plant? Maybe you could work on the production line where it's not so hot, and you wouldn't get so much dirt under your fingernails."

> *"Rich DeVos started from scratch and achieved everything he has by hard work. But he doesn't take credit for his achievements. Instead, he gives credit to God for giving him the ability to work."*
>
> Peter Cook
> Grand Rapids Business and Community Leader

"No, thanks," Harry replied. "I'm doing what I want to do. My calling is to take care of this place and make it look nice."

Harry not only knew what he wanted to do, but he was doing what he felt *called* to do, what he was *supposed* to do. His work was meaningful, and he enjoyed it. He wouldn't have it any other way.

> *"Rich DeVos is a gentleman among gentlemen. He treats everyone with respect and kindness. I've never heard a harsh or disparaging word leave his lips. He's always positive. A special guy."*
>
> CHUCK DALY
> FORMER ORLANDO MAGIC
> HEAD COACH

Rich DeVos believes that a strong work ethic is the key to success in any endeavor—and he has proven it with his own life. Rich's lifelong friend, Boyd Hoffman, told me, "Rich came up the hard way. His parents never had much money, so Rich started out without any worldly advantages in life. He earned his success through hard work and perseverance. His theory of success was simple: 'All you have to do is keep working hard and you will get there.'"

Grand Rapids businessman Bob Israels agrees. "One of Rich's classic statements," he says, "is, 'Try or quit crying.' In other words, don't sit and moan because success isn't handed to you on a silver platter. The world doesn't owe anyone a living. If you want to succeed, you have to try, you have to work hard, you have to go out and get it. If you put everything you've got into everything you're doing, and you keep at it and refuse to give up, you will succeed. Rich DeVos is living proof. He is the Protestant work ethic personified."

Even after his heart transplant, Rich continues to work hard. He believes he still has a lot of unfinished work ahead of him, and he won't quit until the work God gave him to do is done. Rich once told me, "I have a heart of a woman who is forty-four and I'm seventy-six, so that makes my average age somewhere around sixty years young. I still have work to do, and I intend to do it."

"Theologians have said that the need to perform meaningful work is rooted in the God-given urge to be cocreators of the Earth—that by undertaking to improve our world or serve our fellow humans, we share in God's activity. Thus our work assumes a kind of holiness that permeates even the most ordinary of everyday activities."

RICH DEVOS

Crucial character trait no. 6: optimism

Paul Conn, president of Lee University, recalls, "I was twenty-nine years old and a college professor when I first met Rich. He was forty-nine. I was a liberal Democrat; he was a conservative Republican. This whole idea of the power of positive thinking was all new to me. Rich was so consistent and articulate about the optimistic way of life that it impacted me tremendously.

"I was recently at his home in Grand Rapids. It was a cold day in the late fall, and we were watching a football game in the den. It seemed that commercials were coming on after every play, and I griped, 'Let's get on with the game! All these commercials are really getting annoying!'

"Rich looked at me and said, 'Well, Paul, would you like to be sitting at the game right now? It's windy and snowing, the tickets are seventy dollars each, there's all that traffic to fight, and you can't see the game as well in the stadium as you can on TV. You're sitting here in total comfort, it's warm, the game is free, you've got instant replays with slow-motion, and the only price you pay is to put up with a commercial every now and then.'

"That's how Rich views life. While I'm whining about commercials, Rich is saying, 'What a deal! What a great life! Look at all we have to enjoy!' I've learned so much from Rich over the years I've known him, but I still have so much to learn about what it means to be positive, to live your life with an 'upward look.'

"I still have a tendency to grump and complain, but whenever I do, my wife will say to me, 'Paul, if Rich were here, what would he say about your attitude right now?' That's all she has to say. When she puts it that way—'What would Rich say?'—everything pops into focus. Because I know *exactly* what Rich would say."

Rich gives the credit for his unsinkable optimism to his father. "I have always approached everything in life with a positive outlook," Rich says. "My father imbued me with the idea that I could seize opportunity when it came my way, and that approach has helped me maintain an optimism in the face of disappointment."

It is said that pessimists look at half a glass of water and say, "The glass is half-empty." Optimists look at the same glass and say, "The glass is half-full." But Rich is in a class by himself. He says, "Why settle for half a glass? There's lots more water where this came from! Let's go out and get a bucket-full!" There's more optimism in Rich's little finger than most of us have in our whole bodies!

> *"Rich has incredible enthusiasm, and he's a supreme optimist. He never gets down and never gives up."*
>
> Casey Wondergem
> Former Amway Executive

Rich coined a phrase that he has been using for years: "an upward look." He is talking about an optimistic outlook, a positive attitude. "I believe in the upward look," he once said. "I am an optimist by choice as much as by nature." In other words, optimism is not something that people are born with. It's a choice that people must deliberately make.

Life, Rich often says, tends to shape itself according to our expectations. If we expect to be miserable and unhappy, then we will not be disappointed. Our pessimistic expectations will be met. But if we keep an upward look, an optimistic attitude, then—again—we will not be disappointed. Our optimism will be rewarded.

Rich illustrates the power of a person's attitude with an incident that took place many years ago. It was a beautiful, sunny day, and he was feeling on top of the world as he pulled into a service station to gas up his car. The service station attendant came out to his car. (This was in the days when a service station was a real *service* station, before the customer was required to pump his own gasoline.) The young attendant gave Rich a look of concern and asked, "Are you feeling okay, mister?"

"I feel terrific," Rich said with a smile. "Why do you ask?"

"You don't look so good," said the attendant. "You ought to see yourself in the mirror."

Rich tilted the rear-view mirror and was shocked to see himself. His face was a sickly shade of pale yellow. His first thought was, *Oh, no! Jaundice! I've got liver problems, maybe hepatitis!* When Rich pulled out of that service station, he felt miserable and frightened. He was convinced that he had a life-threatening disease—and he actually began to *feel* sick. His entire day was ruined as a result.

> *"Rich DeVos is on our board, and his presence inspires us to aim high and reach for great things. There's a natural organizational mind-set that easily settles for mediocrity. But Rich keeps pushing us to shoot for the moon. He's such a positive person with such an optimistic outlook that he invigorates us all."*
>
> Rick Breon
> Grand Rapids Health-Care CEO

Later, Rich discovered why he had looked so sickly: The service station had just been painted yellow. The light reflecting off the yellow paint made *everyone* who came there look sick and jaundiced. "It is amazing," Rich concludes, "how powerful a single negative thought can be."

The flip side of that story is the fact that, later in life, Rich actually did develop some serious health problems, including a failing heart that needed to be replaced. In every health crisis, through every critical surgical procedure he faced, his amazing spirit of optimism has been a major factor in his recovery. Again and again, Rich's doctors have all told him that it was largely his "upward look" that pulled him through.

Optimism is an essential ingredient of success. It is basic to the American Dream. America was built on a foundation of optimism, hope and a can-do attitude. As Rich puts it, "America has traditionally been a nation of an upward look." Only optimistic, hopeful people dared to leave Europe, cross the Atlantic in leaky wooden boats and come to America, believing they could build a better life for themselves. Pessimists stayed home. Only optimistic, hopeful people dared to believe they could sever the bonds of English taxation and colonial rule, and build a free, democratic nation with liberty and justice for all. Only optimistic, hopeful people dared to venture across the continent in covered wagons, pushing over mountains, across plains and through deserts to settle the western United States.

> *"There are many days when Rich doesn't feel good, but you'd never know it because he never lets on. He never complains about his physical problems. You never see him without a smile. Rich's health may go up and down from day to day, but his optimism never wavers."*
>
> PATRICK BROSKI, LONGTIME EMPLOYEE OF RICH AND HELEN DEVOS

The basic American attitude has always been optimism. In recent years, Rich observes, we have spent too much time and energy tearing ourselves down, criticizing our achievements, finding fault with each other. Certainly, America has its faults. America has had some horrible chapters in its history: slavery, the mistreatment of Native Americans, segregation, and the Vietnam debacle, to name a few.

Yet these tragedies and injustices have been (or are being) overcome because of our long-standing love of freedom, justice, fairness, optimism and hope. Deep down, we believe that the American Dream belongs to everyone. We believe that no one should ever be denied a chance to hope and dream for a better life, and the opportunity to make those hopes and dreams come true. That is what Rich DeVos believes, and that is the optimistic message he has preached throughout his life.

"Rich is unique because of his positive spirit," Jay Van Andel told me. "He's always been such an up guy. No matter how bad a situation was, Rich could always get up in front of an audience and spread hope and optimism. He made it look easy."

Joe Torsella, president of the National Constitution Center, told me, "The most important lesson I've learned from Rich DeVos is the value of optimism. He has met every challenge in his life—and serious challenges they were!—with complete optimism. He has shown that optimism is contagious, and it is a choice we can all make, no matter how difficult things get. We can all be like Rich if we will choose to face the future with confidence and a happy heart."

"To Rich," says John Brown, former Amway executive, "there is no such thing as an average day. Whenever problems came up at Amway, he would say, 'Hey, isn't this great! That's why we are here, right? Our job is to solve problems.' He has a great way of putting everything into a positive perspective. Being around Rich makes you believe that there really is joy to be found at the start of each new day. He is full of enthusiasm for the moment, and you get charged up by just being in his presence."

> *"Rich DeVos is my hero, the person I wish to emulate in life. There's no one I respect more than Rich. He has successfully completed the race of life, and now he's enjoying a victory lap by instilling lessons of life, optimism and the entrepreneurial spirit into the next generation."*
>
> Jon L. Christensen, Former U.S. Congressman

Grand Rapids construction

executive Gary Vos ascribes Rich's success as a business leader to his unfailing optimism. "Rich DeVos is a great leader," says Vos, "because he is an eternal optimist and a great motivator." That same optimism also makes Rich a leader among leaders in the sports world. "Rich DeVos is the perfect sports owner," says Bob Vander Weide, "because he thinks the Magic will win the title every year. He's always had that optimism, even after losses and setbacks."

How can you be like Rich? How can you experience your own amazing success? How can you make your own dreams come true? How can you have the kind of encouraging and uplifting influence that Rich has had on so many lives over the years?

To be like Rich DeVos, you've got to be a leader, a communicator and a salesperson, selling yourself and your dreams. You've got to be wise, and you've got to take bold risks. You've got to be a people person and a life enricher.

To be like Rich, you must love your God, your family, your country and your fellow human beings—and remember to demonstrate that love through your generosity and compassion for others. Most of all, to be like Rich you've got to have these crucial character traits: The will to persevere. A heart of humility and kindness. A strong, determined work ethic.

> *"I believe that life is good, that people are good, that God is good."*
>
> Rich DeVos

Above all, if you want to be like Rich, then keep an upward look. When problems come, smile and thank God for the opportunity to find creative solutions to those problems. When troubles come, remember that life is still good and troubles eventually pass. When people are rude or mean, be patient and forgiving—maybe they're just having a bad day. Say a kind word and move on. As Rich will tell you, most people are decent and good most of the time.

So there you have it. That's how to be like my friend, Rich DeVos. Now you've got the tools, you've got the knowledge, you've got your own dreams.

Now go make those dreams come true!

Afterword: Here's to You, Rich!

THIS BOOK WAS WRITTEN, done, finished. Every chapter was crammed full of stories and insights drawn from the life of my friend, Rich DeVos. There was just one problem: I had more than two dozen stories left over! Some of them just refused to fit a specific category or theme in the book, yet they were too priceless to leave out. So I decided to tuck them into this afterword.

As I was researching and writing this book, I made a fascinating discovery. Out of the literally hundreds of interviews I conducted in the process of creating this book, I didn't hear a single negative word about Rich DeVos—not one! Every person I talked to, from the waitress, the bellhop and the housekeeper to the former U.S. president, had nothing but admiration and appreciation for Rich.

So it is fitting that I close this book with some of the priceless memories and anecdotes that people shared with me. Think of it as a gathering of some of the many friends Rich has made over the years. They are all raising their glasses in a toast.

Here's to you, Rich!

—Pat Williams

The Amway King

Joan Williamson, Amway Employee:

"In the early days of Amway, Rich would be out on the road for long stretches, giving speeches and selling the company. When he returned to the office, it was like a wave of energy shooting through the building. We all could tell when he was back. He would go from desk to desk saying hello to everyone. Everyone knew that Rich loved lemon drops, so many people kept a jar of lemon drops on the desk. Rich always went to those desks first. He would greet everyone—'Hi! How're you doing? What are you working on?' Rich was always comfortable to talk to because he was never like a boss, never above you. He made you feel like you were partners—he made you feel special."

Steve Hiaeshutter, Former Alticor Employee:

"My first real encounter with Rich DeVos was in 1973. I was seventeen and working at my first job as a watchman in the Amway catalog warehouse. I had only been on the job for two weeks, and it was a hot August night. There were a number of entrances to the building, so I set empty aerosol cans above the door. If a door was opened by an intruder, the can would hit the floor and I would hear the noise.

"That night, I heard a clatter, so I went looking for the intruder. Coming around a corner, I saw a well-dressed man walking around in the warehouse. I went up to him and said, 'I'm sorry, but this a restricted area.'

"He said, 'I didn't know that.'

"'I'll have to ask you to leave.'

"'Okay,' he said. And he left without any argument.

"In those days, I was something of a rebel. I had long hair

> *"You'll never hear anyone say a negative word about Rich. That's so unusual about a man who is so successful. Usually people are envious of anyone who has wealth. I never saw that with Rich. People just think, 'Here's a guy who deserves it.'"*
>
> Chuck Daly
> Former Orlando Magic Head Coach

down my back in a ponytail, and I wore blue jeans and moccasins. When I got home, my dad, a law-enforcement officer, asked me about my evening. 'Anything happen? Any visitors?'

"I told him about the man I had kicked out of the building.

"'Do you have any idea who that man was?' my dad asked. 'That was Rich DeVos! You kicked your own boss out of his own warehouse!'

"Rich often strolled around the company grounds at night. After I told him to leave, Rich called my dad and told him what had happened—and Rich thought it was funny. I was amazed—Rich never threw his weight around or asked if I knew who he was. He just let the seventeen-year-old watchman do his job."

Milt Weeks, Retired Amway Employee:

"When I first started with Amway, Rich asked me, 'Milty, how far do you expect to go with Amway?' I replied, 'See that cushy executive chair behind your desk?' Rich grinned and said, 'Welcome aboard.'"

Travels with Rich

Tom Michmershuizen, Retired Amway Employee:

"In 1963, Rich promised the Canadian Amway distributors that he would go to Canada on the first Tuesday of each month. They wanted him to speak at events to help them with their recruiting efforts. I traveled with him on about a half-dozen of those trips.

"The first time Rich and I went to Canada, we flew in a private plane. As we got in the air, Rich said to me, 'Tom, flying is the only way to go! No stop signs, no railroad crossings, no traffic jams—absolutely nothing to slow you down.'

"Sometime later, we were going to fly to Canada, but a freezing rainstorm grounded all the planes in the area. So we got in a car and left Ada, Michigan, at midnight and drove all night long. While we were driving, Rich said to me, 'Tom, driving is the only way to go! You can't trust airplanes in bad weather, but you can almost always get there by car.'

"Later, Amway bought a bus that he was converting into a traveling office. During one of our trips in that bus, Rich turned to me and said, 'Tom, this bus is the only way to go. This thing has restrooms, we have our dictating machines, we can work and not waste any time like we would on a plane or in a car.'

"The point is that Rich was unfailingly positive, no matter what his situation. He always made the most of whatever he had to work with."

William F. Buckley Jr., Founder, *National Review*:

"My most memorable encounter with Rich was when I was flying to Notre Dame to be present at the ordination of Professor Gerhart Niemeyer. Rich was on the same plane. The flight required a stop or two on the way to Indiana, and Rich was getting off at one of those stops and taking a company plane to Grand Rapids. He said to me, 'Why not fly to Grand Rapids with me in my airplane? Don't worry about getting from Grand Rapids to Notre Dame—I'll get you there in one of my planes.'

"I agreed—and I wondered just how many planes he had. We landed, and he took me out to a hangar and showed me his company's 'air force'—if memory serves, there were eight or ten gleaming aircraft, maybe more. It was a grand gesture, but it was done with a simplicity that is so characteristic of Rich DeVos. We've remained in touch since then, and I've acknowledged his generosities many times."

A Friend to Presidents and Governors

Bill Nicholson, Former Amway Chief Operating Officer:

"I met Rich DeVos in the fall of 1974. I was working for Vice President Gerald Ford at the time. On one occasion, he said to me, 'There are two people back in Michigan I want you to meet—Rich DeVos and Jay Van Andel. I have a sense you'll be friends.' It was just eight days after Mr. Ford said this that Richard Nixon resigned the presidency and Mr. Ford became president. That fall, many of Mr. Ford's close friends and allies came to the White House for a dinner, including Rich DeVos. That was the first time I met him. Little did I know what a big part Rich would play in my life."

John C. Gartland, Former Amway Corp. Executive:

"When Gerald Ford was in the White House, he loved to have Rich DeVos and Jay Van Andel visit. The reason he enjoyed having them over was that they never asked for anything. They just talked with him and offered their help and support."

Joe Tomaselli, Vice President and General Manager, Amway Grand Plaza Hotel:

"In the fall of 1992, President George H. W. Bush was making a campaign swing through the Midwest shortly before the election. He was scheduled to stay at the Amway Grand Plaza Hotel, and I was to meet him and welcome him upon his arrival. A half-hour before President Bush was to arrive, Rich DeVos showed up unannounced. The president and Rich knew each other well, and Rich just wanted to greet his friend, George Bush.

"The Secret Service informed us that Mr. Bush was not feeling well—he had a touch of the flu. So the meet-and-greet session that was planned for his arrival had been cancelled. When Mr. Bush arrived at the hotel, Rich and I were standing behind the rope line. Mr. Bush entered and waved to the five hundred or so people who filled the lobby. He wore a raincoat with the collar up.

"How many billionaires will sit down and talk with you and tell you how to become one as well? Rich is a great American who played a significant role in American history. Few people realize how important a role he played. Rich is wealthy and influential, but he's the same humble Rich DeVos that he was at the beginning."

Ron Puryear
Independent Business Owner

"As he was waving and hurrying along, Mr. Bush spotted Rich and stopped in his tracks. He rushed over, stepped over the rope and embraced Rich. This threw the security arrangements totally out of whack because the people all surged toward him. The president invited Rich up to his room for a chat. I thought that was amazing. President Bush was not feeling well, yet just seeing Rich DeVos seemed to invigorate him. The president truly wanted to spend time with Rich. That's the effect Rich has on people. It's refreshing just to be around him."

Paul Kennedy, Orlando Magic TV Announcer:

"At the 1992 All-Star Game in Orlando, I was at one of the Magic parties when Rich came over to chat. He brought a friend along with him, whom he introduced as John. Rich said, 'John, this is Paul Kennedy, and he helps broadcast our games. He does interviews with all the players.' Rich went on and on about how great I was.

"Then Rich said, 'Paul, John is the governor of the state of Michigan.' It was John Engler, and Rich wanted us to meet each other. In Rich's mind, we were on an equal footing and should be introduced to one another."

John C. Gartland, Former Amway Corp. Executive:

"During the Reagan White House years, David Gergen went to Ronald Reagan and suggested that he do a radio show every Saturday at noon. Reagan said, 'Gergen, that's the best idea you've ever had.' So David Gergen contacted all the radio networks—and they all turned him down flat. They said it was too political. One of the networks that said no was the Mutual Network, which Amway owned at the time. Gergen told me what the White House wanted to do and how they had run into a brick wall. So I said, 'Let me see what I can do.'

"I called Rich DeVos directly, and he and Jay said, 'We'll carry that.' They made a decision on the spot. And that's how the president's Saturday radio address got started. Every president since Reagan has kept up the tradition, and those radio talks keep the public informed and often break important news. We can thank Rich and Jay for that because they were not afraid to do the right thing."

Not Unusual at All

Tom Michmershuizen, Retired Amway Employee:

"One time, Gordy, the janitor at our plant, was visibly sad and depressed. Rich asked Gordy what his problem was, and Gordy replied, 'My father is coming to the States from the Netherlands. He doesn't speak any English, and he's going to be stranded in New York by the airline pilots' strike—there's no way to get him out here to Michigan.'

"'I think we can solve that problem,' Rich said. We had Amway meetings lined up in the Northeast. Rich was scheduled to speak at events in Pittsburgh, Philadelphia and upstate New York. We were going to make the trip by private plane, so Rich took Gordy along. When we got to Pittsburgh, Rich had the pilot take Gordy to New York and pick up his father. So Gordy got to pick up his dad and take him back to Michigan. At the end of the visit, Rich had the pilot fly Gordy's dad back to New York.

"Later, I mentioned to Rich that he had gone to a lot of trouble and expense to do a favor for a janitor. But Rich didn't think he had done anything unusual at all. He said, 'Doesn't Gordy deserve the same treatment as you or I?'"

Mister Magic

Chuck Daly, Former Orlando Magic Head Coach:

"When I decided to retire as the Magic coach, I still had $5 million left on my contract—money I would forego if I retired. I called Rich to inform him of my decision, and he asked me, 'Are you sure this is what you want to do?' Rich wanted to make sure I was making the right decision for my family and myself. He knew he could hire a coach for one-fifth of what I was being paid. But at that moment, he wasn't thinking about the money. He was thinking about my needs.

Grant Hill, Former Orlando Magic Player:

"For three years, my injuries kept me on the shelf. Rich DeVos is paying me a lot of money, and I haven't produced for him. Yet he still cares about me as a person and has been completely supportive through the tough times."

Horace Grant, Former Orlando Magic Player:

"I had decided to retire from basketball in the spring of 2002. That summer, I was shopping on Park Avenue in Winter Park, Florida. Wouldn't you know it—I happened to see Rich DeVos. I tried to avoid him because I knew he would try to talk me into playing another year. Well, wouldn't you know it? He spotted me. He came up to me and said, 'Horace, one more year.' Just like that, I knew I couldn't quit. That's why I came back. How could I say no to him?"

Mike Miller, Former Orlando Magic Player:

"When Rich decided to sell the team, he met with the players and told us first. Not many owners would do that. He told us how much the team meant to him and how much he was going to miss it. Later, when he changed his mind and decided not to sell, we were all relieved. There isn't another owner in the league like Rich DeVos."

> *"Rich DeVos is a caring guy who wants nothing but the best for you."*
>
> Bo Outlaw
> Former Orlando Magic Player

Carol Beeler, Former Orlando Magic Employee:

"I was there when Rich DeVos attended his first staff meeting with the Orlando Magic. He listened attentively to various staff members give their reports. The people in charge of Basketball Operations gave a rundown on where the player scout was traveling to look for future players. Several universities were on the list.

"When it was Rich's turn to speak, I wondered if he would give a prepared speech, some sort of 'go-team, rah-rah' pep talk. Instead, he asked a question: 'Where else are we looking?' He was addressing this question to Basketball Operations. The question was surprising because the list seemed extensive. What was he getting at? Had we overlooked some star player or some major university?

"Basketball Operations replied that there were a couple of other universities they were also looking at. Rich said, 'Where else?' The Basketball Ops people looked perplexed. Rich said, 'Are we only looking in colleges?'

"There was a pause in the room.

"Rich continued. 'What if a player is talented,' he said, 'but he can't afford to go to college?'

"Another long pause.

"'The reason I ask is that my family couldn't have afforded to send me to college. Our family had no money, and I had to go to work. And my friend Jay and I started Amway in our basements. I just want to make sure that we aren't overlooking someone just because he can't afford to be in a university.'

"I was stunned. I had expected a canned speech from our new billionaire owner. Instead, I had heard the humble words of a man who was completely unashamed of his meager beginnings. He was real. He spoke what was on his mind. He didn't put on airs. He didn't put on a front. He is real; he's genuine. That's why, at the Orlando Magic, we love Rich DeVos."

> *"When I was in the seventh grade, we had to build a big display on a person who influenced history. I selected my grandfather, Rich DeVos, and I did a full display on him. We had a statewide competition, and I got to the regionals with mine."*
>
> RICK DEVOS
> RICH'S GRANDSON (DICK AND BETSY'S SON)

The Michigan Yachtsman

Bob Vander Weide, Rich's Son-in-Law and Orlando Magic CEO:

"Some years ago, when Australia had the America's Cup, we got involved in an effort to bring the Cup back to America. Rich got behind a syndicate, committing a huge amount of time and money to the effort. Unfortunately, we got hammered and didn't make it into the final rounds. After the defeat, the media approached Rich and started talking about this 'tragedy.' Rich said to them, 'Well, if you don't enter the race, you never will win. That's the way life works. We entered, participated, competed, but we didn't win.' That summarizes Rich's approach to life: You will never win anything unless you are willing to risk failure. Life doesn't always turn out the way you want. Rich is not a spectator. Every day Rich wakes up and plunges into life."

John Bertrand, Sailing Friend:

"Rich was asked by a friend and fellow yachtsman from Michigan to help the New York Yacht Club win back the America's Cup in 1987. Rich was brought in as cochairman of the *America II* syndicate. (The boat was named *America II* after the *America,* which first won the cup in England in 1851.) It was a contentious situation, but Rich was willing to involve himself in it for the sake of the challenge. He was picked for his leadership skills, including his ability to bring different personalities together in a common effort. Amway was one of three sponsors of the team, so Rich had an added reason for wanting the team to succeed.

"In his role as chairman, Rich faced one of his biggest challenges when he arrived in Australia for the challenger trials. The

Australians treated the American team with hostility. The New York Yacht Club had been vilified over the years for their furious defense of the cup, so the Australians viewed the Americans as 'those Yanks' who would do anything to win. The NYYC had held the America's Cup for 132 years before losing it in 1983, and the Australians were justly proud of being the first country other than America to claim the cup. It became 'sport' for the Australians to bash and jeer the Americans. I recall coming through customs in Sydney and being the object of the customs agent's taunts because we had lost the cup.

"But when Rich arrived there, he walked around, shaking hands with people, chatting with them, and demonstrating humility and graciousness wherever he went. People saw that these 'Yanks' weren't such bad guys after all. The *America II* fell short in its bid, and we were eliminated in the challenger trials, but even when Rich loses, he wins. Thanks to Rich's personal warmth, the people of Australia were left with a better impression of our team and our country."

Herb VanderMey, Longtime Friend of Rich DeVos:

"One time I was with Rich on his boat off the coast of Australia. A boat near us indicated there was trouble aboard—the owner captain had a heart attack. Rich sent Tim, one of his security aides, over with a defibrillator. A stewardess, Marianne, went as well, with a couple of extra blankets. Everything was taken care of as much as possible because Rich takes time to care for people in need. Unfortunately, the man couldn't be revived in spite of all Tim's efforts with the defibrillator. So authorities were notified and Marianne stayed aboard for emotional support until they came."

Greg Bouman, Friend of Rich's Son Doug:

"One spring break when we were in high school, six of us guys were staying with Doug at his parents' house in Florida. Late that night, we sneaked out of the house and onto Rich's boat. We got into a bit of mischief, and the police caught us and called Rich. When the police brought us to the house, Rich met us and really yelled at us. We were scared to death, and we felt really awful—Rich is such an even-tempered man and we had never heard him raise his voice before. We all went to bed feeling guilty and miserable.

"The next morning, Rich was up early, making banana pancakes for us. We all apologized to Rich. He just smiled and said, 'Okay, let's go fishing.'"

Patron of the Arts

Stu Vander Heide, Grand Rapids Business Leader:

"One year, Rich and Helen made a multimillion-dollar gift to the Grand Rapids Symphony. That set a leadership tone for the whole organization. Often, when a donor gives a gift of one thousand dollars, they feel entitled to demand a say in what selections are performed and on and on. That sets the stage for a lot of differing opinions and personality clashes. But Rich and Helen are unselfish. They don't use donations to manipulate and get their way. Their philosophy is, 'We're here to support the organization. We want the symphony to be excellent, but we're not going to tell the symphony management what to do or how to do it.' Their unselfish, no-strings-attached approach to giving has had a tremendous effect on the symphony board and on all the supporters of the symphony. Now, the one-thousand-dollar donors know they can't make demands because the million-dollar donor has made no demands. I admire Rich DeVos because he doesn't have any agenda when he donates. He doesn't take advantage of his wealth."

> *"Rich DeVos is a hero. He exemplifies the principle-centered leader described by Stephen Covey. His life is regulated by principles and values, and this enables him to operate as a highly effective human being."*
>
> DR. OLIVER GRIN
> GRAND RAPIDS PHYSICIAN

Theo Alcantara, Former Director, Grand Rapids Symphony:

"Rich wrote a book called *Believe!* He gave me a copy, and I loved it. One day I said, 'Rich, your book is so good—I just love it! When I read that book, I feel so peaceful, I fall asleep.' Rich replied, 'I know what you mean. Sometimes I listen to your concerts and have the same experience.'"

In the Locker Room

Billy Zeoli, President, Gospel Communications International:

"In 1984, the Tigers and the Padres were in the World Series. I did chapel for the teams on Sunday, and Rich went with me. I spoke to the Padres first, then we headed to the Tigers locker room. 'You'll do a better job with the Tigers,' Rich kidded, 'because you want them to win.'

"At the Tigers locker room, Lance Parrish stood up and dedicated the game to my father, who had passed away earlier that year. I was very moved by that. I started into my talk, but after three or four minutes, I just broke down. I was thinking of my dad who was in heaven and the fact that these guys had dedicated the game to him. It just overwhelmed me.

"Rich saw that I was having trouble finishing my talk, so he stepped in front of me and spoke for a few minutes until I had recovered. Then I finished up. Afterwards, pitcher Frank Tanana said, 'That's the first time we've ever had a DP—a designated preacher.'"

Sparky Anderson, Former Major League Baseball Manager:

"Rich DeVos would come to our chapel services in Detroit. That meant a lot to us. He was so busy and successful, yet he would take the time to drive from Grand Rapids to Detroit for our chapel. Sometimes he'd speak to us and encourage the team; sometimes he'd just worship with us. Our players appreciated him being there. It says a lot when a successful person like Rich is so generous with his time."

Handy Around the House

Scott Reininger, Friend of Rich's Son Doug:

"I was seven the first time I spent the night at Doug's house. Doug had gone down the hall to brush his teeth, and I was in his bedroom alone. At this point, Doug's dad walked into the room. I had never met Rich DeVos before. He had come in to change a lightbulb, so I asked, 'What are you doing?' He said, 'I'm the maintenance man.' I said, 'What's your name?' He said, 'My name is Rich. What's yours?' I told him, and he finished changing the bulb, then he left.

"The next morning, Doug and I were sitting at the table, eating breakfast. Rich walked into the room and kissed Helen. I turned to Doug and said, 'Does the maintenance man always kiss your mom?'"

Thelma Vander Weide, Bob Vander Weide's Mother:

"At Christmastime, whenever presents are opened, Rich runs around and immediately picks up all the wrapping paper. He can't stand to have anything lying around, not even for a second. After a meal, he heads to the kitchen to clean up. I once ran into him in the kitchen when he was rinsing dishes and putting things way. I told him, 'This is my job.' He said, 'I'll help you.'"

A Class Act

Harvey Gainey, Grand Rapids Business Leader:

"When I first started in the trucking business, we carried a lot of freight for Amway Corporation. Later, Amway brought in an executive who changed the arrangement so that all of the billing went through a Texas-based firm. When the Texas company ran into financial trouble, we stopped getting paid. When the account had gone ninety days past due, I went to see this Amway executive about the money that was due us. He was uncooperative and rude, and he told me to leave his office.

"I was livid, so I put in a call to Rich. He was vacationing on Peter Island in the Caribbean. I was amazed and impressed when he called me right back. I told him my problem, and a check was delivered to my desk the very next day—paid in full. I don't know what happened to the executive who treated me so shabbily, but I do know that Rich wasn't happy about the way he'd handled things. Rich bent over backwards to make it right, and there is no one in the world that I admire more than Rich DeVos."

Master of Ceremonies

David M. Hecht, Grand Rapids Attorney:

"I have known Rich for more than thirty years, and I am continually amazed at his ability to do and say exactly the right thing in any situation. On one occasion, Rich served as emcee at an award ceremony in which an elderly award recipient—a man in his nineties—started to give a lengthy acceptance speech. He began reading his remarks off of a stack of pages, and it was clear that this was going to go on for quite some time. Worse yet, he lost his place and started rereading his speech!

"In that infinitely kind and compassionate way he has, Rich stepped up and said, 'I think you got your pages out of order. Let me help you.' It was a great relief to the audience, and Rich saved the speaker from a lot of embarrassment. This is exactly the kind of wise and compassionate act that we have come to expect from Rich DeVos."

Rich the Pastry Snitch

Esther Brandt, Alticor Employee:

"One time, on a flight aboard the corporate jet, I heard some noise from the kitchen area. I went to check it out, and there was Rich DeVos, rummaging around in the food pantry. I looked at him and he looked at me, and we both knew what he was doing: looking for food that his doctor said he shouldn't be eating! He looked like a kid with his hand caught in the cookie jar.

"'I don't want a doughnut,' he said with a sheepish grin, 'but if you were a doughnut, where would you be hiding?'

"'I thought doughnuts weren't on your diet,' I said.

"'Oh, I don't want one,' he said. 'I just thought I would check.' I left him there, rummaging in the pantry. Sometime later, I came back and checked the shelf where the doughnuts were kept. Three of them were gone."

Joe Tomaselli, Vice President and General Manager, Amway Grand Plaza Hotel:

"One day, Rich DeVos walked into the kitchen at Bentham's restaurant. He picked out a roll from the basket, broke off a piece and started eating. Some of the employees didn't recognize him and were startled. You could see it on their faces. They were thinking, *Who does this guy think he is?*

"Rich grinned at them and said, 'The way I'm behaving, you'd think I owned the place.'"

The Trusting Soul

Dr. Luis Tomatis, One of Rich's Doctors:

"I've been Rich's doctor for many years. I've been faced with a number of life-and-death decisions with him, which means the responsibility on me is enormous. When I think of Rich, the word that comes to mind is *trust.*

"In 1983, Rich was having heart trouble. I explained the problem to him, and he looked at me and said, 'Luis, do you think I have to have this surgery?' I said, 'Yes.' Rich replied, 'Well, let's do it.' That surgery was done in Grand Rapids.

"In 1992, Rich needed more work done on his heart. We went to the Cleveland Clinic, and after the doctors reviewed his case, they recommended more surgery. Rich asked my opinion. I said, 'We need to do it.' Rich said, 'Okay, let's do it.'

"Then infection set in. This required three more operations. Rich was very sick throughout this period, but every time I laid out the case for the next surgery, he would ask, 'Do you think I should do it?' I'd say, 'Yes.' And he would say, 'Okay, let's do it.'

"A few years later, we knew his heart was failing and a transplant would be his only hope. Dr. Rick McNamara and I met with Rich's son, Dick DeVos, and Dick's wife, Betsy. At one point, Dick asked, 'Do you think we have to do this?' I thought, *The apple doesn't fall far from the tree.* Then Dick, Betsy, Dr. McNamara and I flew to Manalapan, Florida, to meet with Rich.

"Rich asked me a series of questions about the heart-transplant procedure. He had a good grasp of the situation, including the risks. Then he said, 'Okay, let's do it.' Rich trusted us as physicians. That's the way Rich has always conducted himself. He chooses people he can trust, people he has confidence in. Then when they advise him, he trusts their advice and says, 'Okay, let's do it.'"

"Rich DeVos has a lot of wisdom. The only way to explain it is his relationship with God. God has made him wise."

BARB VAN ANDEL GABY
JAY'S DAUGHTER

A Final Word from the Author—and from Rich

I CAN'T THINK OF a better way to end this book than to let Rich have the last word:

"I'm humbled by all the wonderful stories, but let's be honest! No one can be that *good! So, let me tell you once again what I really am: I'm a sinner, saved by the grace of God. If some of the things related in this book are helpful to you, I'm thankful—and wish you the very best as you pursue your dream."*

RICH DEVOS

Acknowledgments

WITH DEEP APPRECIATION I acknowledge the support and guidance of the following people who helped make this book possible:

Special thanks to Bob Vander Weide and John Weisbrod of the Orlando Magic.

A huge thanks goes to the entire DeVos family for welcoming me into their homes and lives, and for sharing so many special memories of Rich. The stories you shared with me are priceless and added so much to this book. I am forever grateful for your generosity.

I owe deep gratitude to my former assistant, Melinda Ethington, for all she did for me over the years and to my intern, Doug Grassian, who has poured his heart and soul into this book.

Hats off to three dependable associates—my advisor Ken Hussar, Hank Martens, formerly of the Orlando Magic mail/copy room, and my ace typist, Fran Thomas.

Hearty thanks are also due to Peter Vegso and his fine staff at Health Communications, Inc., including my editor Susan Heim, and to my partner in writing this book, Jim Denney. Thank you all for believing that I had something important to share and for providing the support and the forum to say it.

Two Rich DeVos associates, Jill Grzesiak and Kim Bruyn, went way beyond the call of duty in helping me research this book. I am also thankful to Kim Bruyn and Marc Longstreet for taking the time to review the manuscript and for generously sharing their valuable insights with me.

Special thanks and appreciation go to my wife, Ruth, and to my wonderful and supportive family. They are truly the backbone of my life.

Finally, I wish to thank all of the people listed below who took the time to share their stories and reflections on the life and character of Rich DeVos. Their contributions we invaluable in helping me paint the portrait of this very special person.

Lorie Adrianse
Richie Adubato
Theo Alcantara
Marty Allen Jr.
Nick Anderson
Sparky Anderson
Darrell Armstrong
Ted Arzonico
John Avellan
Nick Barbetta
Charles Bartlett
Richard Bartlett
John Batts
Carol Beeler
Bud Berends
Ken Bergsma
John Bertrand
John Bissell
Jeff Bissey
Debbie Blozinski
William Boer
John Boerema
Roger Boerema
John Bouma Sr.
Greg Bouman
Sue Brandsen
Esther Brandt
Rick Breon
Sherri Brewer
Dr. Bill Bright
Bill and Peggy Britt
John Brockman
Jim Brooks
Patrick Broski
Dee Brown
John Brown
Kim Bruyn
William F. Buckley Jr.
Donald Buske
Pat Butler
Semyon Bychkov
Dr. Gaylen Byker
John Canada
John Canepa
Jon L. Christensen
Jerry Colangelo
Paul Collins
Charles W. Colson
Paul Conn
Missy Conroy
Peter Cook
Craig Courts
Jan Courts
Lynne Courts
Todd Courts
Dr. Stephen R. Covey
T. Kenneth Cribb
Trammell Crow
Carol Cunningham
Lenny Currier
Kevin Cusack
Chuck Daly

Robert Davidson
Karen DeBlaay
Arnaud de Borchgrave
Andrew DeClerq
Dennis Delisle
Max DePree
Andrea DeVos
Betsy DeVos
Cassandra DeVos
Dalton DeVos
Dan DeVos
Dick DeVos
Doug DeVos
Elissa DeVos
Helen DeVos
Maria DeVos
Micaela DeVos
Pam DeVos
Rick DeVos
Ryan DeVos
Jim DeVoss
Marvin DeWinter
David Doezma
Jim Dornan
Joe Louis Dudley Sr.
Lou Dykstra
Howard Edington
Vern Ehlers
John Eldred
Joseph Elliott
Ken Ellis
Gov. John Engler
John Ensign
Rev. Jacob Eppinga
Larry Erhardt Sr.
Dr. Jim B. Fahner
Bill Fay
John Faye
Dr. Larry Feenstra
Dr. Edwin J. Feulner Jr.
Rick Fiddler
Tim Foley
President Gerald R. Ford
Charlie Freeman
David Frey
John Gabriel
Barb Van Andel Gaby
Arlen Gaddy
Harvey Gainey
Pat Garrity
John C. Gartland
Joel Glass
Paul Gordon
Julie Gory
Arie Goudswaard
Horace Grant
Dr. Oliver Grin
Jill Grzesiak
Larry Guest
Matt Guokas
Jim Hackett
John Haggai
Gen. Alexander M. Haig Jr.
Ron Hale
Danny Hamby
Bernice Hansen
Penny Hardaway
Ernie Harwell
Ralph Hauenstein
Dick Haworth
Matt Heard
David M. Hecht
Joyce Hecht
Don Held
Melanie Held
Dr. Louis Helder
Jimmy Hewitt
Bernice Heys
Bruce Heys
Glenn Heys
Randy Heys
Steve Hiaeshutter

Bob Hill
Brian Hill
Grant Hill
Jayne Hodgson
Peter Hoekstra
Boyd Hoffman
Jack Hogan
Earl Holton
Robert Hooker
Wayne Huizenga
Rev. Bill Hybels
Swiss Imfeld
Robert Israels
Irwin Jacobs
Mike Jandernoa
Sid Jansma Jr.
Greg Johnson
Kevin Kabat
Chris Kaiser
Fred Keller Jr.
Jack Kemp
Shawn Kemp
D. James Kennedy
John Kennedy
Paul Kennedy
Bob Kerkstra
Kurt Kimball
Birgit Klohs
Wally Knack
David Koetje
Mark Koetje
Ken Koldenhoven
C. Everett Koop
Mark Koster
Todd Krause
David LaClaire
Dr. Richard Lapchick
John Loeks Jr.
John Logie
Gordon Loux
Marc Lovett
Jennifer Lowe
Arend Lubbers
Josie Luster-McGlamory
Rich MacKeigan
Don Maine
Alex Martins
Rev. Stan Mast
Charlie McCallum
Clebe McClary
Philip McCorkle
Ken McDonald
Tracy McGrady
Dr. Rick McNamara
Peter McPherson
Jerry Meadows
Edwin Meese III
Fred Meijer
Tom Michmershuizen
Mike Miller
Paul Miller
Harry Mitchell
Tom Monaghan
Mark Murray
Eric Musselman
Hon. Sue Myrick
Rev. David Nicholas
Bill Nicholson
Michael Novak
Jon Nunn
Neil Offen
Shaquille O'Neal
Arnold Ott
Bo Outlaw
Jim Payne
Bob Pew
Rev. Neal Plantinga
Howard and Adele Postma
Rodney Powell
Ben Prawdzik
Elsa Prince-Broekhuizen
Ron and Georgia Lee Puryear

Jack Reid
Scott Reininger
Tony Renard
Bobby Richardson
Orlando Rivera
Doc Rivers
Chuck Royce
Rick Santorum
Robert Schierbeek
Brian Schmitz
Dr. Robert A. Schuller
Dennis Scott
Audrey Sebastian
Peter Secchia
Doug Seebeck
Bill Seidman
Beurt SerVaas
Jim Shangraw
E. Clay Shaw Jr.
P. J. and Ann Shooks
Diana Sieger
Cynthia Smith
Dan Smith
Fred Smith
Gale Smith
Hyrum Smith
Mick Smith
Kevin Solon
John Spoelhof
Alan Spoon
Pattie Stacy
Glenn Steil
Tom Sterner
Chuck Stoddard
Mike Sullivan
Art Susan
Flutie Tolonen
Joe Tomaselli
Dr. Luis Tomatis
Jerry Tubergen
Dave Van Andel
Jay Van Andel
Steve Van Andel
Marvin Van Dellen
Jay Van Houten
Fred Vandenberg
Ginny VanderHart
Stu Vander Heide
Guy Vander Jagt
Herb VanderMey
Dave Vanderveen
Art and June Vander Wall
Bob Vander Weide
Cheri Vander Weide
Dave Vander Weide
Hannah Vander Weide
Katie Vander Weide
Thelma and Roger Vander Weide
John Varineau
Carl Ver Beek
Helen Verburg
Helyne Victor
Jody and Kathy Victor
Mike Volkema
Dan Vos
Gary Vos
Tom Walsh
Vicki Weaver
Milt Weeks
John Weisbrod
Dan and Bunny Williams
Joan Williamson
Casey Wondergem
Bob Woodrick
Prof. Sir Magdi Yacoub
Dexter and Birdie Yager
Chuck Yob
Bill Youngberg
Billy Zeoli
James Ziglar

❧ ❧ ❧

You can contact Pat Williams at:

Pat Williams
c/o Orlando Magic
8701 Maitland Summit Blvd.
Orlando, FL 32810
407-916-2404
pwilliams@orlandomagic.com

If you would like to set up a speaking engagement for Pat Williams, please call or write his assistant, Diana Basch, at the above address or call her at 407-916-2454. Requests can also be faxed to 407-916-2986 or e-mailed to *dbasch@orlandomagic.com*.

We would love to hear from you. Please send your comments about this book to Pat Williams at the above address or in care of our publisher at the address below. Thank you.

Health Communications, Inc.
3201 S.W. 15th Street
Deerfield Beach, FL 33442
fax: 954-360-0034